IMAGES
of America

The Upper Merrimack Valley to Winnipesaukee by Rail

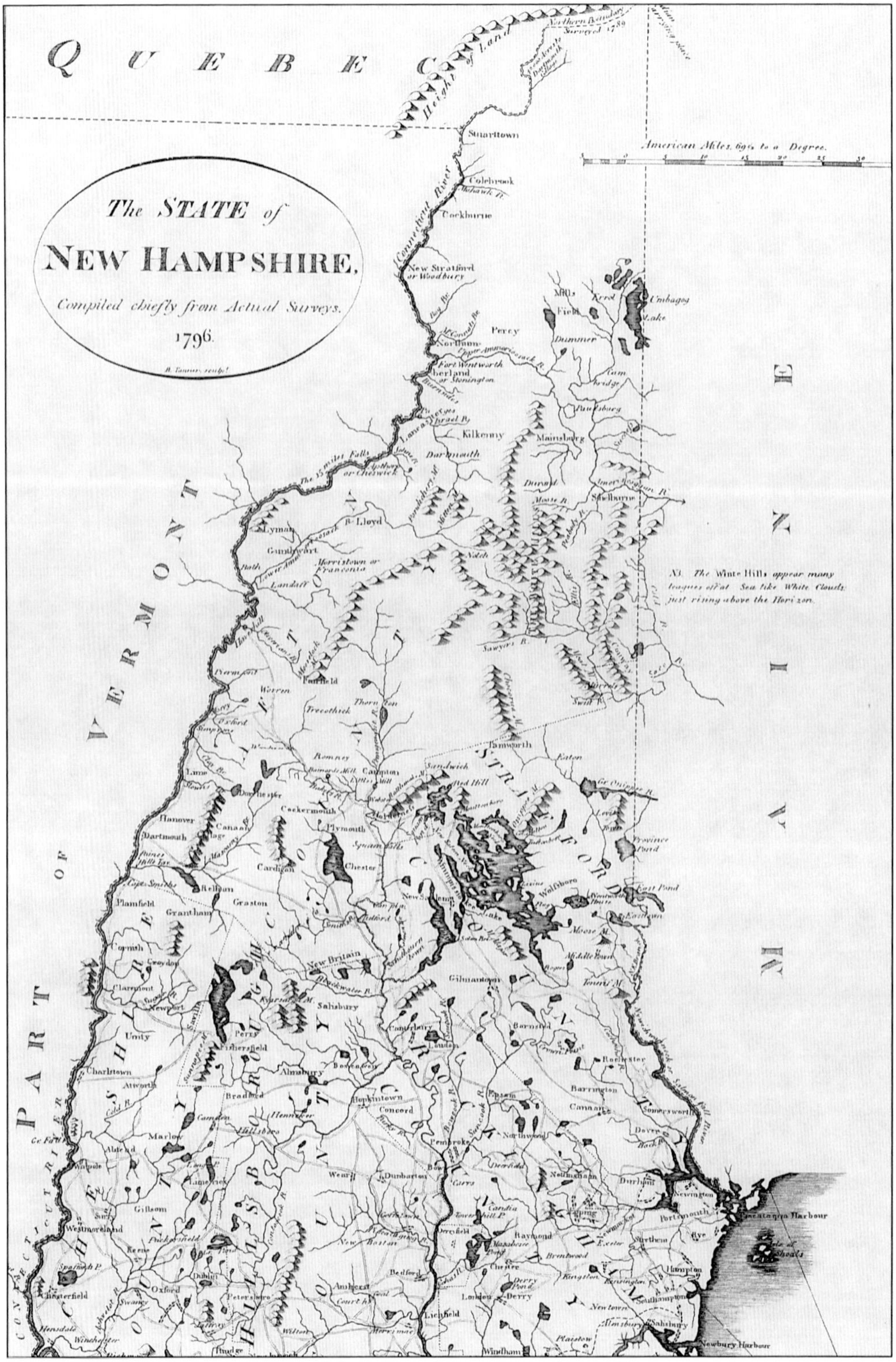

A map of the state of New Hampshire, 1796.

IMAGES
of America

The Upper Merrimack Valley to Winnipesaukee by Rail

Bruce D. Heald and Joseph A. Bush Sr.

ARCADIA
PUBLISHING

ISBN 978-0-7385-6478-4

Published by Arcadia Publishing
Charleston, South Carolina

Printed in the United States of America

Library of Congress Catalog Card Number: 2009921969

For all general information contact Arcadia Publishing at:
Telephone 843-853-2070
Fax 843-853-0044
E-mail sales@arcadiapublishing.com
For customer service and orders:
Toll-Free 1-888-313-2665

Visit us on the Internet at www.arcadiapublishing.com

Contents

Acknowledgments

Special thanks is extended to the following societies, companies, and individuals for their contribution to this volume: the historical societies of Ashland, Boscawen, Bristol, Concord, Franklin, Holderness, Laconia, Manchester, Penacook, Plymouth, and Tilton, New Hampshire; the Concord & Montreal Railroad; the Boston & Maine Railroad; the Winnipesaukee Flagship Corporation; *The Weirs Times and Tourist Gazette*; *The Granite State Monthly*; the Lakes Region Association; *The New Hampshire Troubadour*; Mr. Robert Lawton; Beth Lavertue; Charles Lane; and the countless others who have given of their time and effort.

Introduction

The rivers of New England have been celebrated in prose and verse since they first became known to man, and among them all none have proved more strongly attractive, more inspiring of noble and appreciative sentiment, than has the Merrimack. To sing the praises of this majestic stream, the poet John Greenleaf Whittier returned again and again, lavishing upon this feature of Northern New England scenery the encomiums that Bryant similarly bestowed upon the mountains and hills of the Berkshire, the pure-souled Whittier viewing the natural charms of his loved Merrimack from every possible standpoint, and responding in varied notes of the music thus stirred within him.

Born among the mountains that surround the Pemigewasset Valley, and holding its course in swift and most beneficent flow from Winnipesaukee to the shore of Massachusetts, this river was one of the major waterways of New England's material agencies, as well as one of the most beautiful streams that has been bestowed upon man.

In this state the "Merrimack Valley" had a significant and beneficent influence in natural and material affairs that the localities of but few watercourses can equal. It is almost uniformly characterized by rural, pastoral scenery, and its distinguishing natural qualities are those of quiet restfulness. Along its banks are towns and villages, isolated estates, institutions, and businesses, the abiding and sojourning places of populations that represented the best development and outgrowth to the life of the New England region. During the summer months, this whole valley is, par excellence, of the country, and too much cannot be said in setting forth its merits.

Through the Merrimack Valley the railroads had planted a steel highway, and united its services as a transportation, developed and ministered agent with those naturally furnished by this watercourse. Indeed, the Upper Merrimack Valley Route, which we shall take in this volume, to its source, shall be one of reflection and reminiscence of those days gone by, but which shall endure in our hearts for a very long time.

To preserve this legacy of the Merrimack Valley, we have tried to capture some of the characteristics of a place that give us so much pleasure.

This rare photographic journey through time is intended to enrich our reminiscences of the early railroads, the romance of the river valley, the landmarks, and the quaint hamlets as we trek northward from Manchester, to the White Mountains of New Hampshire, the "Merrimack Valley."

This volume has been assembled by the private collections of the authors for the sole purpose of preserving this legacy.

Bruce D. Heald, Ph.D.
Joseph A. Bush Sr.

One

Indian Lore and Early Settlements

The Merrimack River Valley to Lake Winnipesaukee

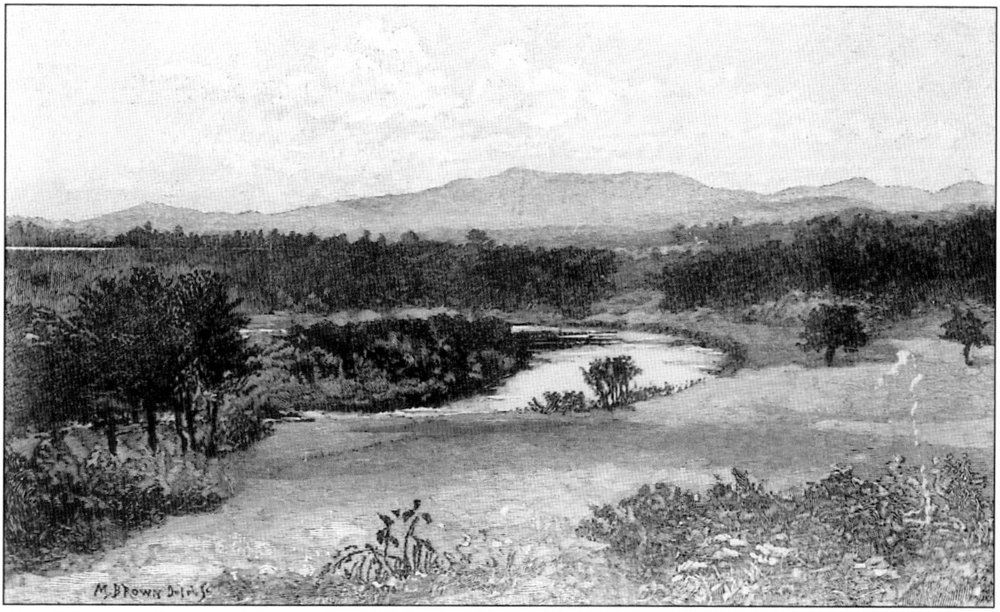

The Merrimack near to Nature. This river was a favorite byway for the Native Americans. It is said that those of the interior gave it its present name, which signified "a strong or swift current," while the Massachusetts Indians call it Merrimack, meaning "a place, or water, of islands," from the many beautiful islands it contains. Others give a different derivation: coming from the union of the Pemigewasset and Winnipesaukee Rivers.

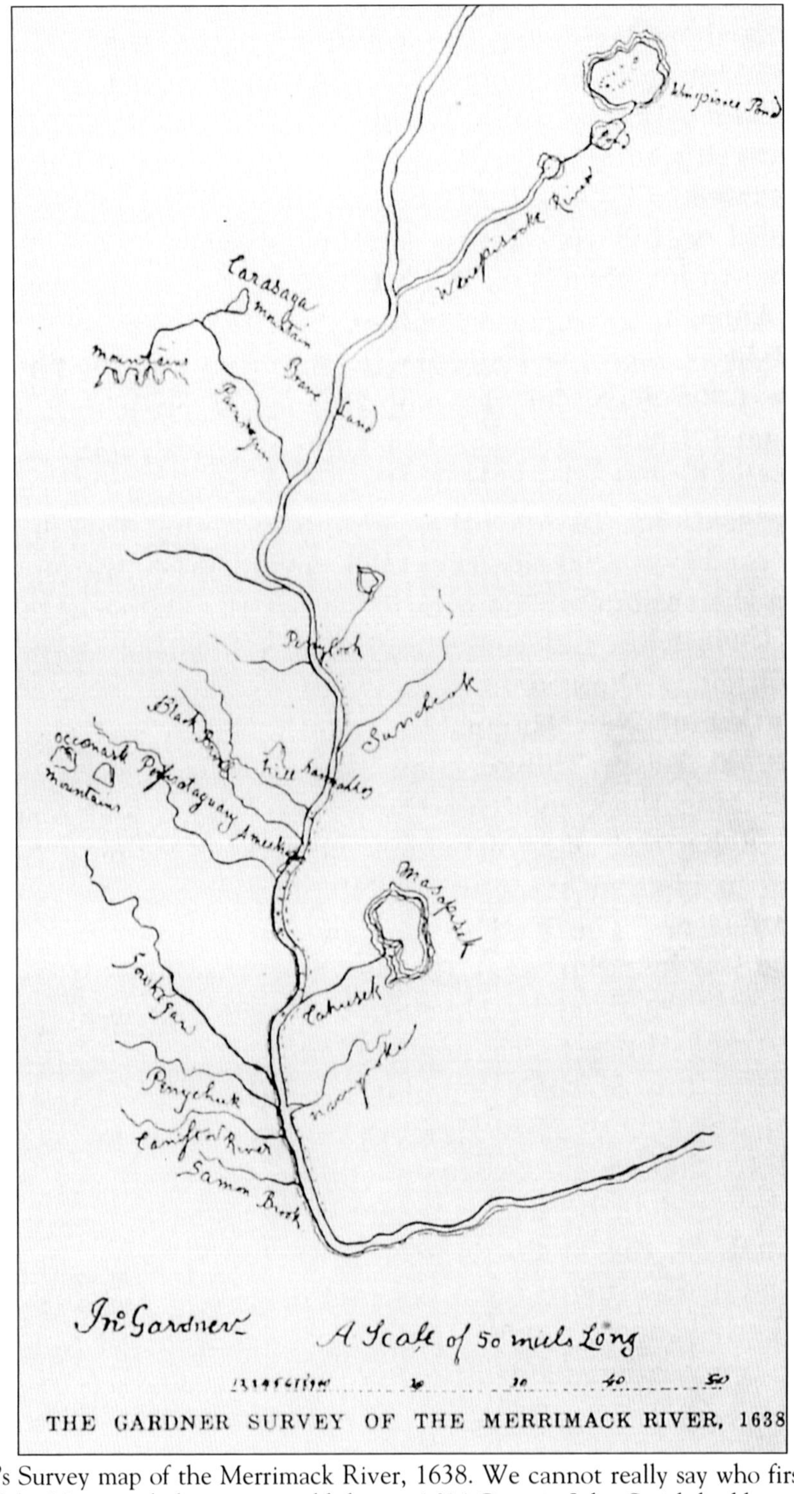

Gardner's Survey map of the Merrimack River, 1638. We cannot really say who first saw the waters of the Merrimack, but we are told that in 1614 Captain John Smith had heard of it. He called it a "great broad river or bay," and said: "The river's name is Merrimack as I take it."

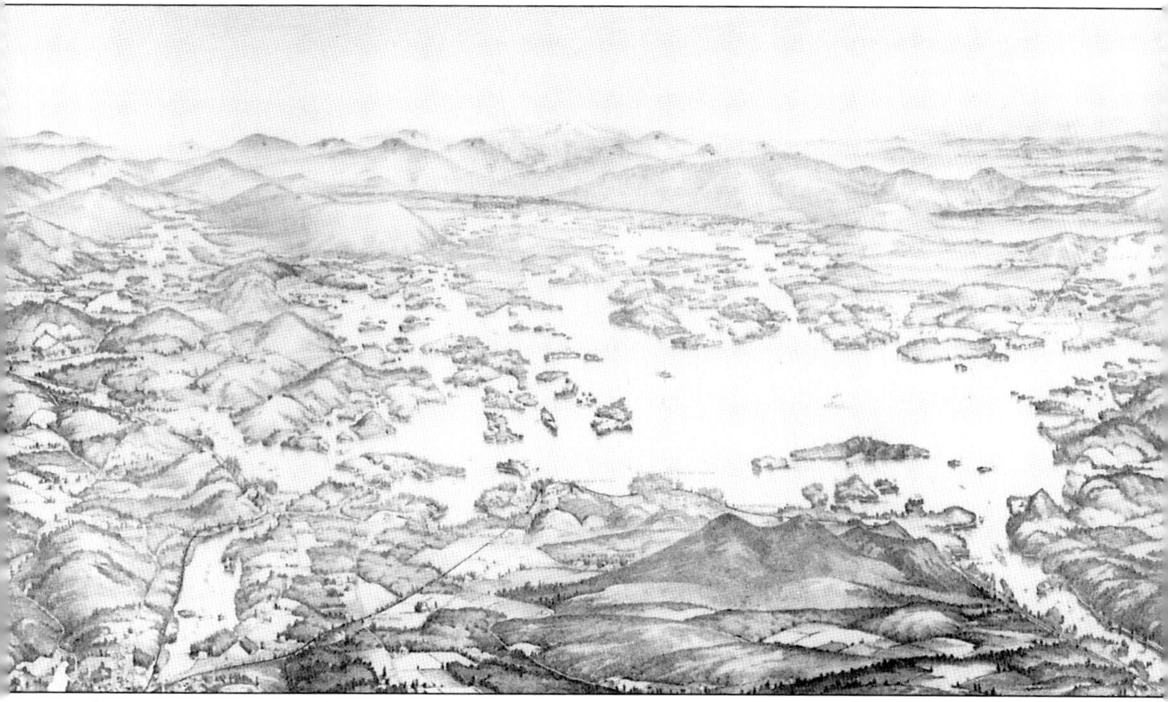

Lake Winnipesaukee map, Boston & Maine Railroad, 1909. New Hampshire's largest lake, covering 72 square miles with a mainland shoreline of 186 miles, is dotted with 274 habitable islands and surrounded by the foothills of the White Mountains. The lake is 504 feet above sea level, 23.5 miles long, and from 1 to 15 miles wide. It was named by the Native Americans as "The Smile of the Great Spirit," indicating that they recognized that omnipotence had placed the seal of its crowning glory upon this sparkling lake. It is safe to say that Winnipesaukee is one of the three largest fresh water lakes in the continental United States which lies wholly within the boarder of one state.

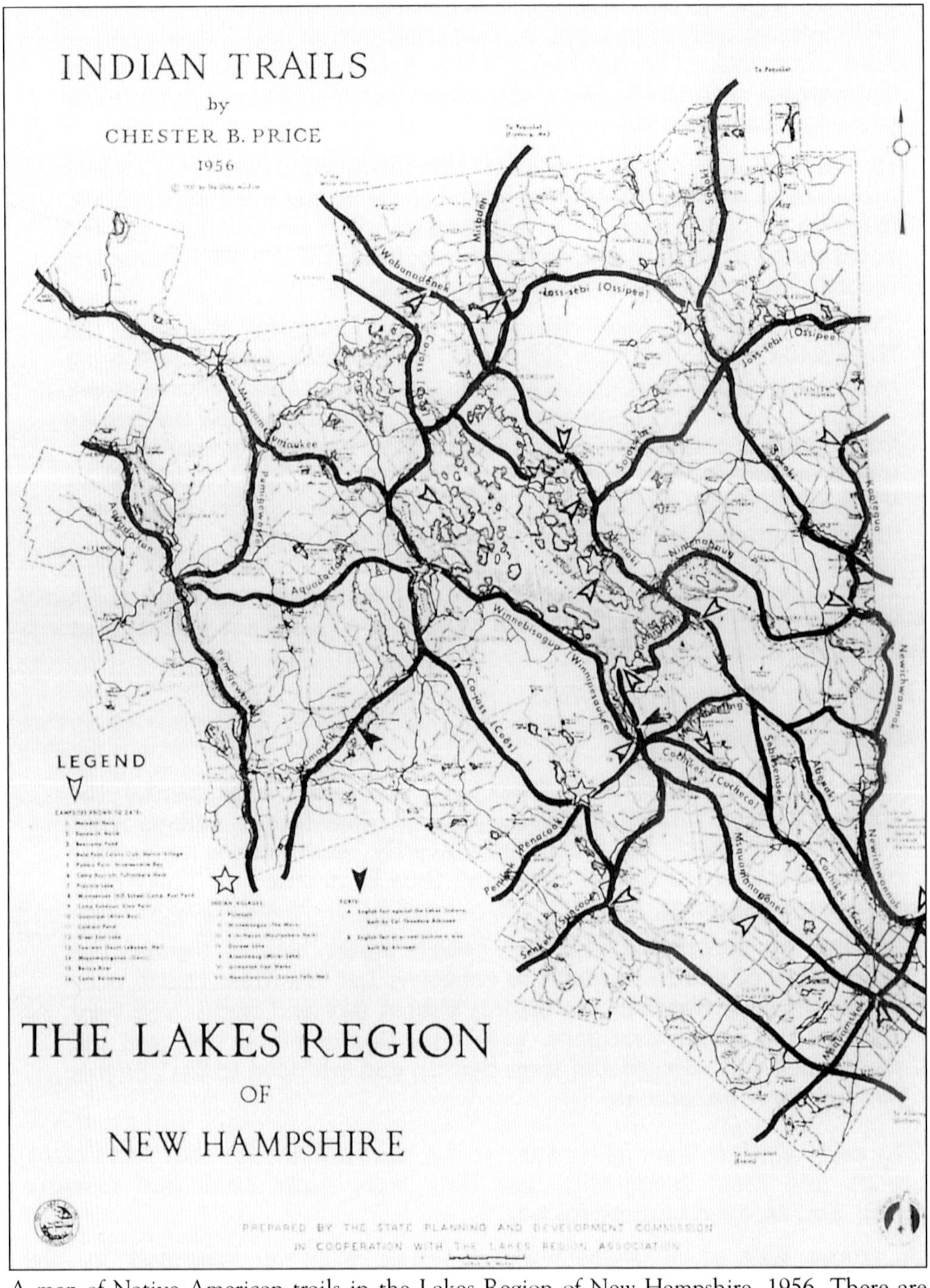

A map of Native American trails in the Lakes Region of New Hampshire, 1956. There are conflicting stories about this early name, Merrimack. One writer maintains that it was Kaskaashadi, ". . . the place of broken waters." Another gives Cabassauk, ". . . the place of the sturgeon," and a third suggests that it was Morodemak, a word which is made up of old Abnaki syllables meaning a ". . . deep or profound river."

"The Bow of the River Bend." It was Winnipurkit, a Sachem of Saugus, who married a daughter of the great chief of the Penacooks, whose principal location was where Concord now stands. There was a great feast, and then the bride was accompanied to Winnipurkit's home at Saugus, on the sea coast, by a band of prominent citizens. After a season she went to her father's home for a visit, and was escorted by some of her husband's chiefs; but when she was ready to return, a falling out occurred between Passaconaway, her father, and Winnipurkit, her husband, over a matter of native etiquette; neither would send an escort with or for her. At last she was determined to return alone, and at the time of the spring freshet, she set out in a canoe on "the troubled stream," and met her fate in the Amoskeag Falls in Manchester.

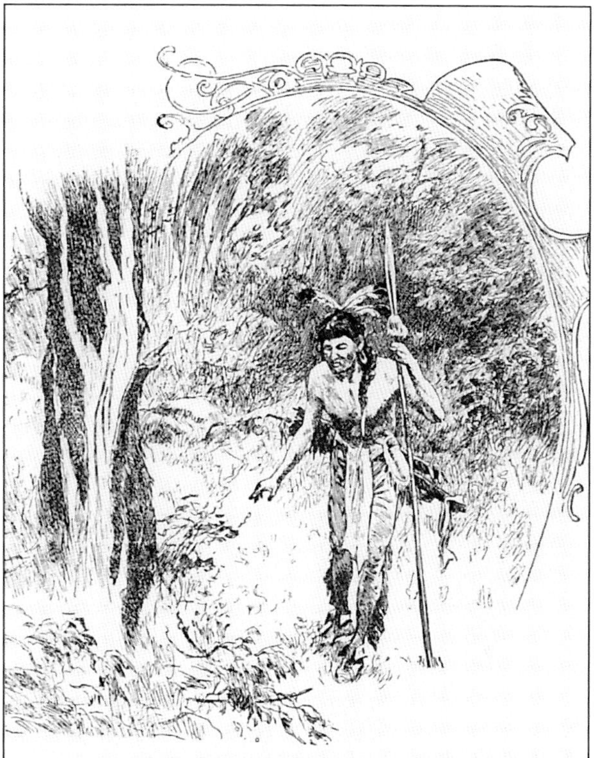

BOW OF THE RIVEN OAK

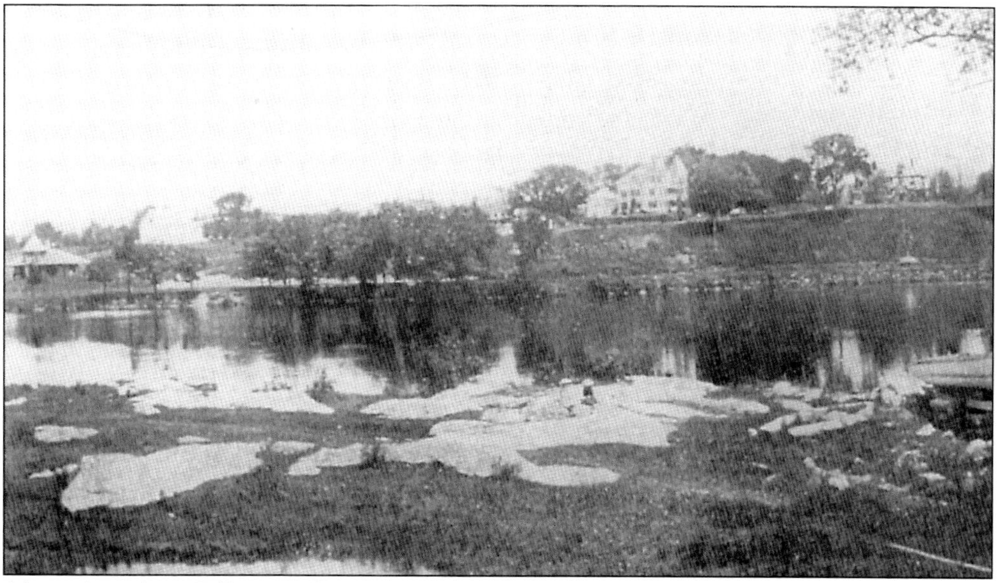

Above Amoskeag Falls. Manchester was a favorite meeting place for the Native Americans long before the European settlers came, due to the excellent fishing at Namaske Falls and around Lake Massabesic, "Place of Much Water."

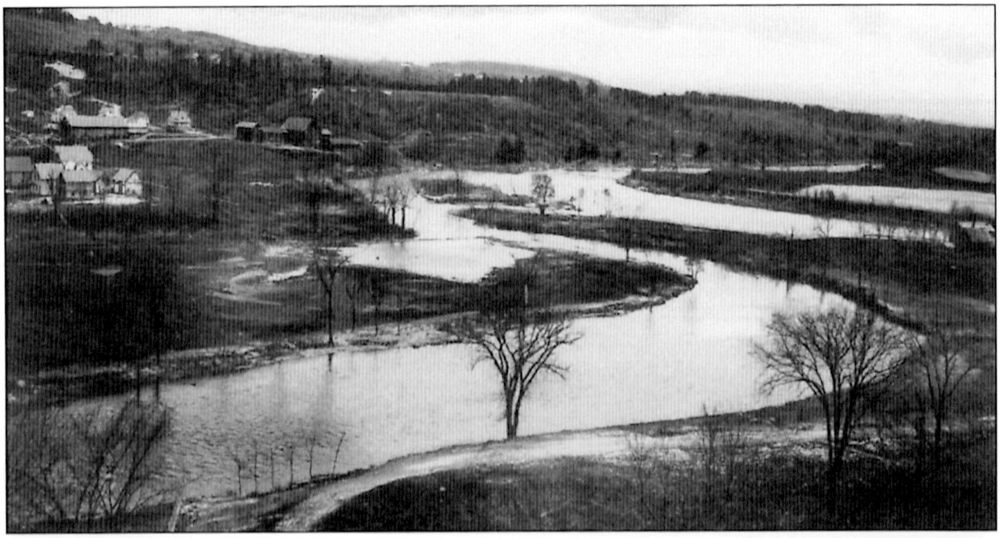

The junction of the Pemigewasset, Winnipesaukee, and Merrimack Rivers, Franklin, N.H., 1909. The region extending from old Dunstable to Pennycook was surveyed as early as 1638. One August day, about twenty years later, an expedition to find the source of the Merrimack started upstream "in botes." The members of that party were quite upset when they came to the "forks" in the present city of Franklin and found two streams instead of one leading into the wilderness. The following was recorded by Jonathan Ince: "But taking notice of both these rivers and knowing that we must make use of but one, I called the Indians to inform us which was Merrimack; their answer was the river which was next to us—that came from the easterly point, which river we followed unto the Lake."

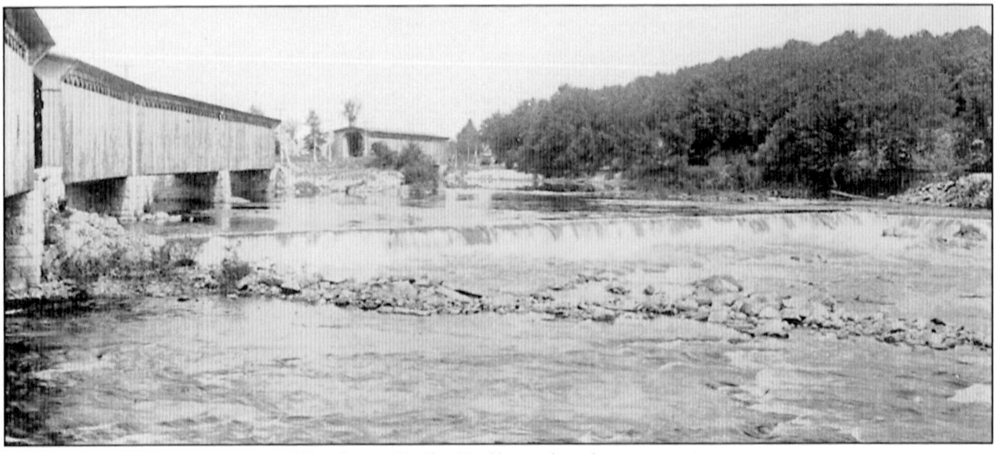

Hooksett Falls. Roll on, bright stream!
And ever thus, from earliest time, thou'st leaped,
And played amid these caverned sounding rocks,
When the long summer's sun hath tamed thy power
To gentleness; or, roused from thy long sleep,
Hast cast thy wintry fetters off, and swept,
in wild, tumultuous rage, along thy course,
Flinging the white foam high from out thy path
And shaking to their very centre earth's
Foundation stones.

By the shores of inland waters. In 1629, Passaconway, a great chief, sold the territory extending from the Piscataqua to the Merrimack River, and from the line of the Massachusetts Bay Territory 30 miles into the country, to Rev. John Wheelwright and his associates. The deed was signed by Passaconaway, the Sagamon of Pennacook; Runnawit, the Chief of Pawtucket; Wahangnonawit, the Chief of Squamscot; and Rowls, the Chief of Newichewannock, and properly witnessed.

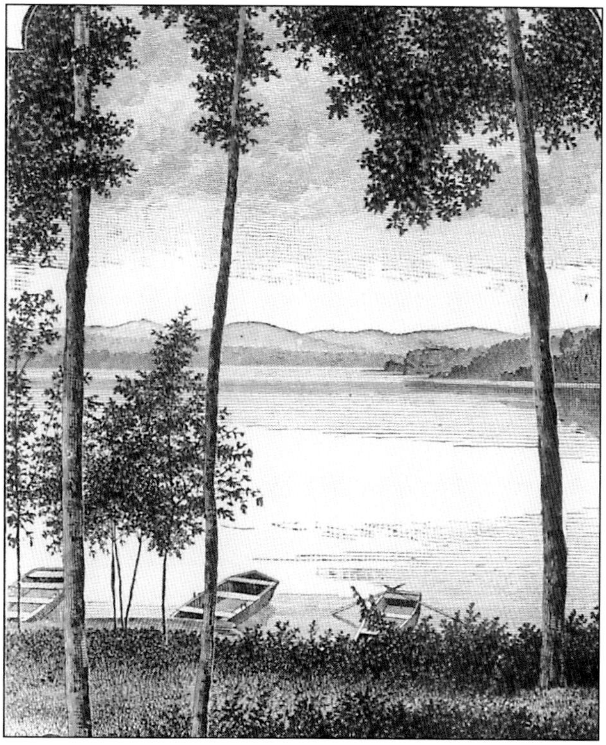

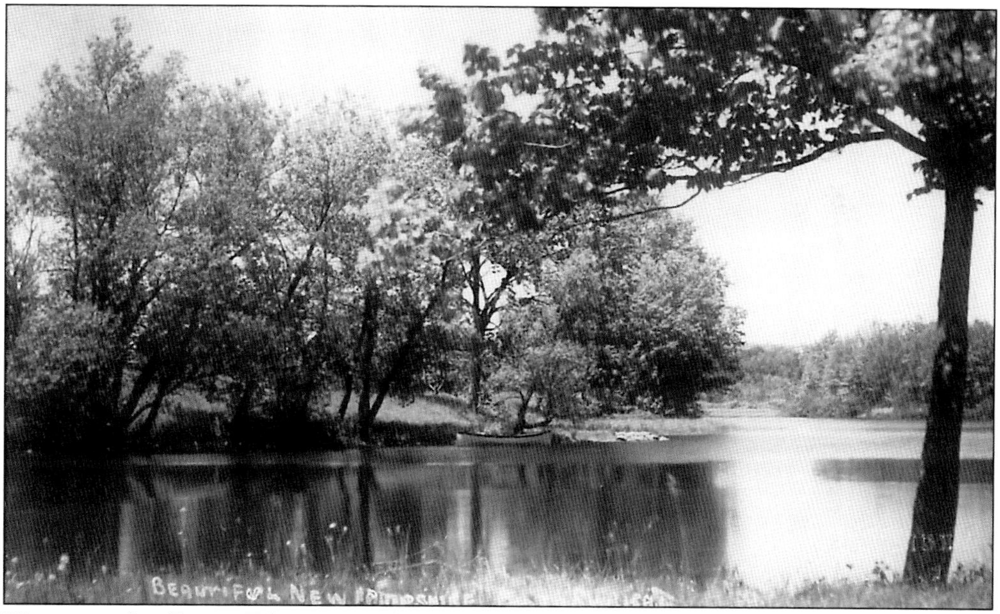

Winnipesaukee River, Tilton, N.H. One can hardly wonder where Massachusetts Bay Colony would have set its boundary marker if the surveyors and their Native American guides had followed the salmon up the Pemigewasset instead of the shad up the Winnipesaukee River, for it was on Endicott Rock in Lake Winnipesaukee that the surveyors placed that line at the village of Aquadoctan, which is now the Weirs, and marked it on the boulder now enshrined there, 1652.

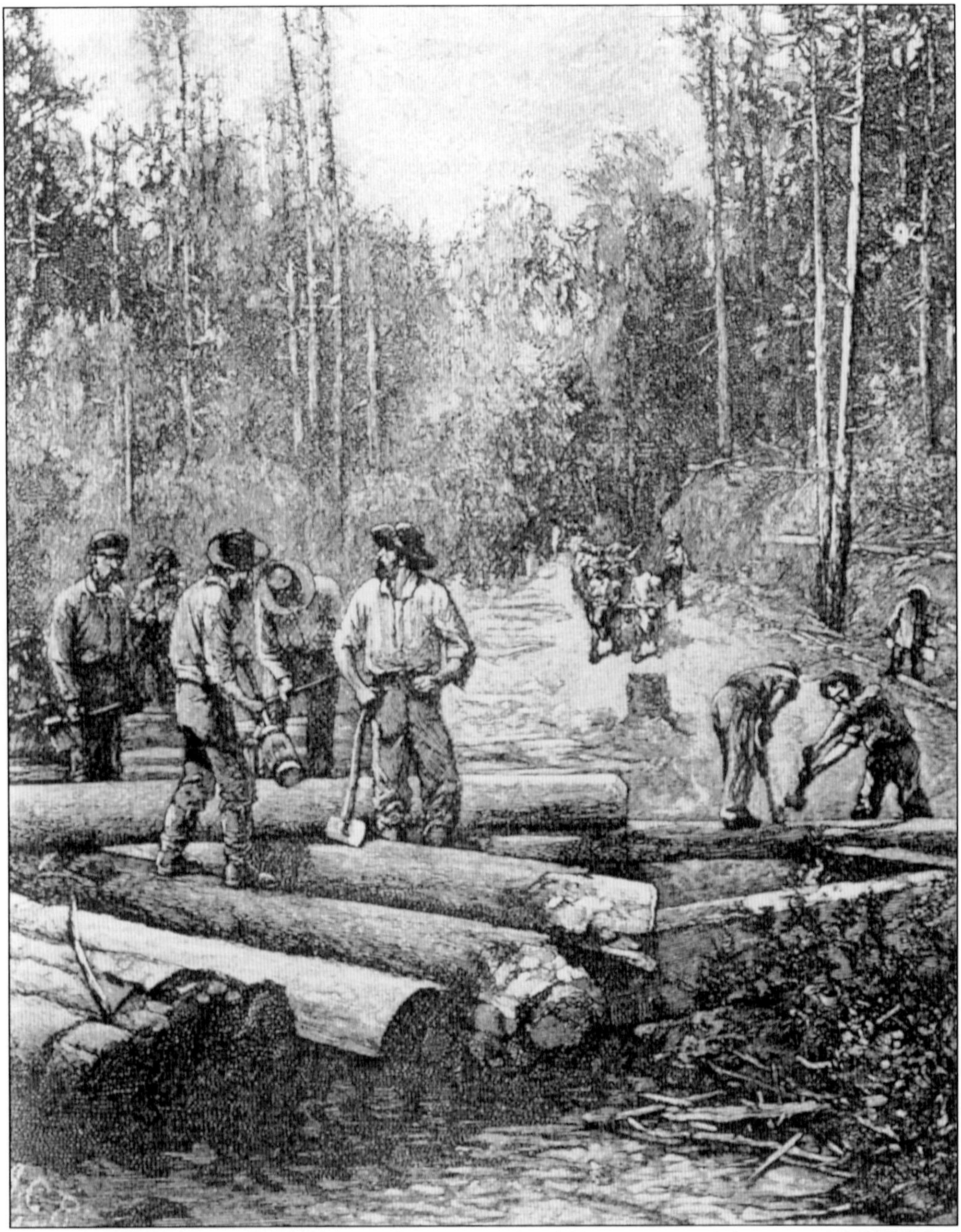

Harvesting the woods—lumbering on the river. It should be mentioned that some of the largest and most valuable pines were floated down the river for masts for the King's Navy. Lumber for spars, bowsprits, and masts were rafted down the Merrimack or were allowed to drift the Contoocook during high water. From the very first settlement of Boscawen, getting out ship timber and rafting them to Medford was the town's major industry.

There was shipbuilding on the river. Most of the timbers of the largest ships ever built in America, such as the four-mast clippers ship the *Great Republic* were prepared in the Nashua shipyard of Luther Robey, who furnished the material for more than one of the famous "ocean flyers."

Two

The Heart of the Valley
Manchester, Concord, Penacook, and Boscawen, New Hampshire

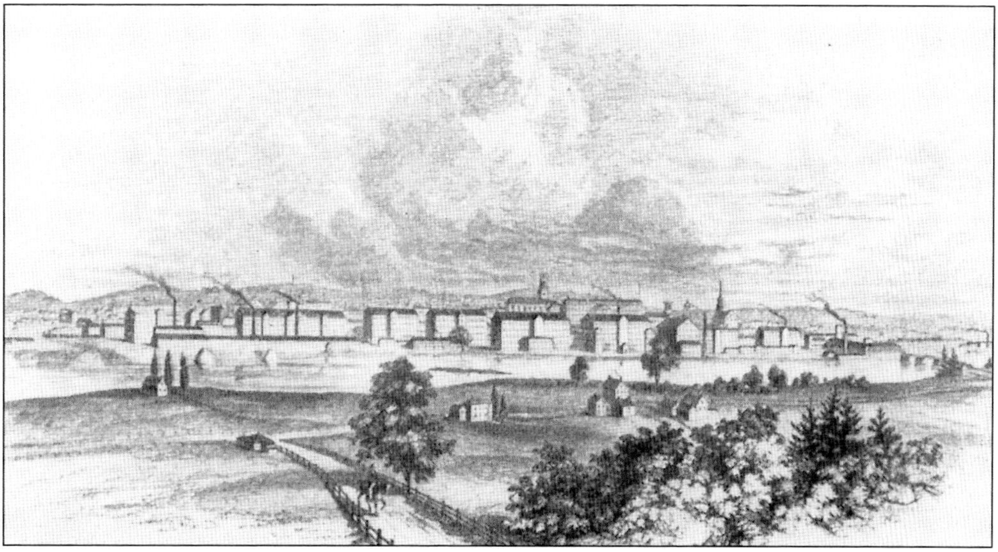

Manchester in 1855. This is an old print of Manchester taken from the west bank of the Merrimack River. During this period, Manchester became a leading industrial center of the Merrimack Valley. The first sawmills, built before the opening of the century by Blodget and Stark, were succeeded by the first of the mills that were destined to inaugurate one of the greatest manufacturing industries in the world, which has been instrumental in the building of this metropolis of New Hampshire.

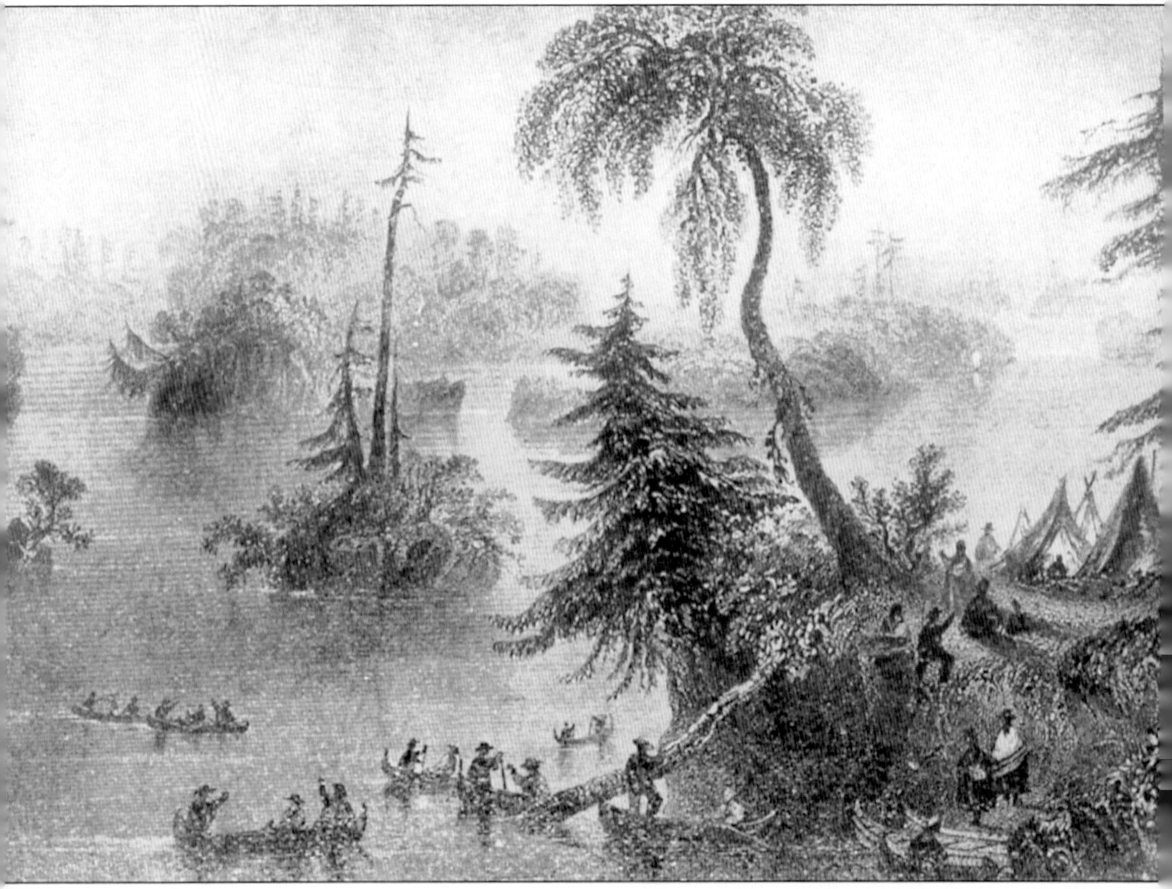

In the days of the voyageurs.The first white settler to build a dwelling in this territory was John McNiel, who was sent to the Falls to look after the interests of the Scotch-Irish people in Londonderry, *c.* 1722. No permanent settlement was made, however, until the grant of Tyng Township in April 1735. From that date a slow but certain growth followed until 1751, when upon September 3, a town was incorporated under the name of Derryfield. This name remained through the long and sanguinary years of the French and Indian War, the Revolutionary War, and the Reconstruction and Constitutional period following the struggle for independence. (A Bartlett Print)

Samuel Blodget. In 1810 this town became known as Manchester, so called after Manchester, England, upon the suggestion of Hon. Samuel Blodget, and its era of prosperity may be said to have dawned. Blodget's Canal had been completed three years before, and for thirty-five years the Merrimack was the maritime highway of business enterprise.

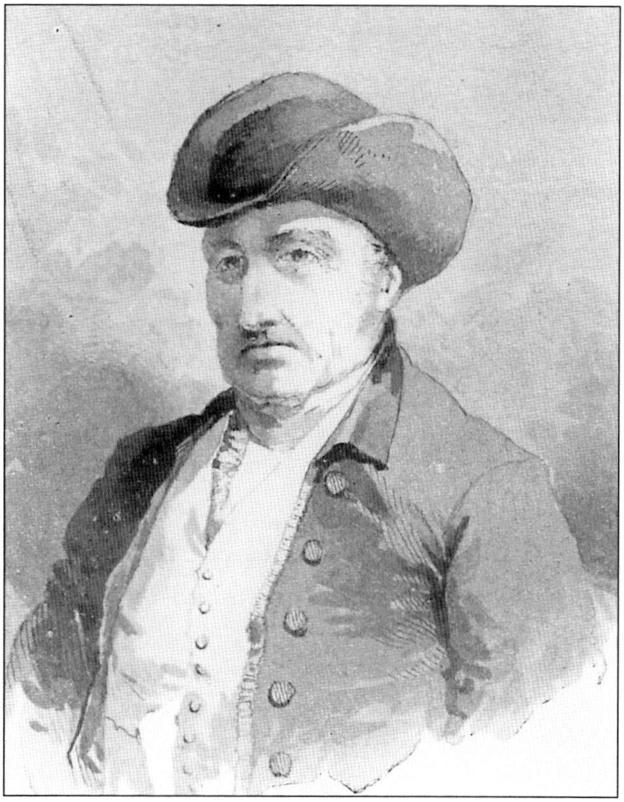

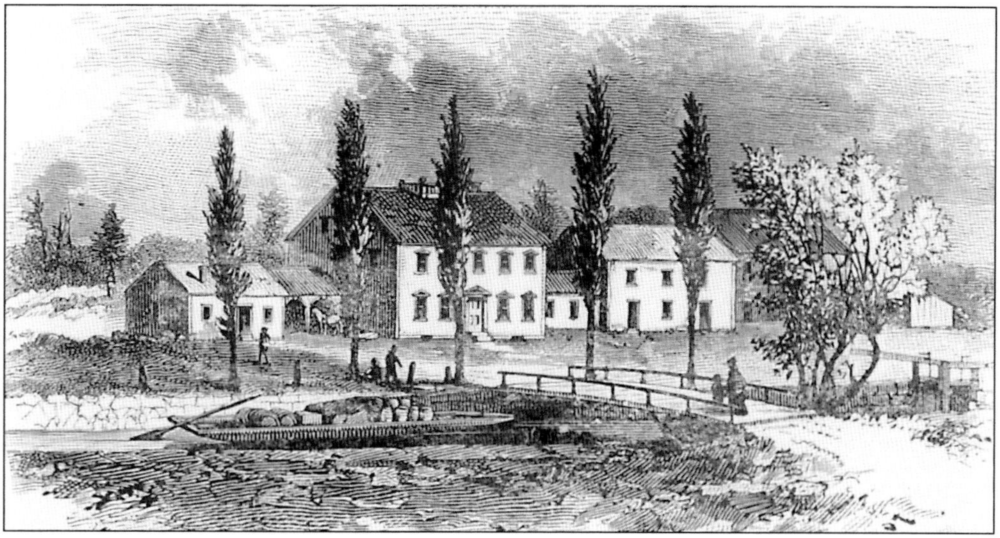

The Blodget Homestead, Manchester, N.H.

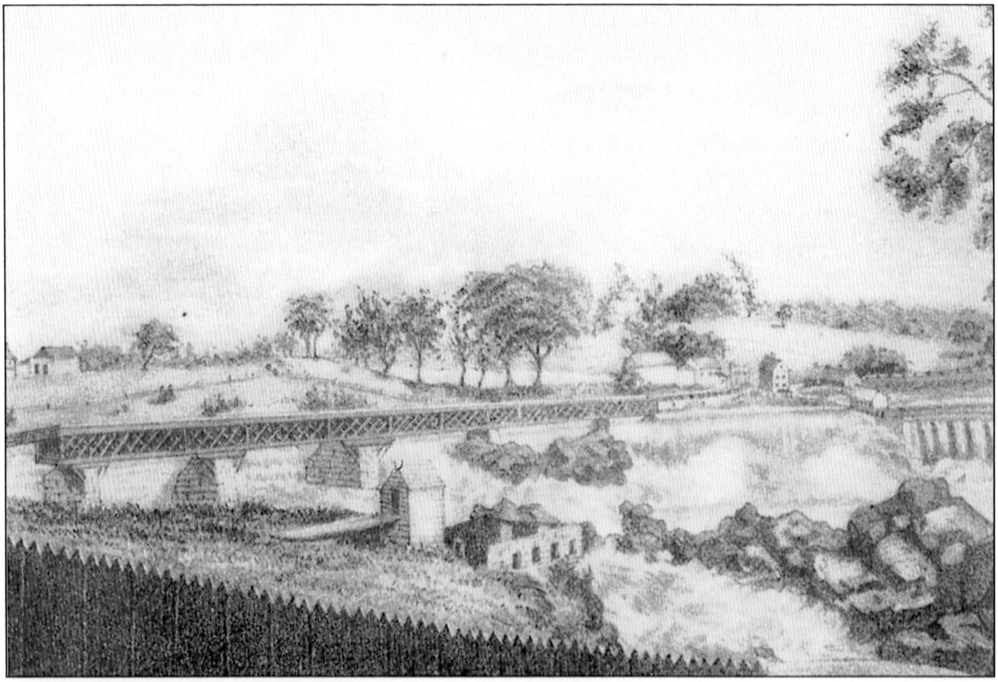
Amoskeag Falls from an old print.

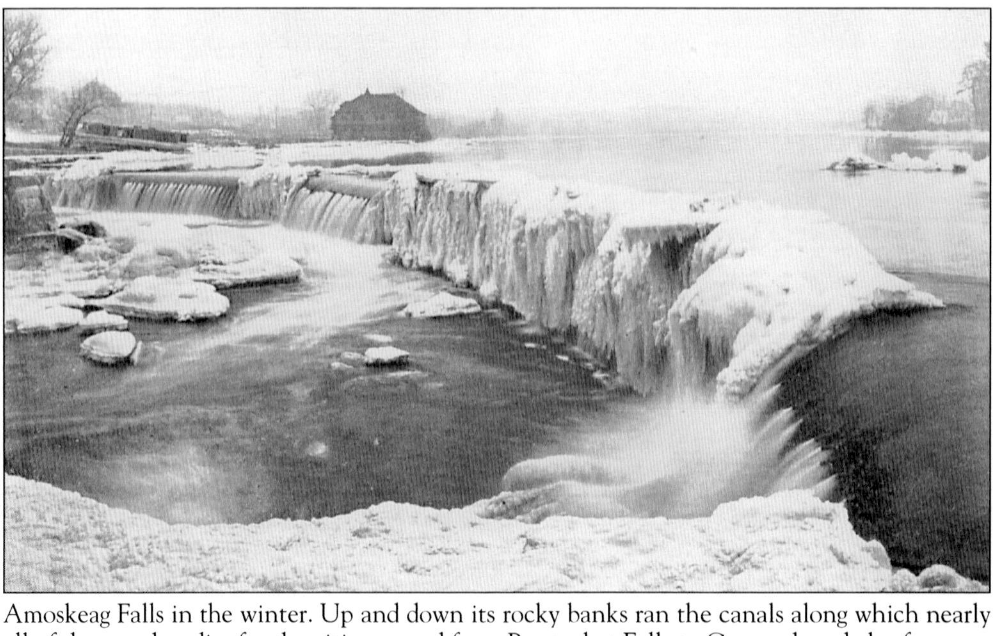
Amoskeag Falls in the winter. Up and down its rocky banks ran the canals along which nearly all of the merchandise for the cities moved from Pawtucket Falls to Concord, and also for some of the interior towns in the state.

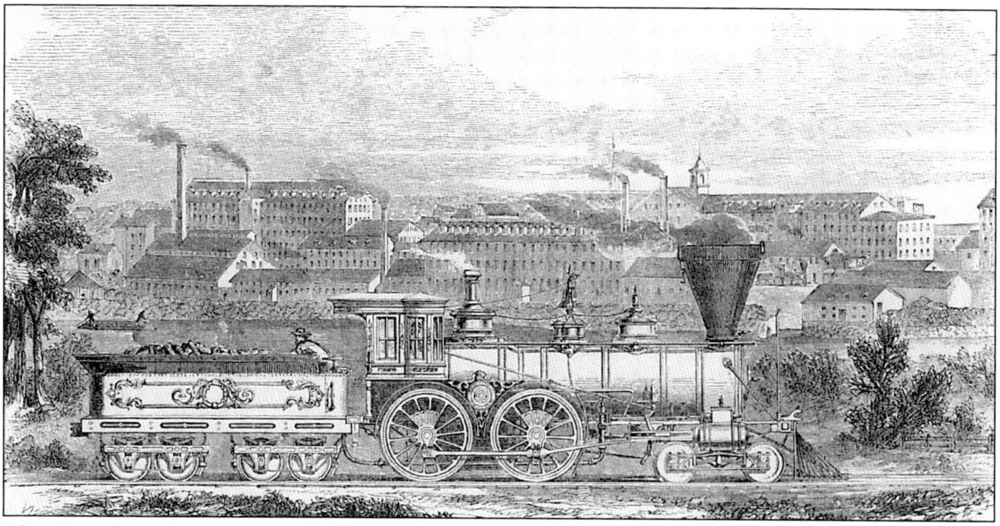

The Amoskeag Locomotive works. The Amoskeag Manufacturing Co., Manchester, N.H, was one of the largest and most flourishing in the U.S. Its charter empowered it to manufacture "woolen, cotton, iron, and other goods," and the apparently meaningless Native American name of Amoskeag was sent on bales of cotton, sheetin, and the like, to the farthest limits of America. The company was divided into five distinct departments, known as the Land and Water-Power Co.; Amoskeag New Mills; Amoskeag Machine Shop and Locomotive Works; the Amoskeag Batting Mill; and The Hooksett Co., at Hooksett. The construction of these works dated from about the year 1840.

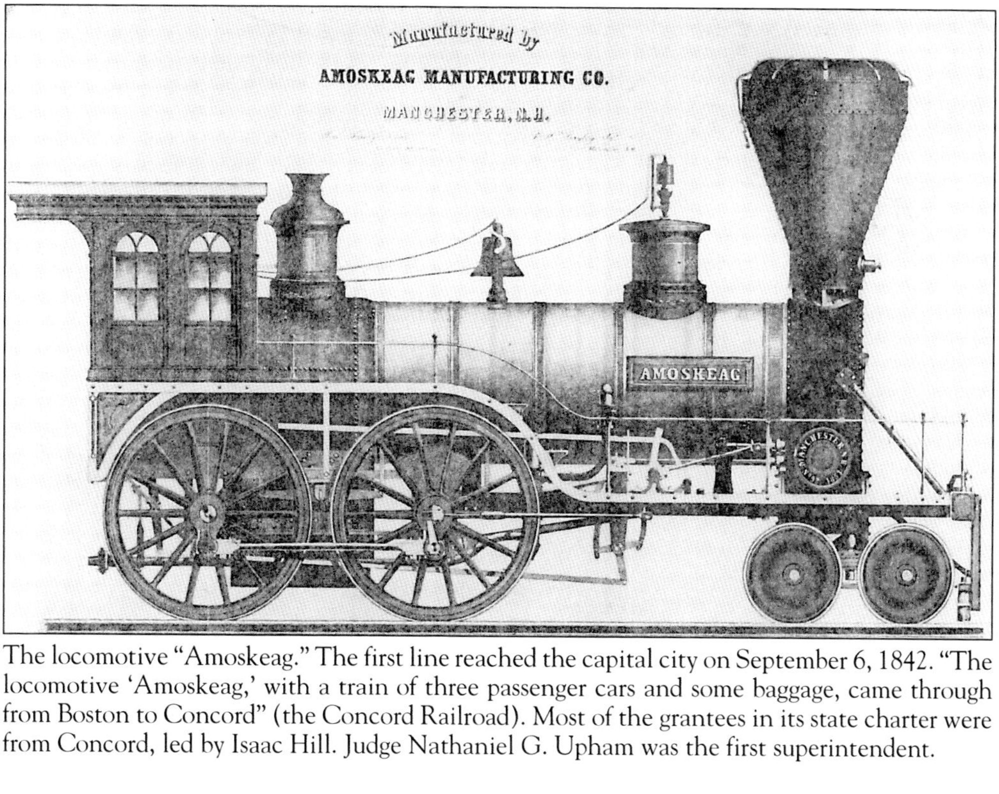

The locomotive "Amoskeag." The first line reached the capital city on September 6, 1842. "The locomotive 'Amoskeag,' with a train of three passenger cars and some baggage, came through from Boston to Concord" (the Concord Railroad). Most of the grantees in its state charter were from Concord, led by Isaac Hill. Judge Nathaniel G. Upham was the first superintendent.

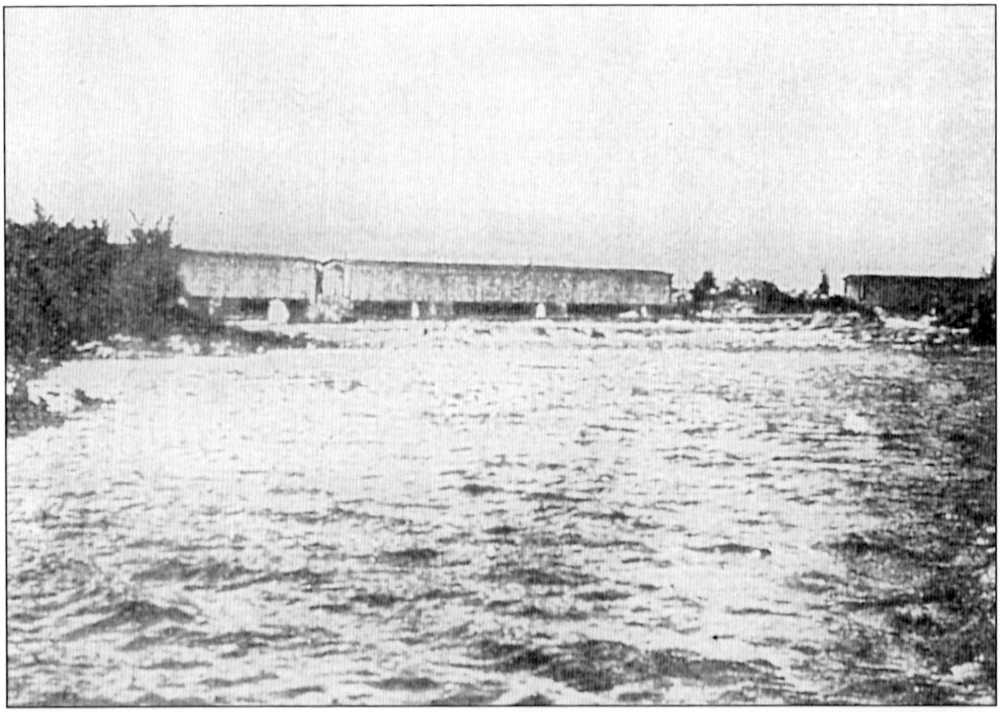

Hooksett Bridge, 1903.

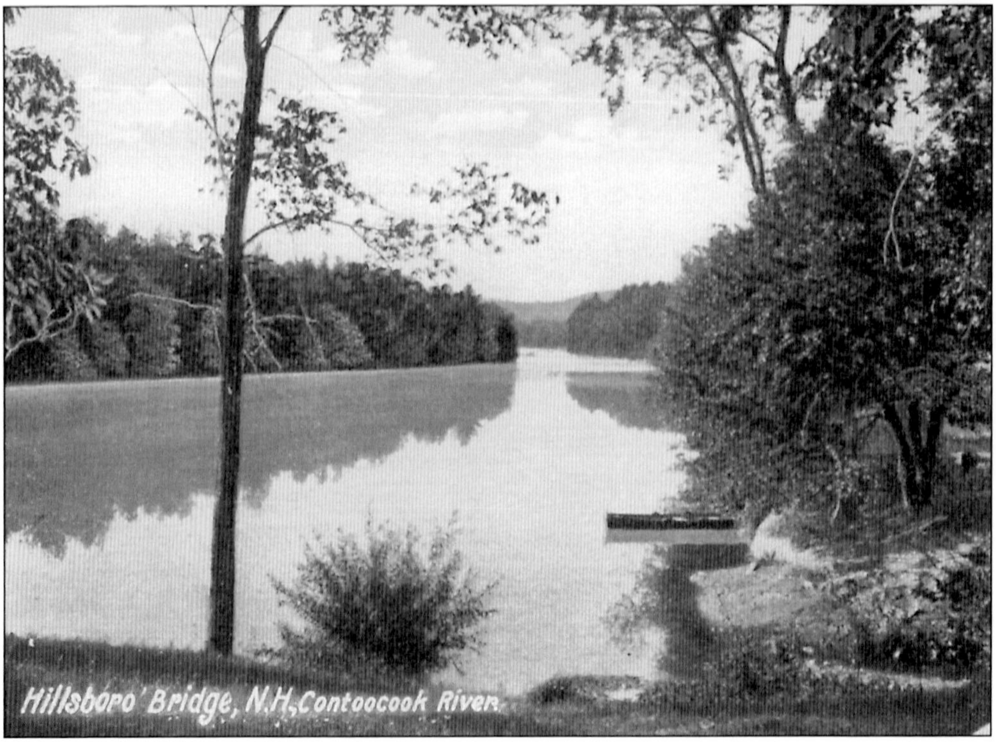

Hillsboro Bridge, Contoocook Pinnacle, 1903.

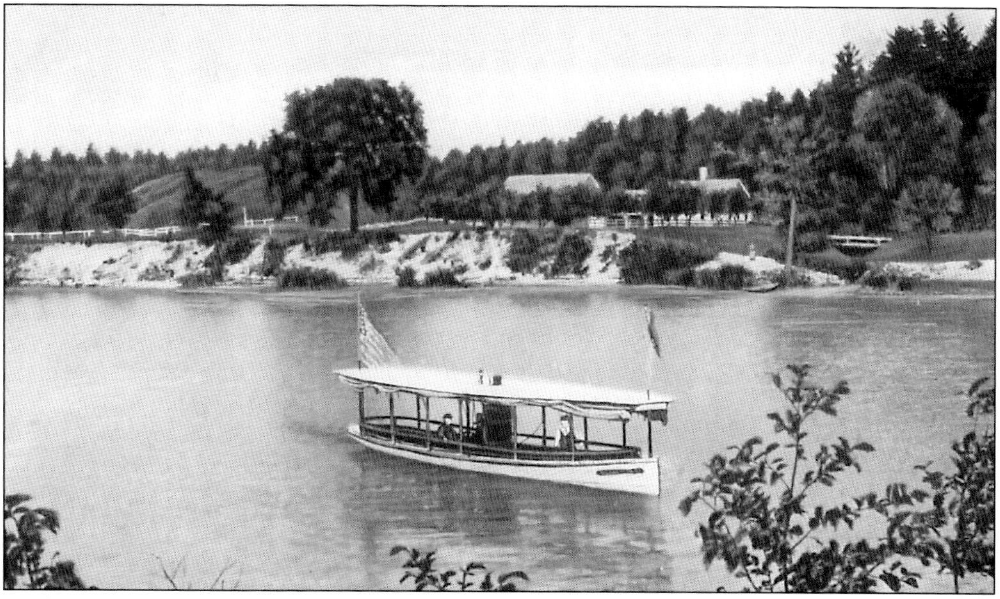

A pleasure steamboat cruising the Merrimack, November 9, 1909. Steamboating was a favorite pastime for the more elite in the vicinity.

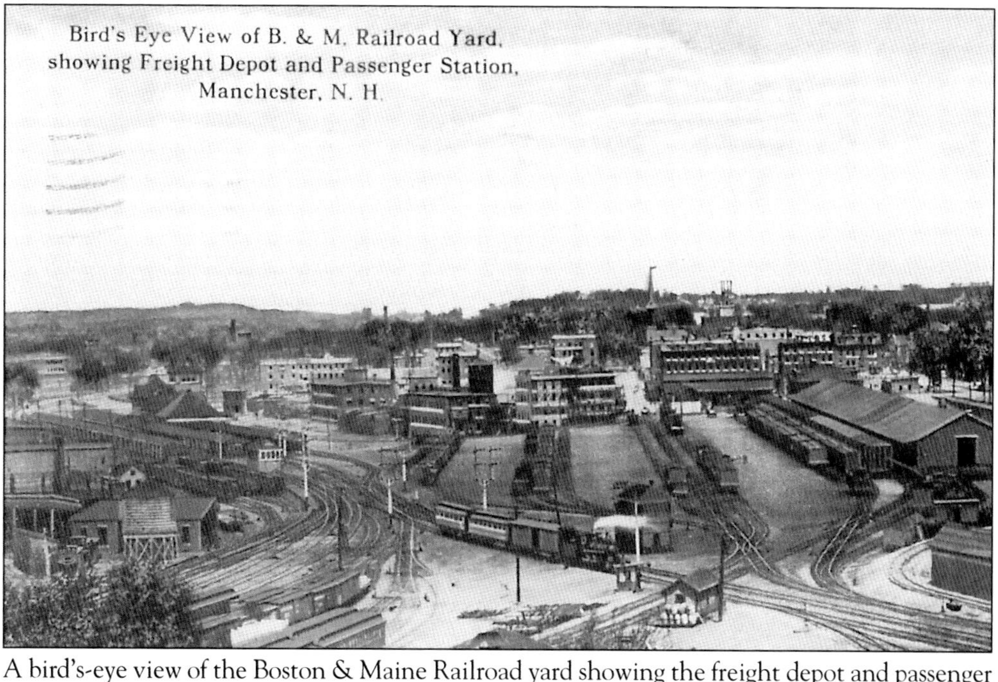

A bird's-eye view of the Boston & Maine Railroad yard showing the freight depot and passenger station, Elm Street, Manchester, N.H., 1920.

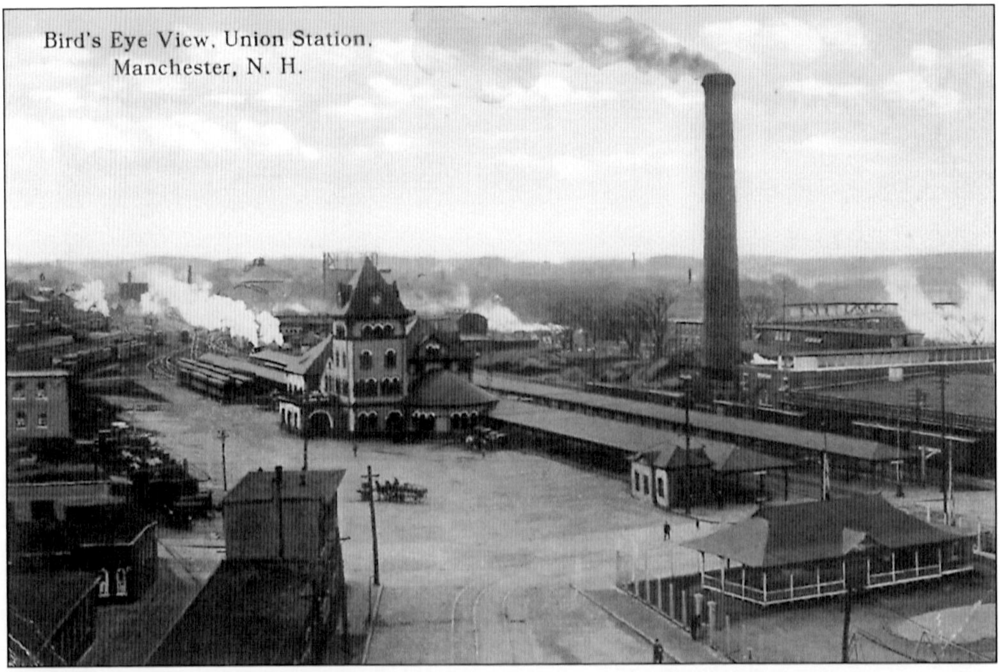

A bird's-eye view of the Manchester Union Station and rail complex, Manchester, N.H., 1915.

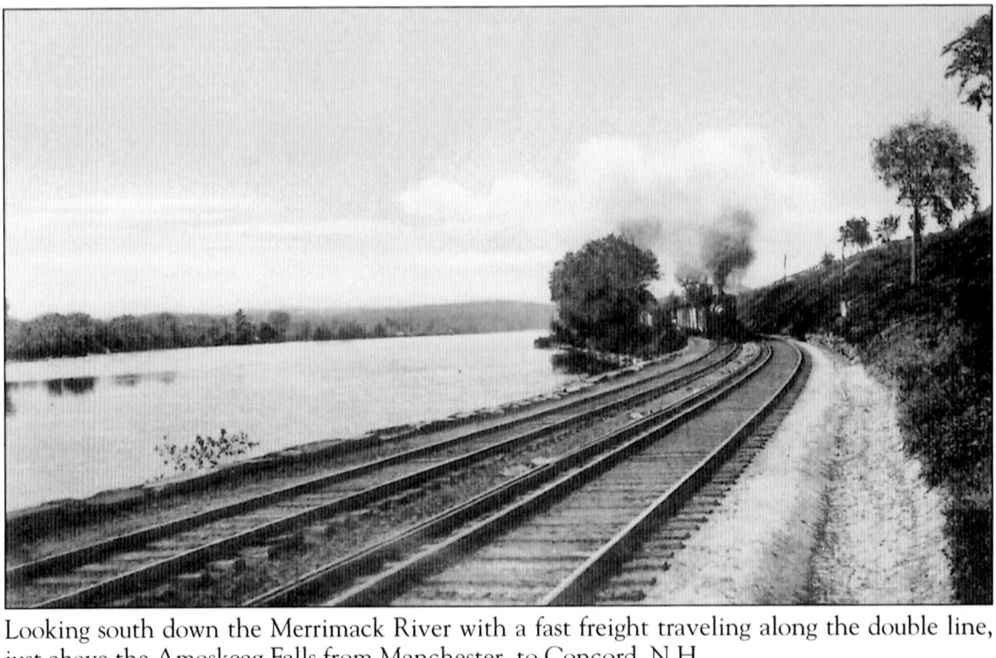

Looking south down the Merrimack River with a fast freight traveling along the double line, just above the Amoskeag Falls from Manchester, to Concord, N.H.

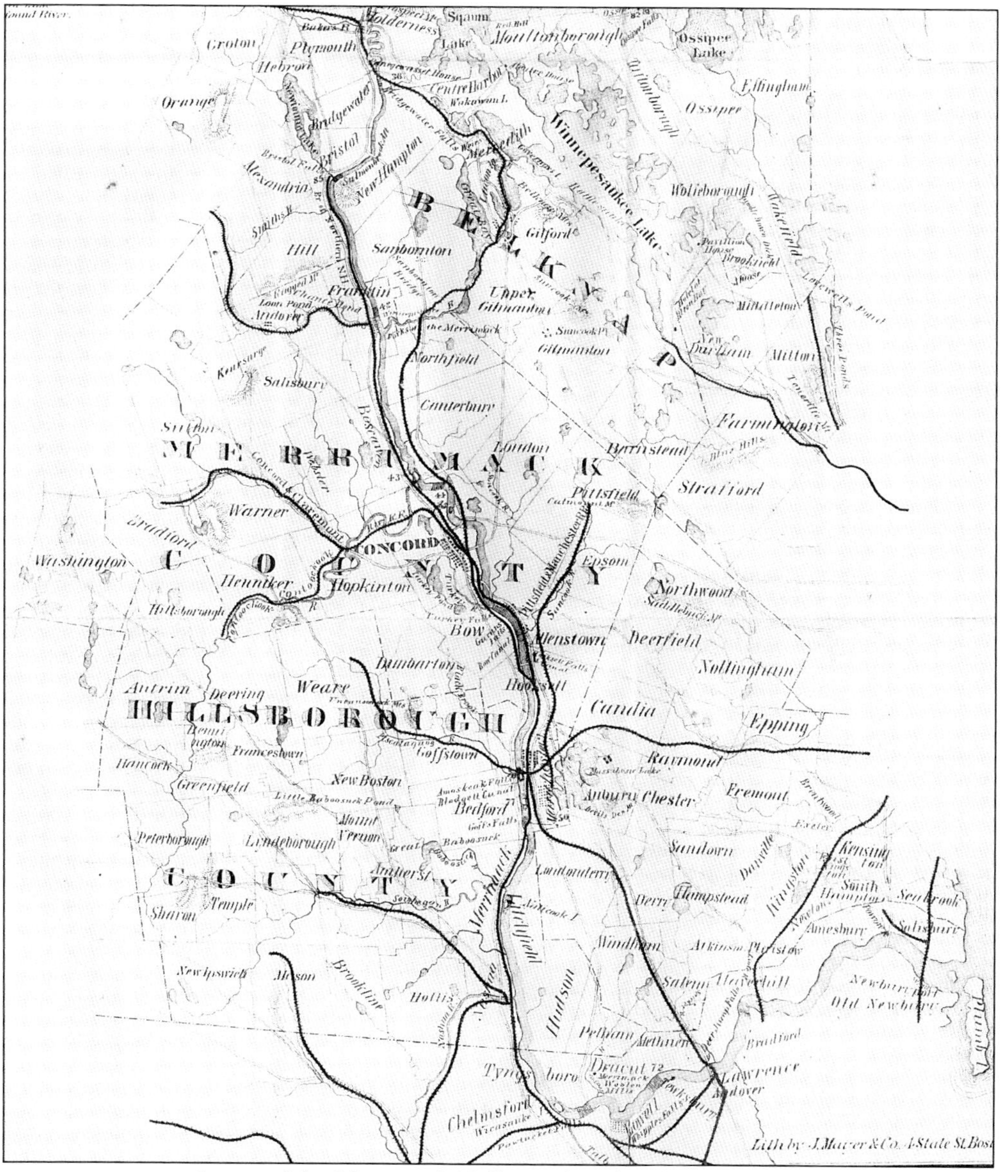

A map of the Merrimack Valley with railroad routes, 1872.

BOSTON TO WINNIPESAUKEE AND WHITE MOUNTAINS.

THROUGH SCHEDULE, IN EFFECT JUNE 28, 1886.

Miles.	STATIONS.	No. 51 Local.	No. 29 Mail.	No. 53 Mont'l Exp.	No. 75 Mt. Exp.	No. 145 Mont'l Exp.	No. 189 Local.	No. 285 Mont'l Exp.
		A.M.	A.M.	A.M.	A.M.	P.M.	P.M.	P.M.
....	Lv. Boston .... B. & L. R.R.	......	7.30	8.30	9.30	1.00	3.00	7.00
....	" Salem .... " "	......	......	7.50	9.10	12.40	......	6.50
....	" Lawrence (via Lowell) " "	......	......	8.15	9.30	12.05	3.15	6.40
26	" Lowell .... " "	......	8.30	9.20	10.14	1.48	3.53	7.48
40	" Nashua Junction... " "	......	9.00	9.46	10.40	2.13	4.20	8.20
57	" Manchester....... Concord R.R.	......	9.48	10.15	11.10	2.43	5.02	8.54
75	Ar. Concord .... " "	......	10.30	10.50	11.40	3.12	5.42	9.25
....	Lv. Concord .... B. & L. R.R.	6.55	11.00	10.55	11.42	3.17	5.50	9.30
84	" Canterbury .... " "	7.14	11.21	......	......	......	*6.17	*
88	" Northfield.......... " "	7.22	11.28	......	......	......	*6.24	*
93	" Tilton .... " "	7.32	11.39	11.27	......	3.50	6.35	10.11
97	" East Tilton.......... " "	7.39	11.47	......	......	......	*6.43	*
102	" Laconia .... " "	7.49	11.58	11.43	12.25	4.08	6.55	10.30
104	" Lake Village........ " "	7.54	12.03	11.50	......	4.12	6.59	10.35
109	" Weirs .... " "	8.03	12.13	12.00	12.36	4.23	7.09	10.46
119	Ar. Centre Harbor.......... Steamer	......	......	1.00	......	5.10	......	......
125	" Wolfboro'.............. "	10.10	......	3.05	......	7.00	......	......
113	Lv. Meredith .... B. & L. R.R.	8.10	12.21	12.08	......	4.32	7.16	10.55
121	" Ashland............ " "	8.28	12.38	12.28	......	4.51	7.34	11.14
126	Ar. Plymouth .... " "	8.38	12.50	12.40	1.05	5.02	7.45	11.26
....	Lv. Plymouth .... B. & L. R.R.	8.50	......	......	1.38	5.20	P.M.	......
128	Ar. Livermore Falls.... " "	8.55	......	......	1.51	5.26	......	......
130	" Blairs .... " "	9.05	......	......	1.55	5.30	......	......
134	" Campton Village... " "	9.14	......	......	2.03	5.38	......	......
135	" Thornton........... " "	9.22	......	......	2.07	5.42	......	......
140	" West Thornton .... " "	9.38	......	......	2.18	5.53	......	......
143	" Woodstock .... " "	9.49	......	......	2.25	6.00	......	......
147	" North Woodstock.. " "	10.00	......	......	2.35	6.10	......	......
154	" Flume House .... Stage	11.45	......	......	3.50	7.40	......	......
159	Ar. Profile House............. "	12.45	......	......	4.50	8.40	......	......
126	Lv. Plymouth .... B. & L. R.R.	8.48	1.40	1.15	1.35	5.17	......	11.36
131	Ar. Quincy .... " "	8.59	1.52	......	......	......	......	......
134	" Rumney............ " "	9.04	1.57	......	......	*	......	*
137	" West Rumney...... " "	9.11	2.04	......	......	......	......	*
142	" Wentworth......... " "	9.20	2.15	......	......	......	......	*
146	" Warren............ " "	9.28	2.23	1.50	......	5.50	......	12.23
155	" East Haverhill ..... " "	9.48	2.45	......	......	......	......	*
160	" Haverhill.......... " "	9.58	2.55	2.16	......	*6.18	......	*
163	" North Haverhill.... " "	10.05	3.03	......	......	*	......	*
....	" White Mt. Transfer " "	......	3.11	......	2.50	6.32	......	......
168	" Woodsville......... " "	10.15	3.15	2.30	......	6.38	......	‡1.20
....	Lv. Woodsville......... " "	10.40	4.00	—	......	......	......	‡7.05
173	Ar. Bath................ " "	10.57	4.13	P.M.	......	*6.42	......	7.16
178	" Lisbon............. " "	11.10	4.27	......	3.15	6.53	......	7.28
184	" North Lisbon ...... " "	11.23	4.42	......	......	......	......	7.41
189	" Littleton .... " "	11.35	4.54	......	3.37	7.14	......	7.52
195	" Wing Road......... " "	11.50	5.10	......	3.50	7.25	......	8.05
199	Ar. Bethlehem Junc.... " "	12.04	5.26	......	4.04	7.37	......	8.17
201	Ar. Maplewood...... P. & F. N. R.R.	12.15	5.40	......	4.16	7.50	......	8.32
202	" Bethlehem ...... " " "	12.20	5.45	......	4.21	7.55	......	8.37
209	" Profile House ... " " "	2.18	6.05	......	4.40	8.13	......	8.55
203	Ar. Twin Mt. House.... B. & L. R.R.	12.15	5.38	......	4.16	7.48	......	8.31
207	" White Mt. House... " "	12.23	5.48	......	......	......	......	8.43
208	" Fabyan's........... " "	12.25	5.50	......	4.28	8.00	......	8.45
209	" Mt. Pleasant House " "	12.35	5.55	......	4.35	8.05	......	9.25
213	" Crawford House... P. & O. R.R.	......	6.00	......	5.00	8.30	......	9.20
217	Ar. Summit Mt. Wash... Mt. W. Ry	......	......	......	6.30	......	......	11.00
195	Lv. Wing Road .... B. & L. R.R.	11.55	5.15	......	4.00	7.27	......	8.28
200	Ar. Whitefield.......... " "	12.08	5.28	......	4.13	7.36	......	8.43
210	" Jefferson........... W. & J. R.R.	12.30	5.55	......	4.40	8.00	......	9.10
202	" Scott's .... B. & L. R.R.	12.14	5.34	......	4.19	7.42	......	—
204	" Dalton.............. " "	12.18	5.37	......	4.23	7.46	......	......
206	" South Lancaster... " "	12.23	5.43	......	4.29	7.50	......	......
211	" Lancaster.......... " "	12.35	5.55	......	4.40	8.00	......	......
217	" Guildhall........... " "	......	6.50	......	6.50	......	......	......
221	Ar. Groveton .... " "	......	7.00	......	7.00	......	......	......
		P.M.	P.M.		P.M.	P.M.		A.M.

* Stops on signal to take, or on notice to Conductor, to leave passengers.

Boston to Winnipesaukee and the White Mountains, Boston & Lowell Railroad schedule, 1886.

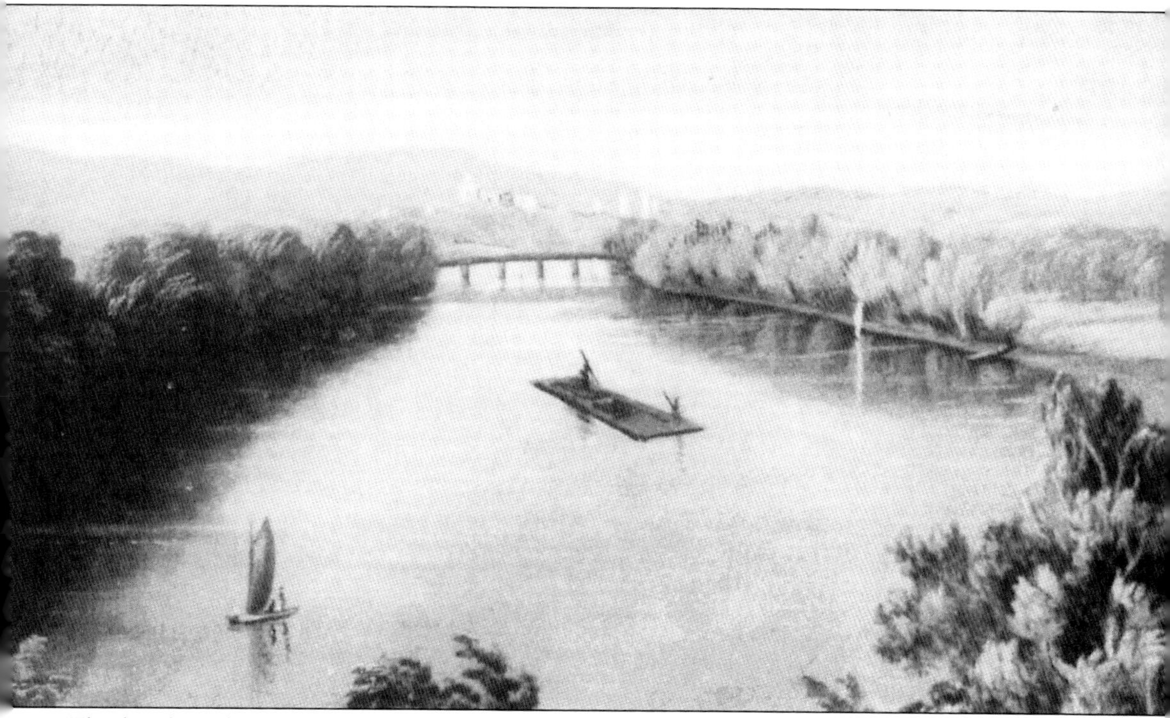

The bend in the river, Concord, N.H. The first white settler in this territory was Captain Ebenezer Eastman, who built a block house here in 1727. The territory was granted by the Massachusetts Bay Colony on January 17, 1725, to Benjamin Stevens and ninety-nine others. The following year the town was laid out to measure 7 square miles. Captain Eastman was one of the grantees. At first the Native Americans (the Pennacooks) were friendly, but for nearly twenty years (1744–62) there was a great deal of tension between the two sides, which kept the inhabitants awakened to a sense of their dangerous situation.

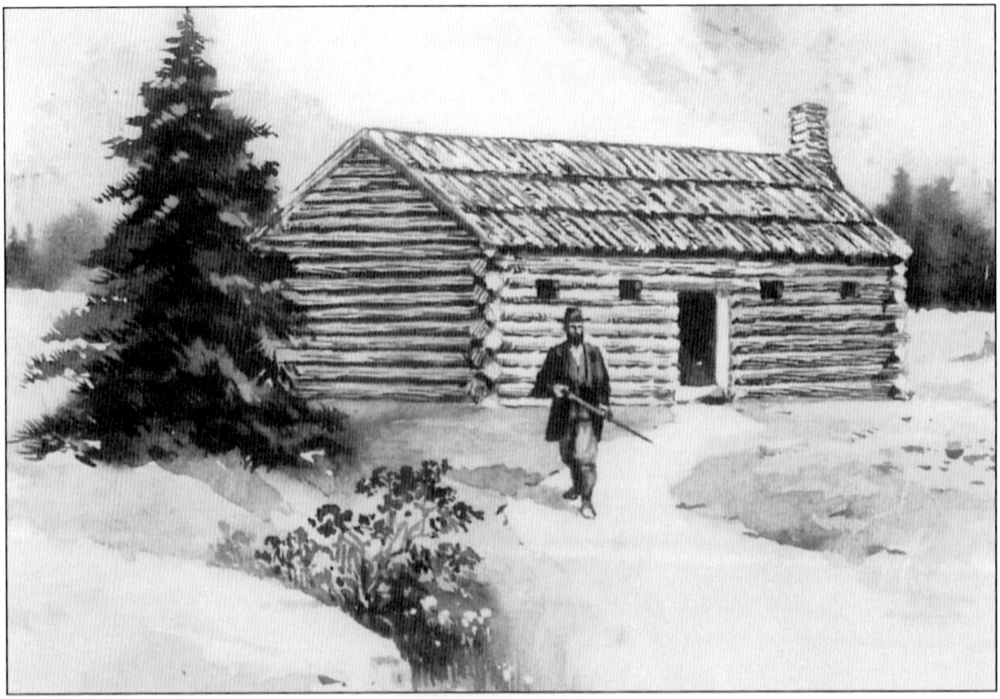

The first meetinghouse and blockhouse. As granted, the settlement had legal status as "The Plantation of Pennycook." Having erected a village and set up a government, the settlers secured incorporated township status from Massachusetts in 1734. The new town was named Rumford, since some of the settlers had been born in a parish of that name in England.

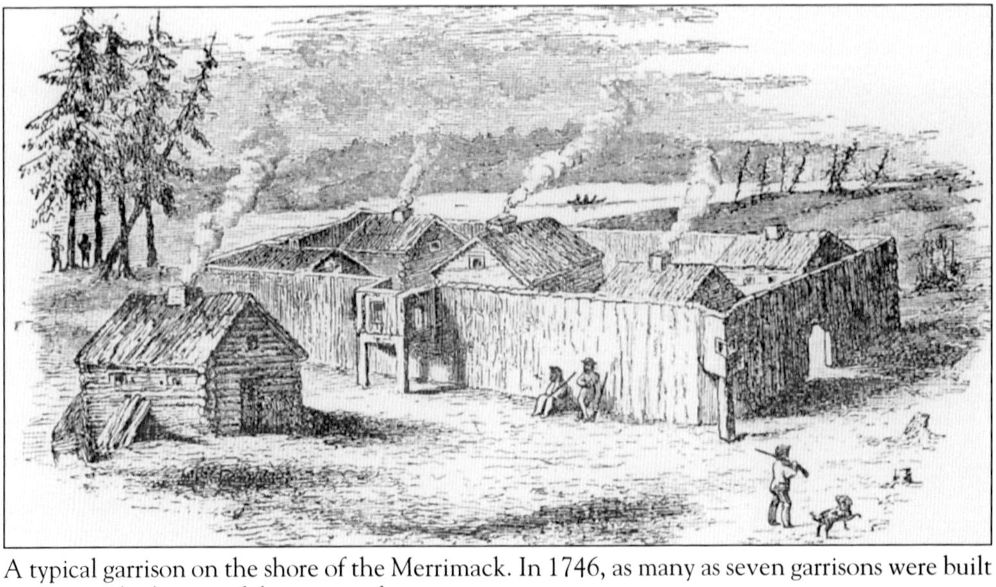

A typical garrison on the shore of the Merrimack. In 1746, as many as seven garrisons were built to protect the homes of the new settlers.

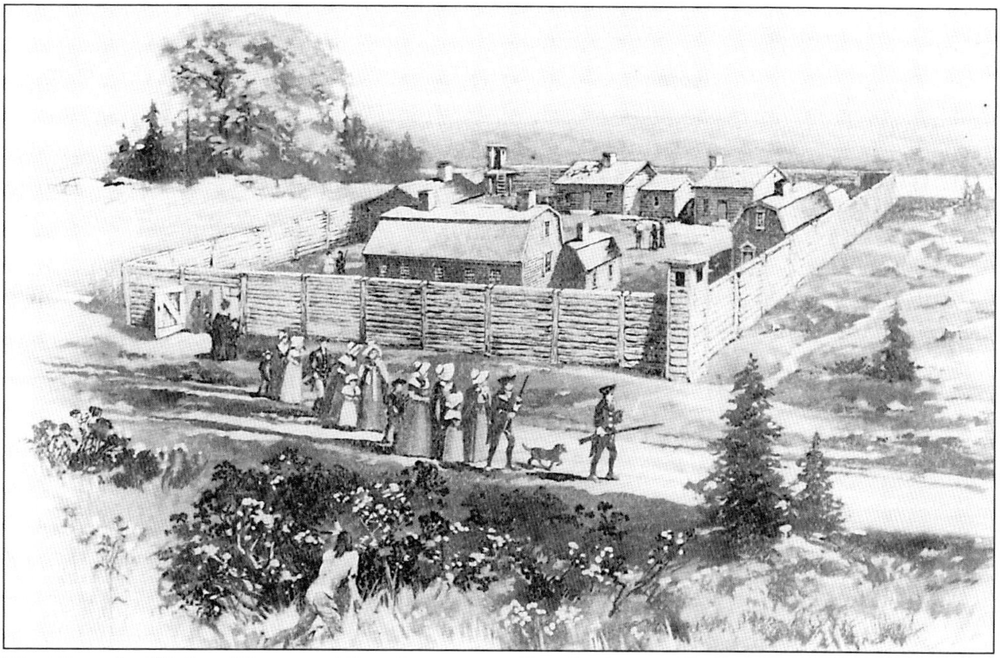

The Timothy Walker House and Fort (garrison at Rumford, now Concord, N.H.), 1734. Despite these precautionary measures, an attack from Native Americans took place on August 11, 1746. Five men were killed and two were carried off as captives.

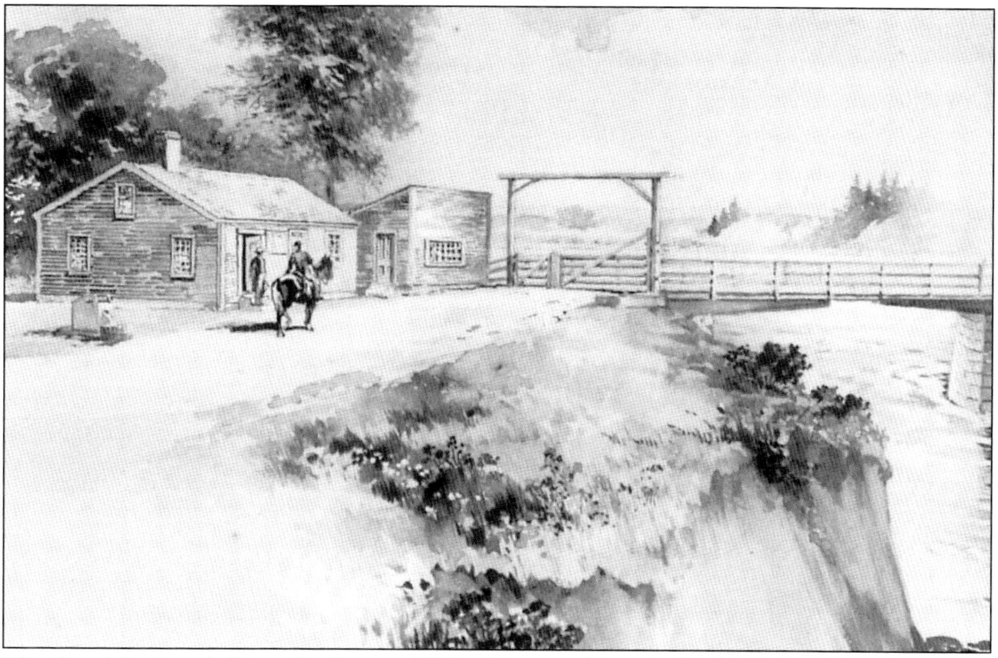

The first Merrimack River bridge, *c.* 1700s. Merrimack's west bank was reached by canoes; horses and oxen swam across. For many years ferries were the only means of crossing the river and when someone suggested bridging the Merrimack, there was ". . . great consternation up and down the valley. The shad would be frightened away! Navigation would be obstructed. There would be an interference of the normal movement of the tides."

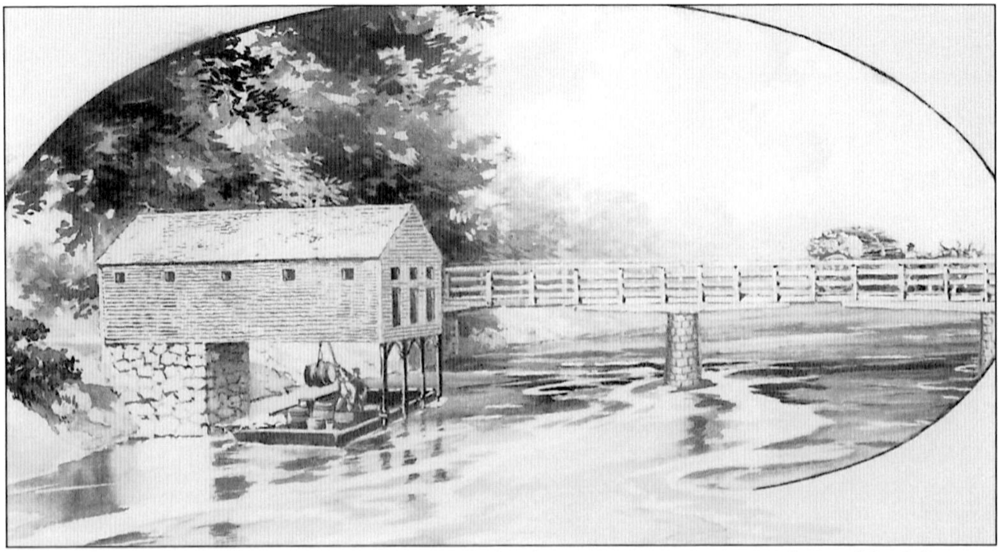

The Boston Boat Line terminal, at the lower bridge. In 1729, a new road, roughly following Manchester Street, was cut from the Gashouse area to connect with the first road, near the "Broken Bridge" spot on the Soucook. Until Henry Rolfe put in a ferry here, the Soucook had to be forded. A boat furnished ". . . fit to carry people and creatures" was ordered by the townsmen for use at Main Street's lower end. John Merrill was the first ferryman.

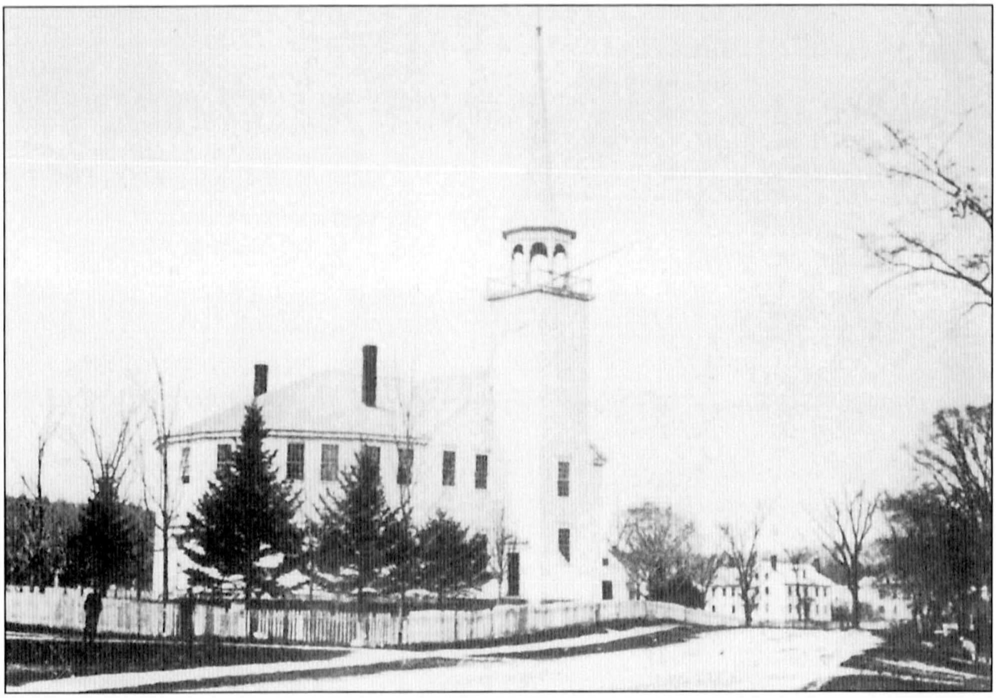

The Old North Meeting House. Concord assumed self-government again in 1766, with the first town meeting since 1749. In 1778, Concord was picked by the legislature as the site for a constitutional convention, to draft a replacement for the statute whereby New Hampshire became a state in 1776. The new state constitution became effective June 2, 1784, and Concord was selected as the seat of government for inauguration of the governor and the legislature.

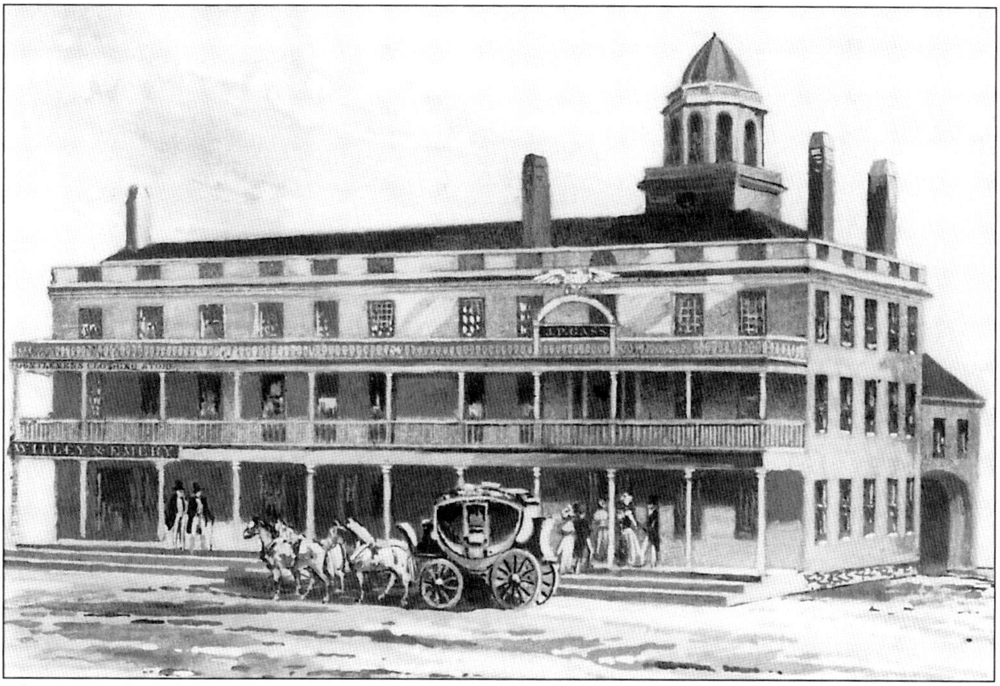

The original Eagle Coffee House, built in 1827. It was in the Grecian Hall of this inn that many events were held, political and otherwise; it was the heartbeat of the social elite of the state.

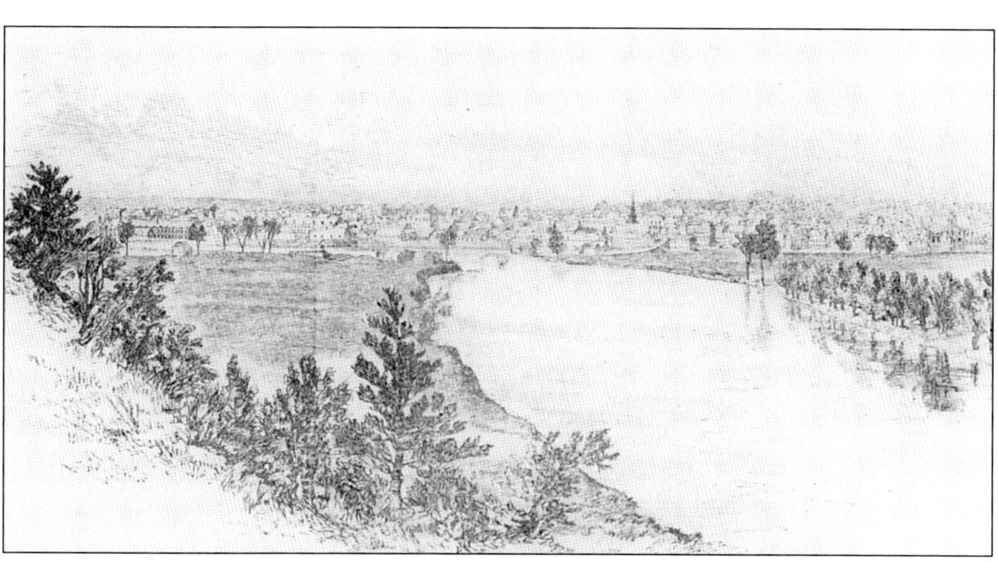

Concord in 1855 as seen from the bend in the river.

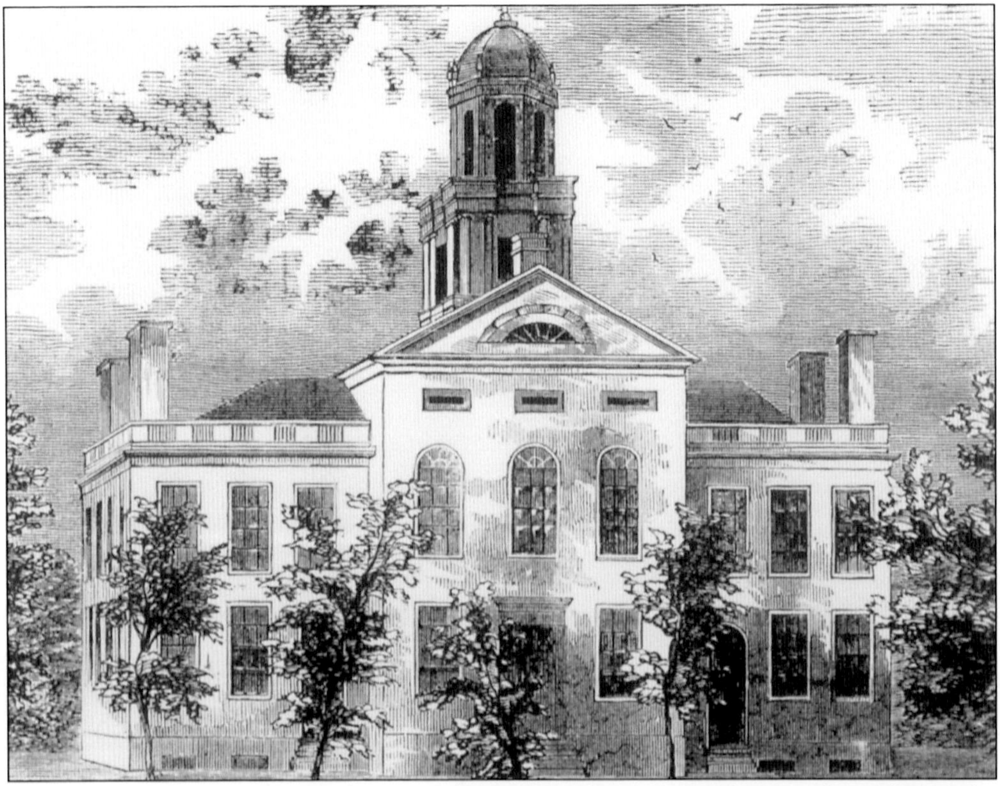

New Hampshire's State House, 1816–19. New Hampshire's State House is the oldest in the nation with a legislature still occupying its original chambers. The capitol was originally a two-story parallelogram which was surmounted by a silo-like dome. The center of the building is 50 in front by 57 feet in depth; the wings are each 38 feet in front by 49 feet in width, with the addition of a projection in the center of each front. "It is two stories above the basement, which rose five feet above the surface of the ground; the first story being 19 feet; the second, 18 feet in the wings and 31 feet in the center."

"When the State House opened in 1819, the House had a membership of 192 and there were 12 members in the Senate. The Speaker's stand was on the west side and there were six seats to each for the Senate to sit when in joint session."

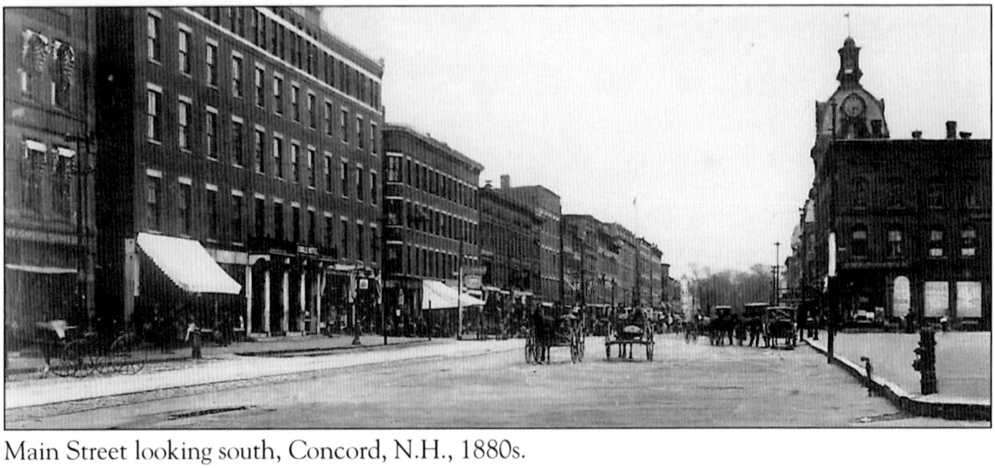

Main Street looking south, Concord, N.H., 1880s.

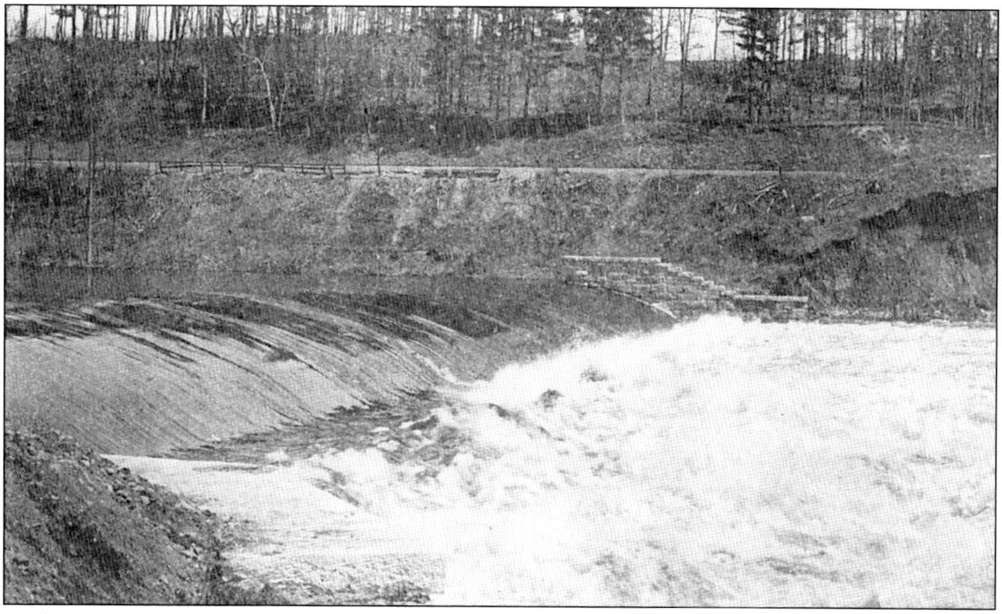

High water on Merrimack River at Sewalls Falls near Concord. The dam is 497.5 feet long, and at flood stages the water is 14 feet deep.

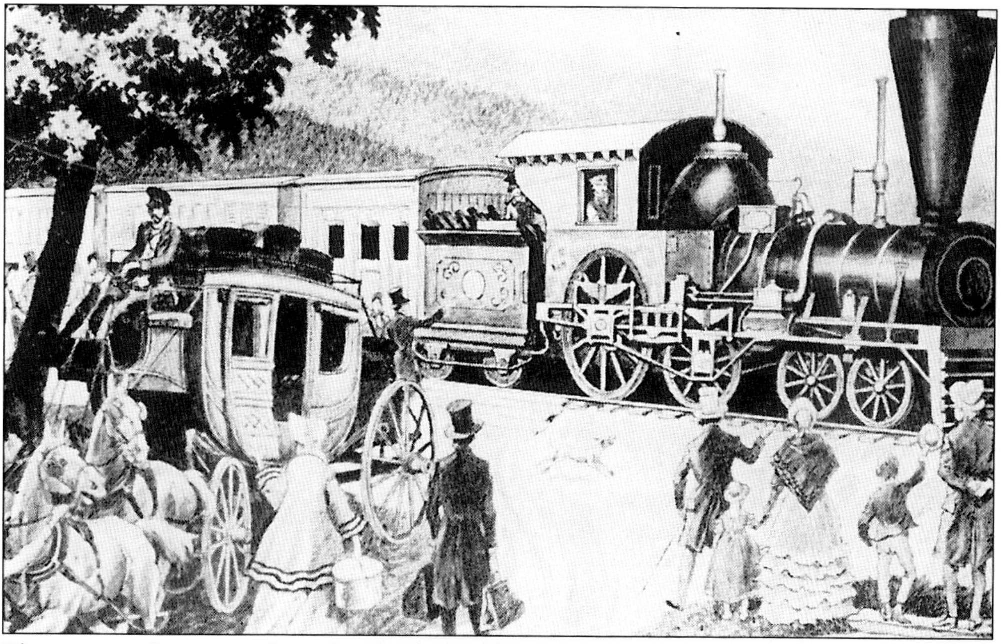

The stagecoach meeting the railroad. The building of railroads soon put the the stagecoach out of business for traveling in those early days was at the speed of 20 or 30 miles an hour; thereby leaving the stagecoach far behind. Pictured is the arrival of such an early train, c. 1849. "The engine came up in grand style, and when opposite our village, gave one of its most savage yells, frightening men, women and children considerably." The objections to the building of railroads sound ludicrous to many: "The farmers would be ruined"; "Horses would have to be killed because wholly useless"; "There would be no market for oats or hay"; "There would be constant fires from sparks from the engines"; "It would cause insanity."

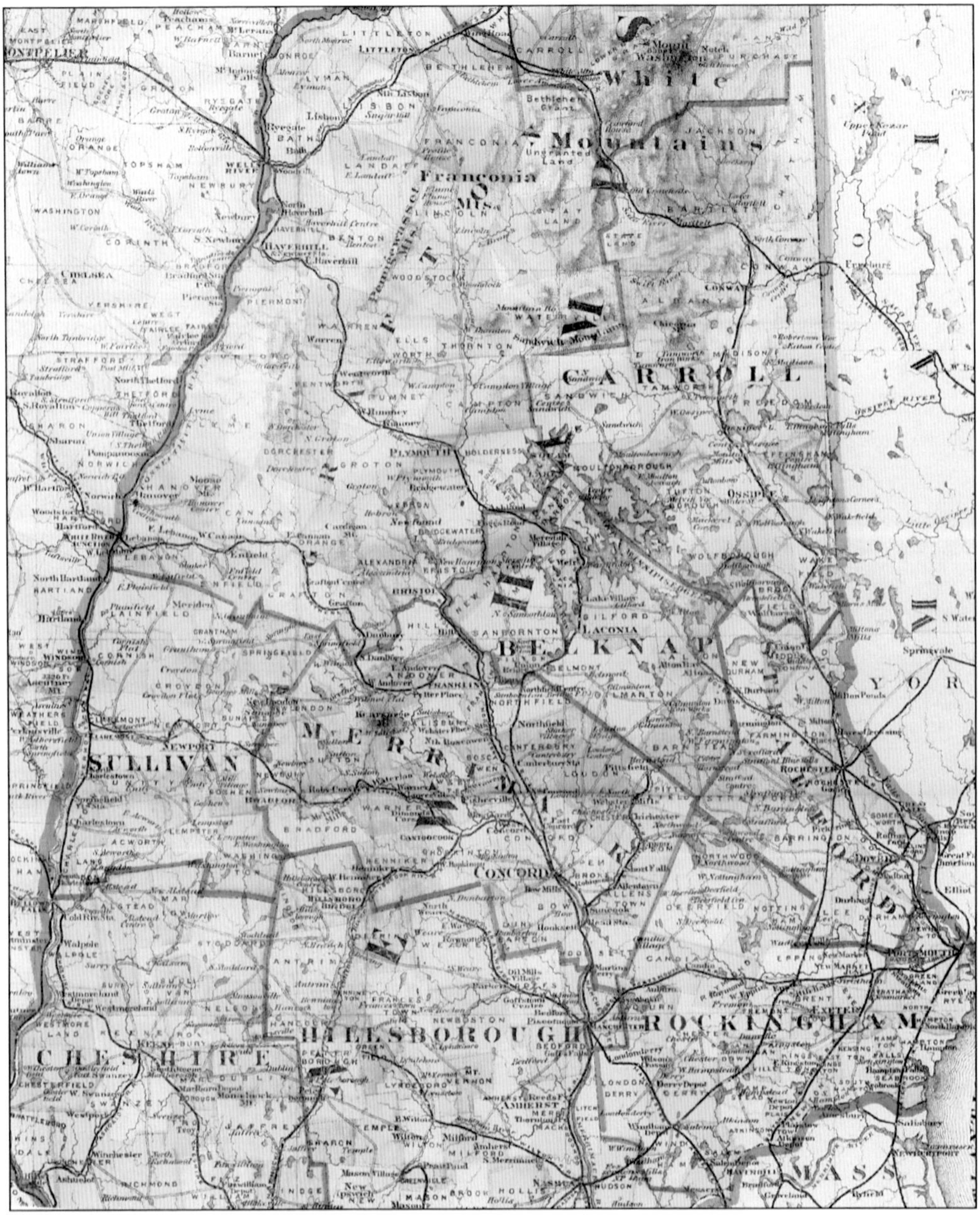

A detail from a railroad and post office map of New Hampshire, 1877.

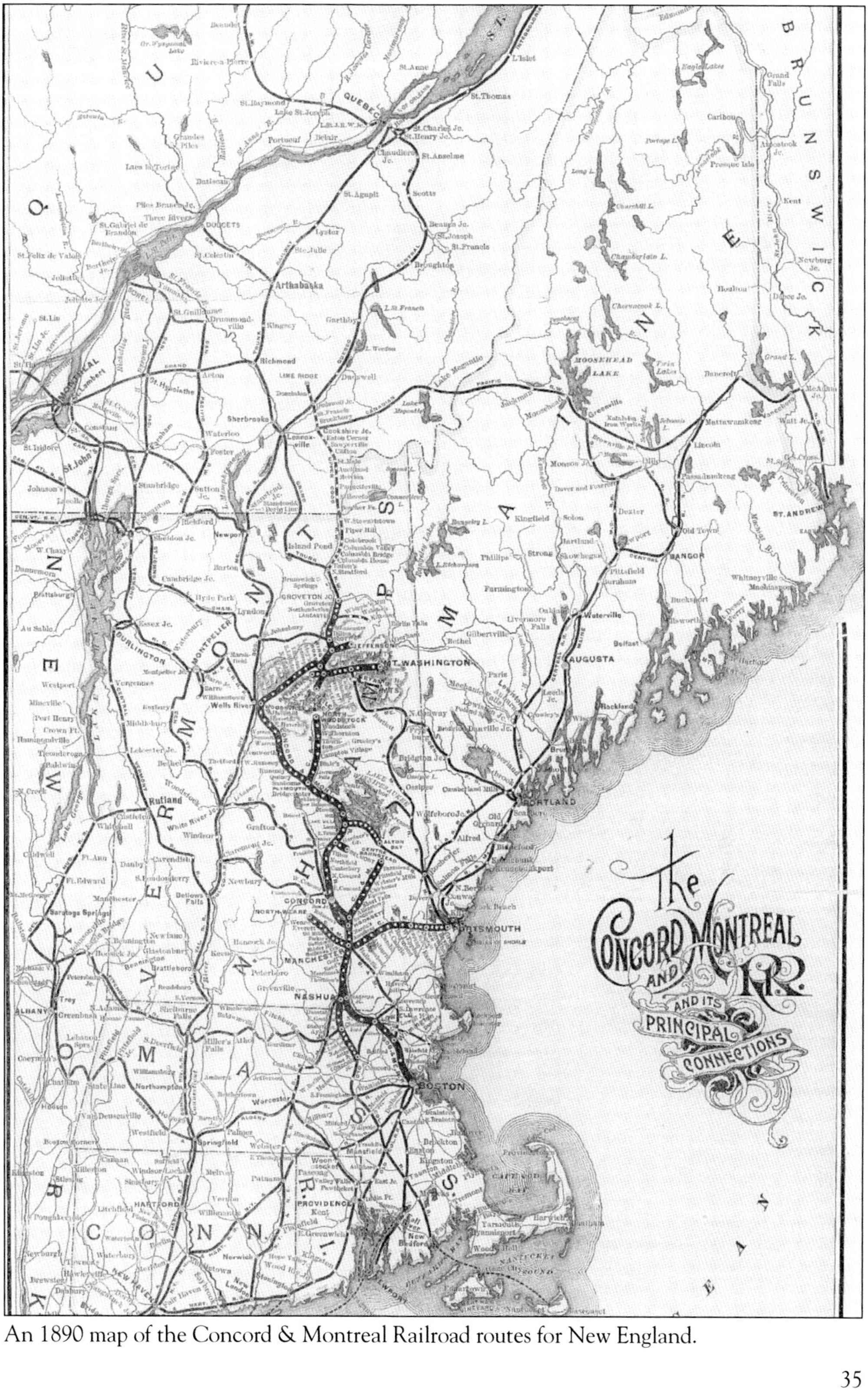

An 1890 map of the Concord & Montreal Railroad routes for New England.

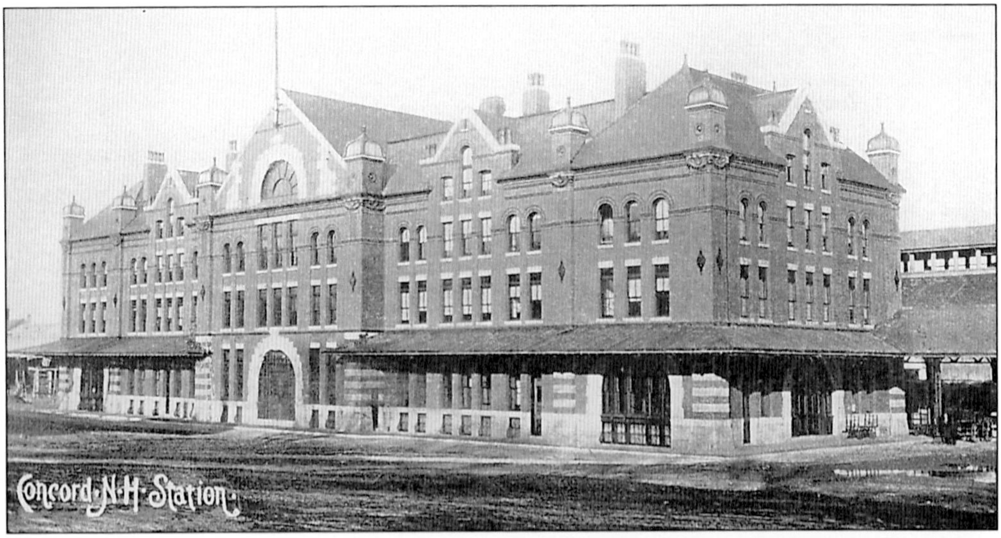

Concord & Montreal Railroad station, Concord, late 1880s. This passenger station was one of the finest edifices of its kind. The entire establishment occupied upwards of 2 acres of land. The style was that of the English Renaissance. The main building was 280 feet long and 65 feet wide, and contained three completely furnished stories, a basement, and an attic. It was constructed of dark red brick, with base-walls and window sills of Concord granite. The rotunda in the center measured 60-by-65 feet and divided the building into two wings.

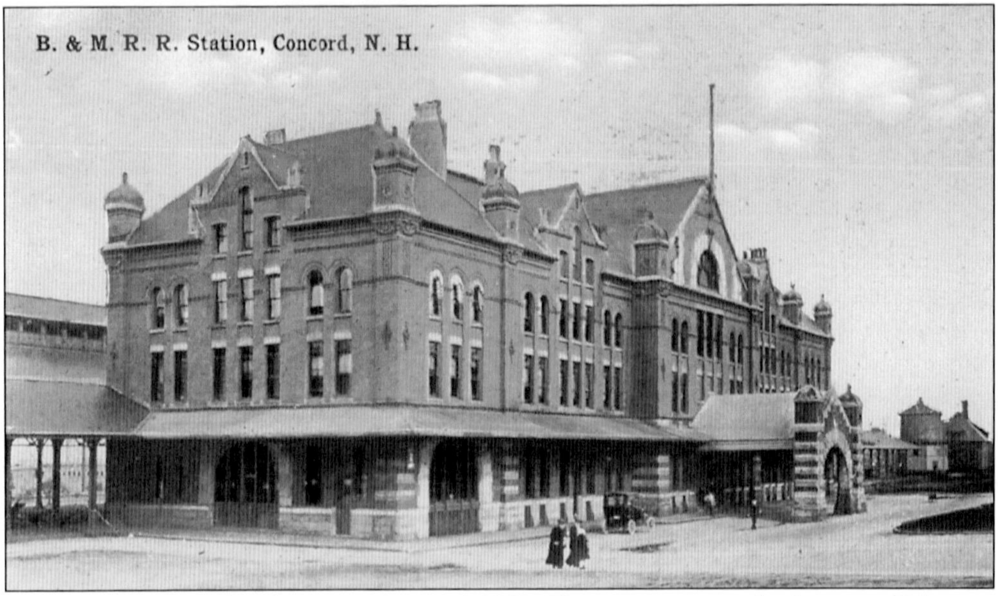

Boston & Maine Railroad station, Concord, N.H. This station sat at the bottom of Pleasant Street. The railroad era flourished for more than a century. It multiplied population, paid millions in wages and taxes, and made the community a freight transfer and "make-up" point. "Railroad Square" was once the largest building in northern New England. Passenger engines such as "Tahanto," "Souhegan," "Penacook," "General Stark," Ixion," and "Rob Roy" traveled up and down the tracks hauling "the cars" north, south, and west. The ponderous station is gone, along with Railroad Square; in the early 1960s, it was supplanted by a shopping center, a retailing town within a city.

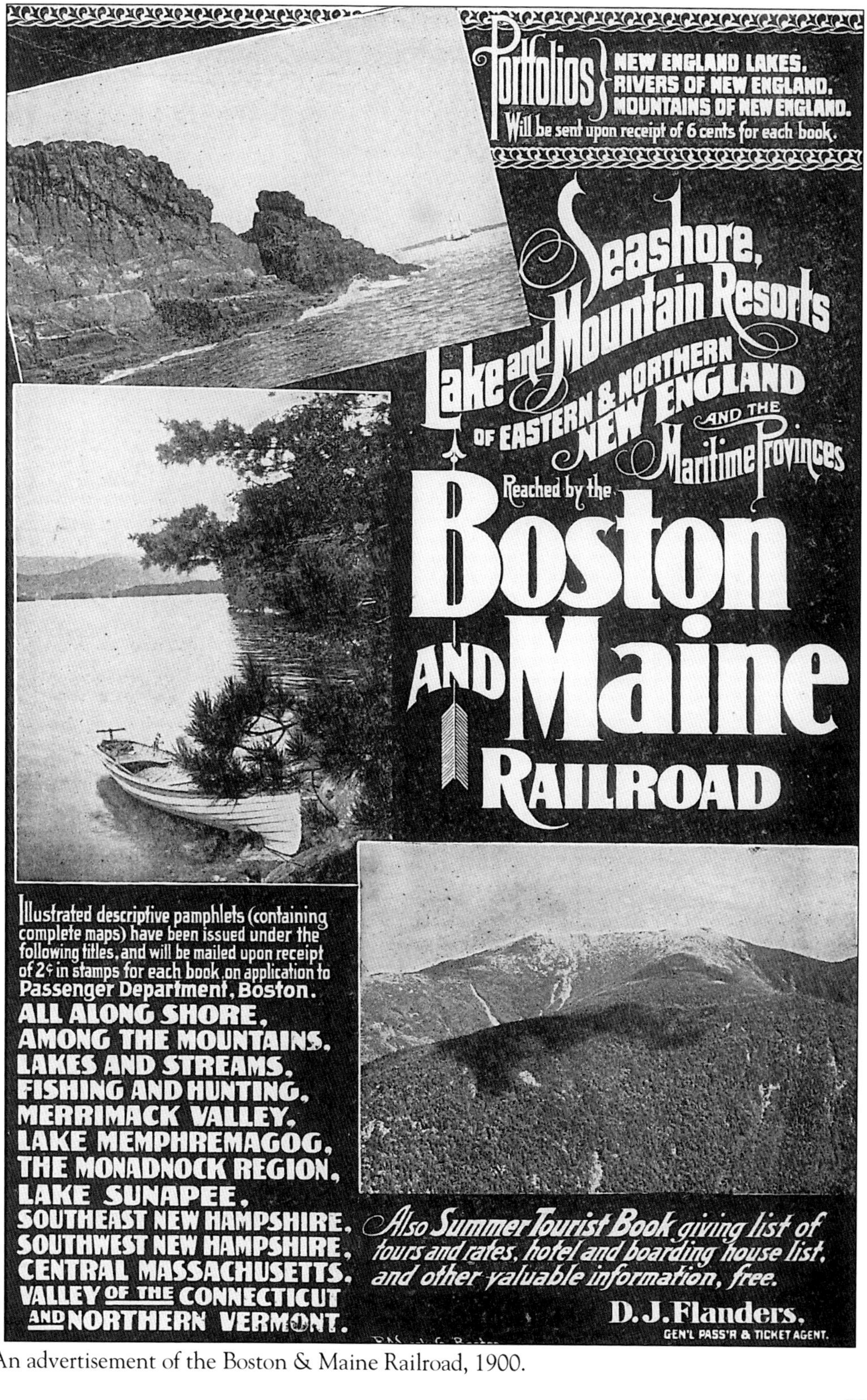

An advertisement of the Boston & Maine Railroad, 1900.

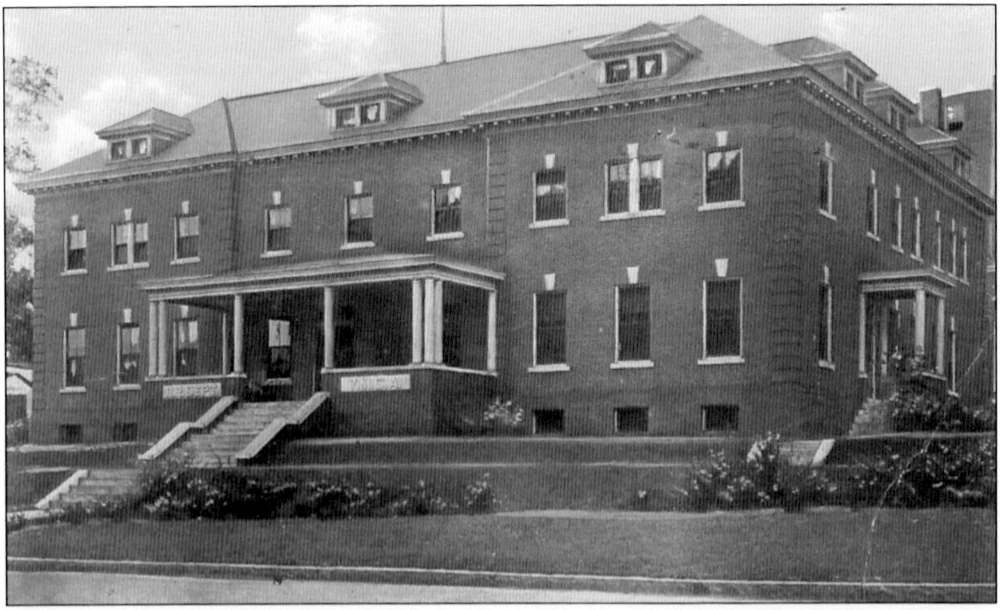

The Concord Railroad YMCA, located in front of the railroad station. The building has been replaced by a parking lot, *c.* 1900.

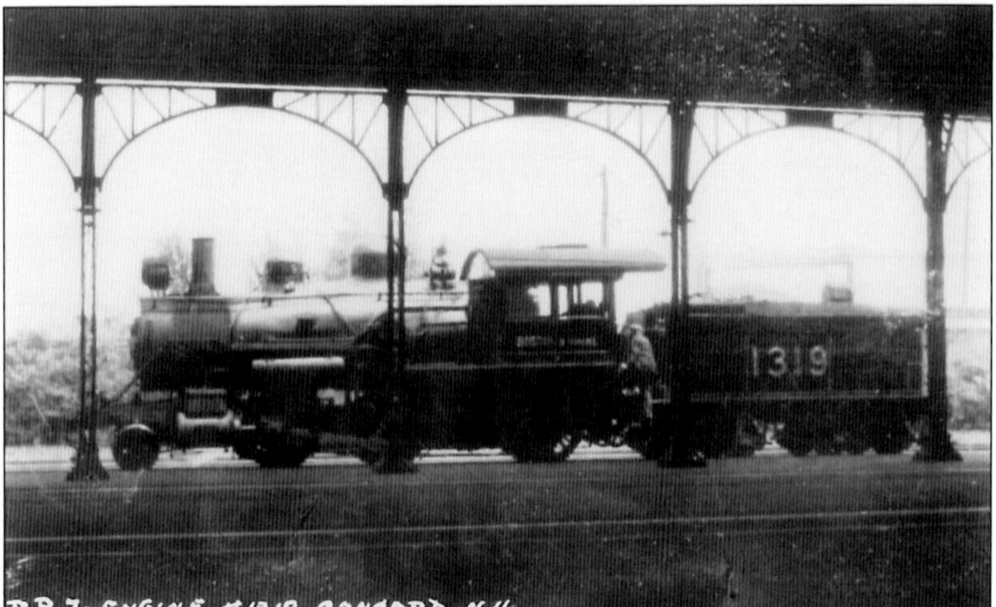

The Boston & Maine Railroad Engine No. 1319 as it sits at the railroad station in Concord, N.H. Note the engineer stepping into the cab for a daily run.

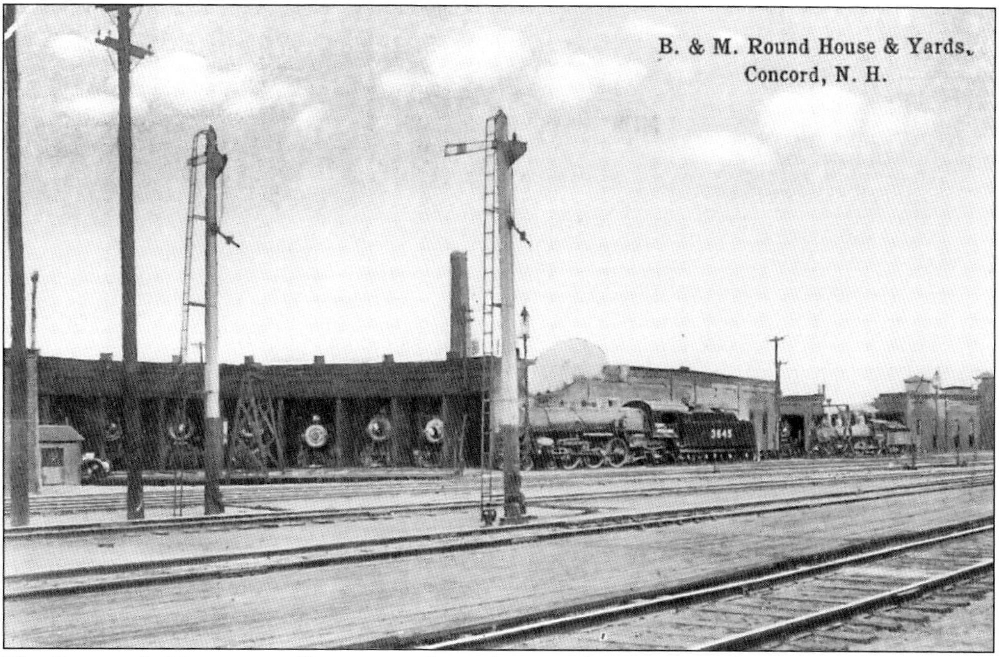

The Boston & Maine roundhouses, yards, and repair shops just north of the railroad station, c. 1892.

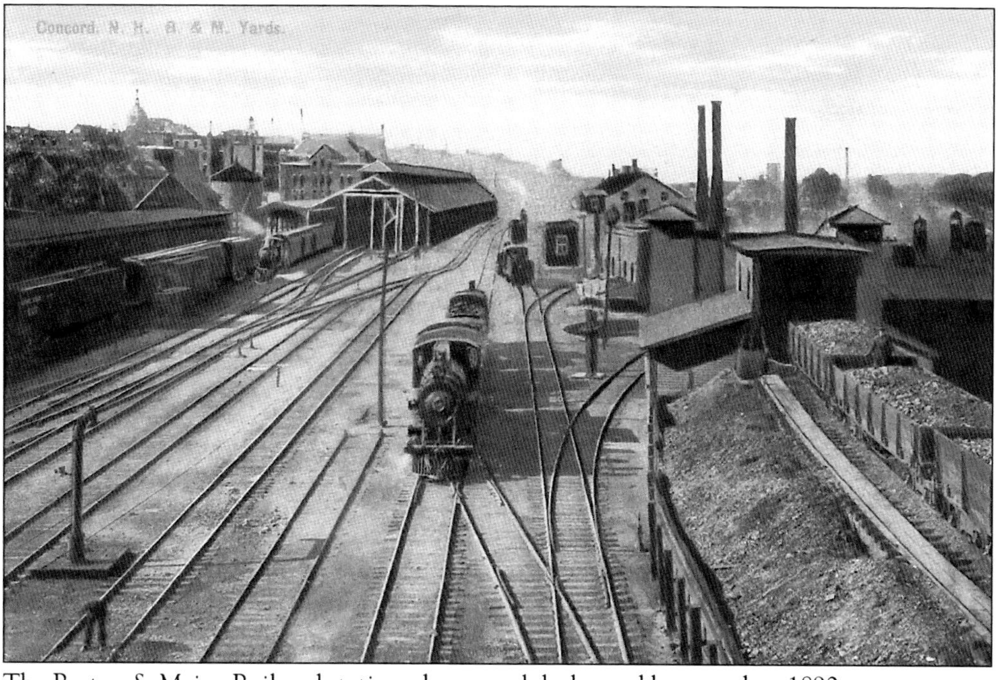

The Boston & Maine Railroad station, shops, coal decks, and busy yard, c. 1890.

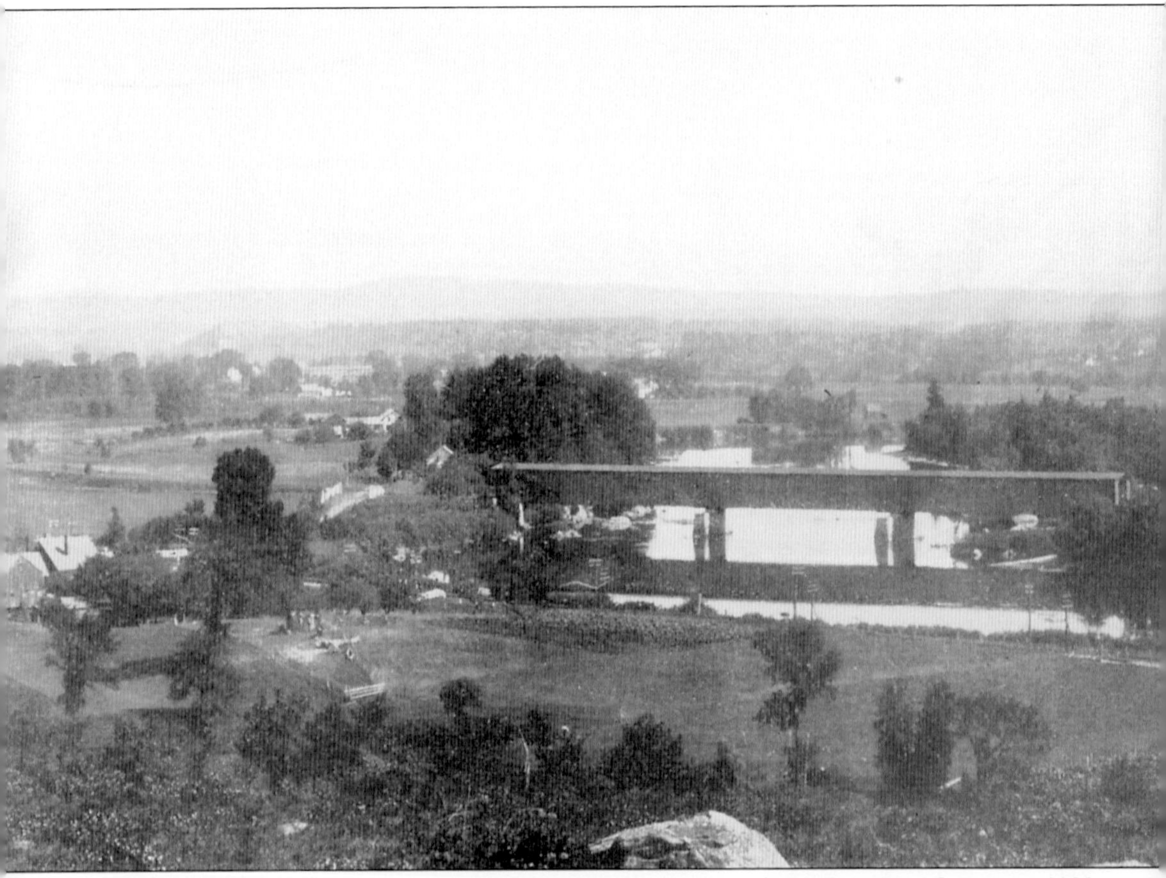

The Boston & Maine Railroad bridge crossing the Merrimack River at Bow Junction, 1900. Quickly accepted as a prime mover for both passengers and freight, the railroads spread rapidly from Concord. A primary route was to Laconia, Plymouth, Woodsville, and Wells River. The Boston, Concord & Montreal opened in 1853; to White River Junction, Vt., via Franklin and Lebanon, the Northern, in 1848; to Claremont Junction via Lake Sunapee, by 1872, and soon spurs ran to Bristol, Hillsboro, and other towns in the Merrimack and Winnipesaukee Valleys.

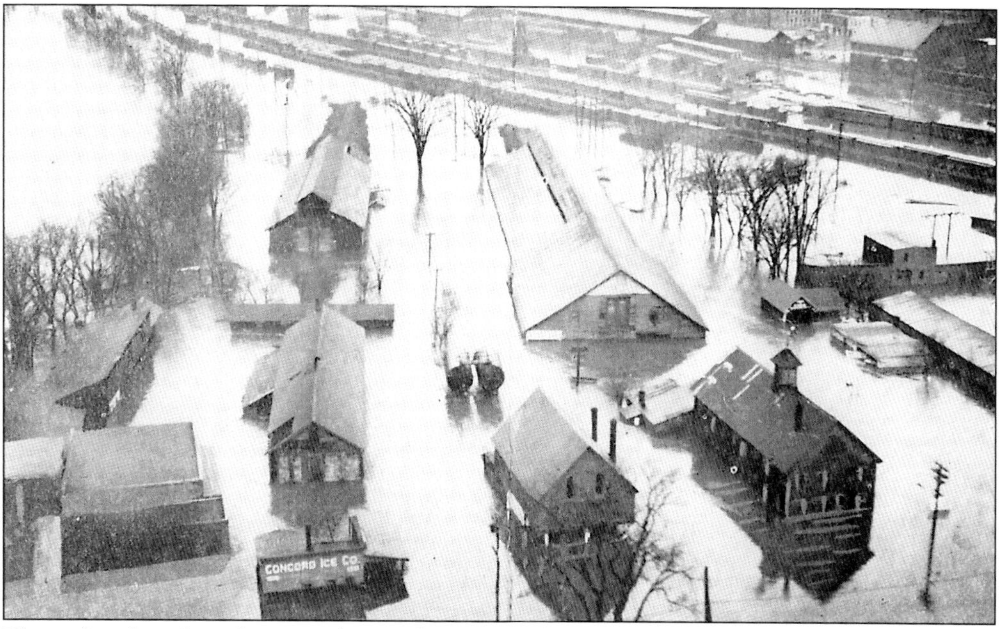

The railroad yards underwater during the spring of 1936, when the Merrimack River flooded over the yard and shop property at the Concord station.

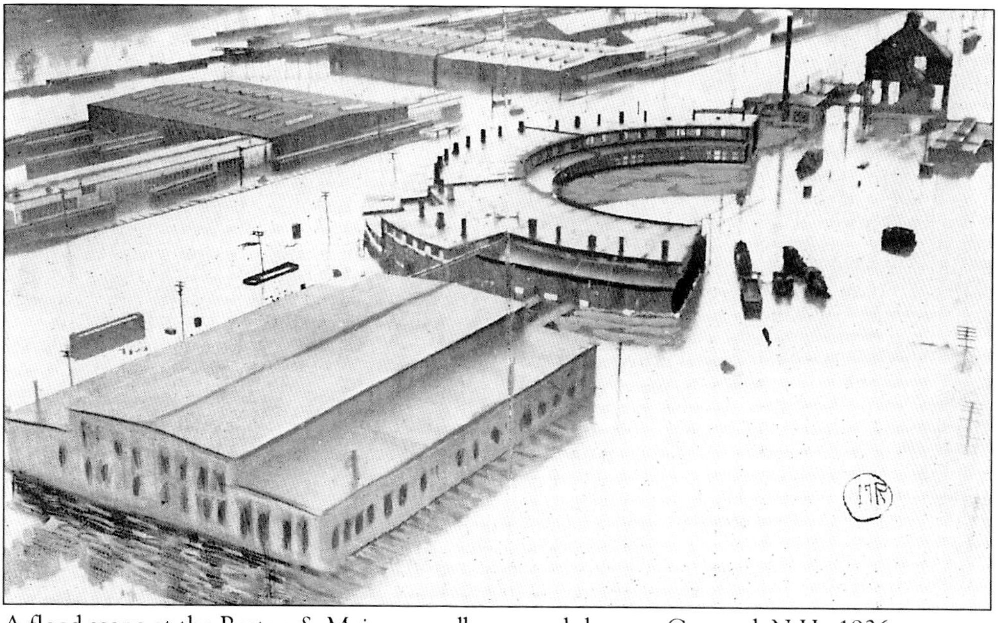

A flood scene at the Boston & Maine roundhouse and shops at Concord, N.H., 1936.

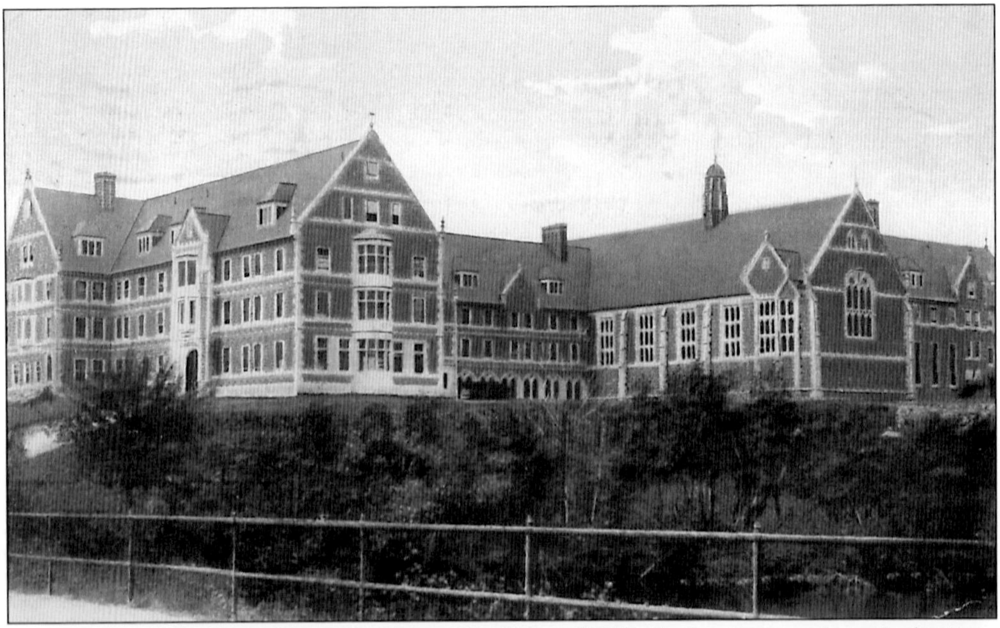

St. Paul's School, Concord, 1911. In the small village of Millville, 2 miles west from the business district of Concord, is located St. Paul's School.

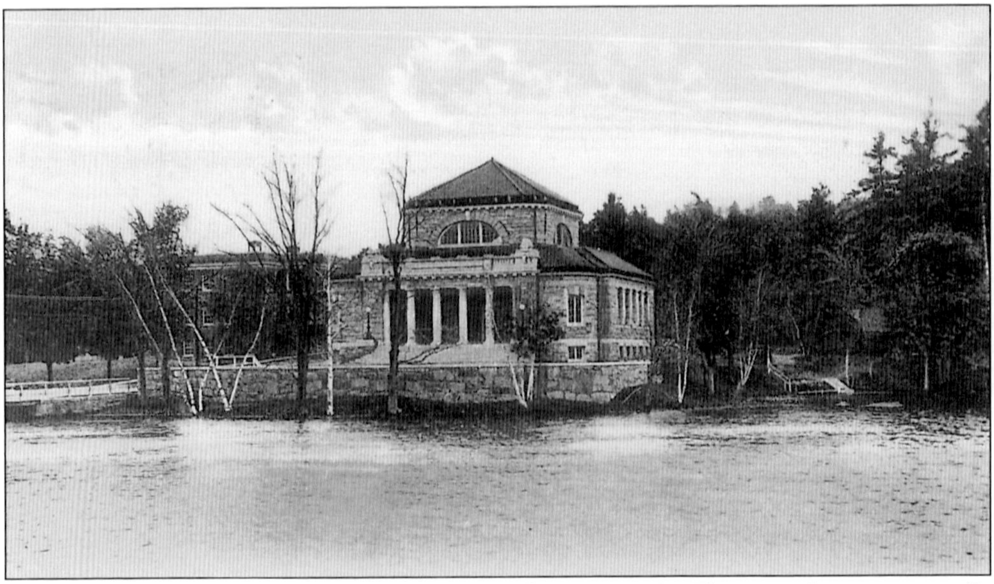

The Sheldon Library, St. Paul's School, Concord, N.H., 1907. The grounds were originally known as the "Shattuck Farm," and were given to the school at its founding in 1855 by Dr. G.C. Shattuck, of Boston, Massachusetts. It is considered to be one of the finest preparatory schools in the nation.

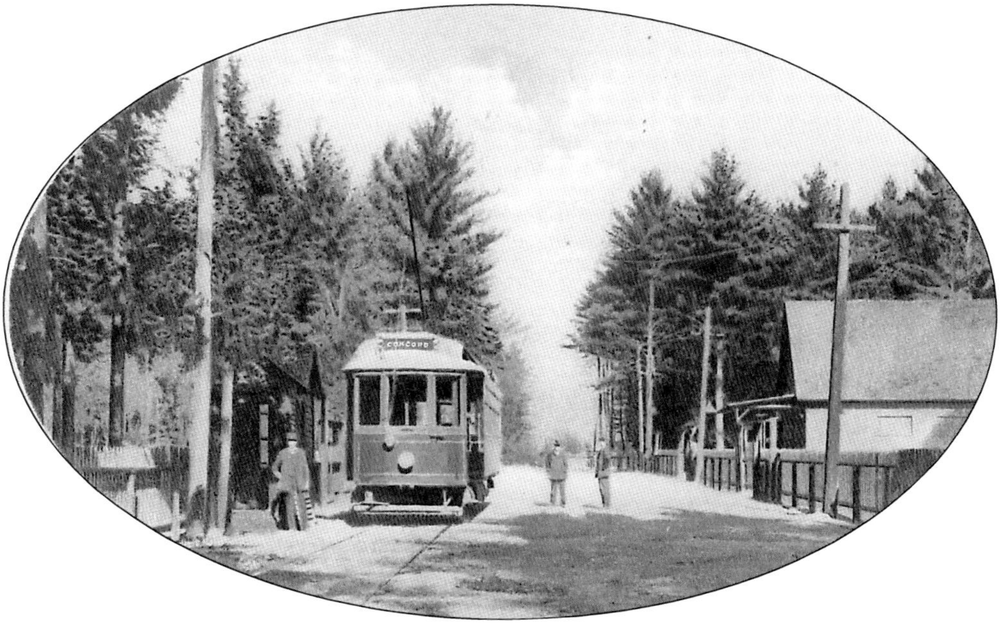

A Concord Trolley Car Co. trolley coming into the Contoocook River Park.

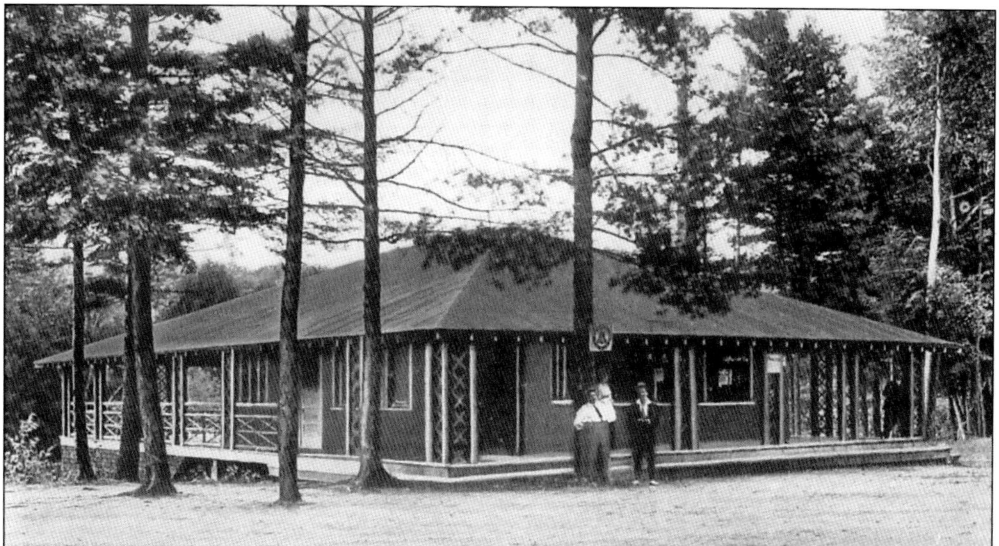

The bungalow at the Contoocook River Park, Penacook, early 1900s.

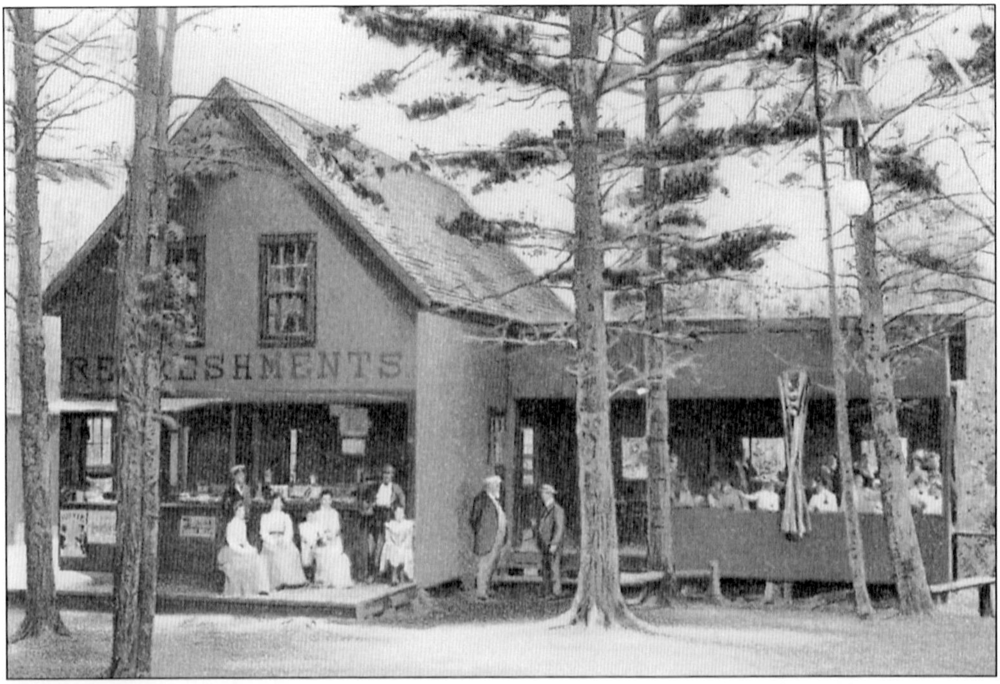

The refreshment stand and dining area at the Contoocook River Park, early 1900s.

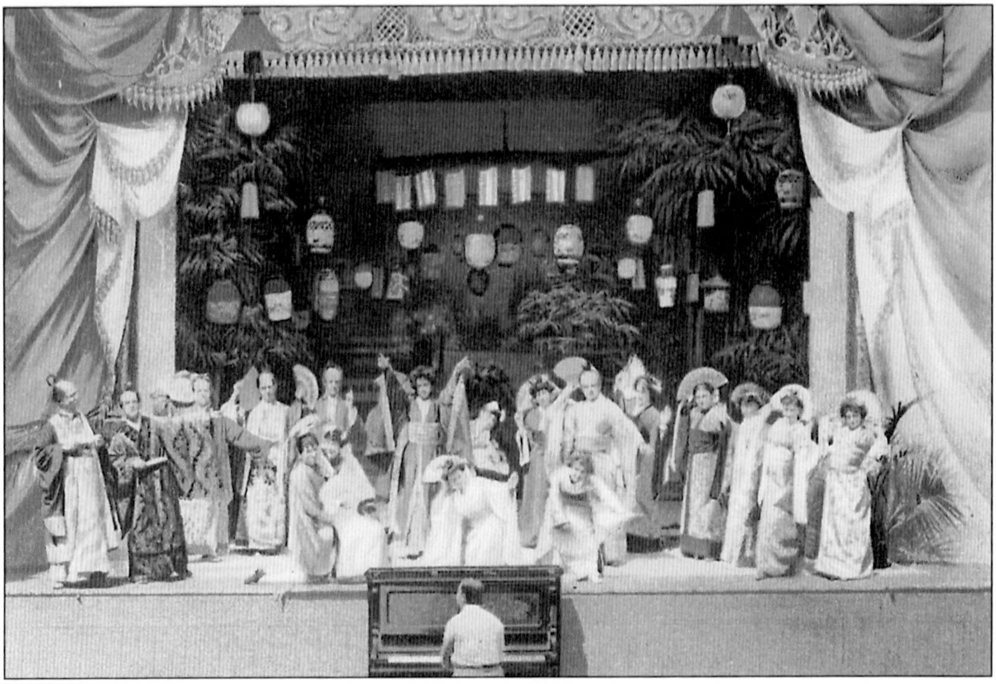

Close up of a play being performed at the Open Air Auditorium at the Contoocook River Park, early 1900s.

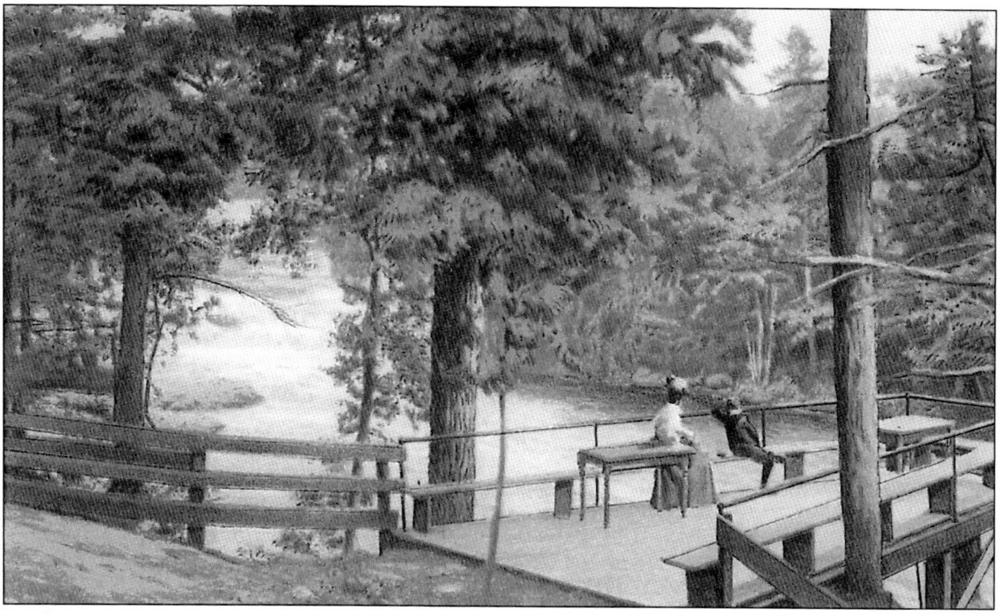

Looking west toward the dam at Look Out Point at the Contoocook River from the Contoocook River Park side of the river, 1900s.

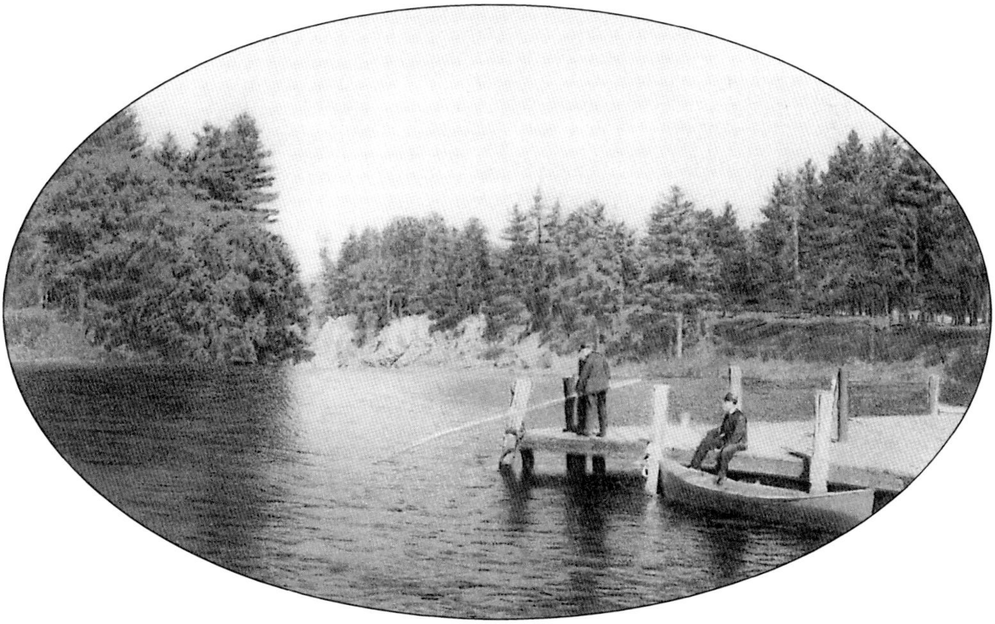

Men fishing at a boat landing. Looking east toward the dam on Look Out Point at the Contoocook River Park, 1900s.

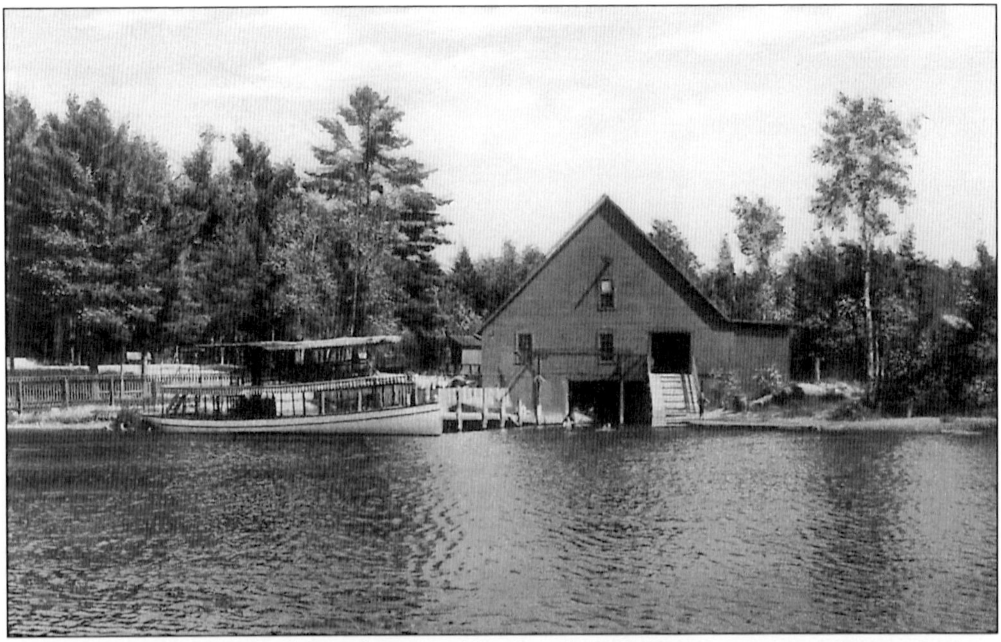

The Contoocook River Park boat house and landing, late 1890s.

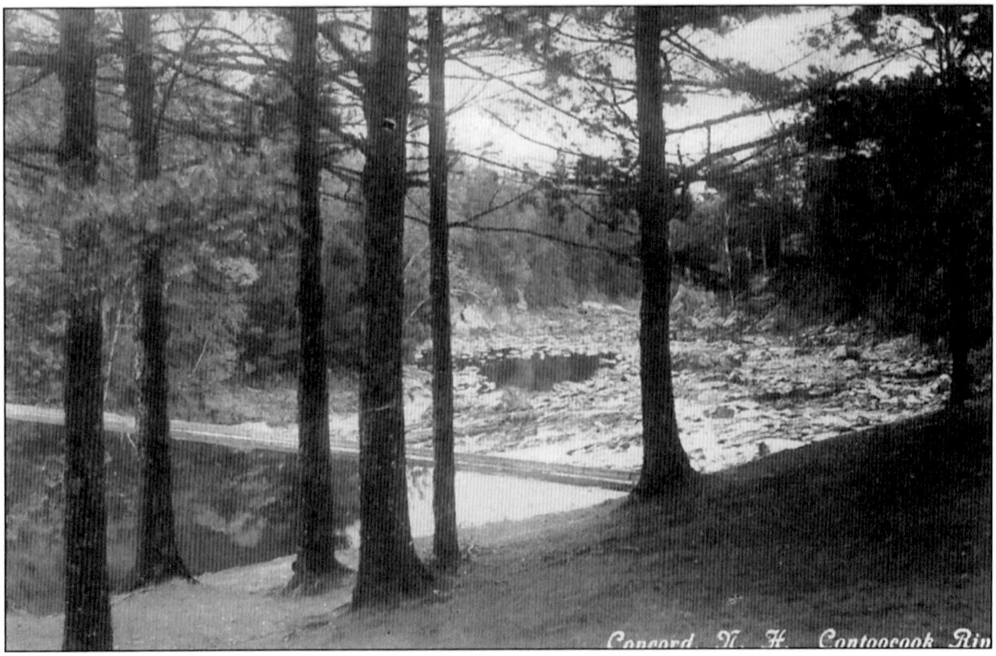

Gorge and Look Out Point as seen from Contoocook River Park, early 1900s.

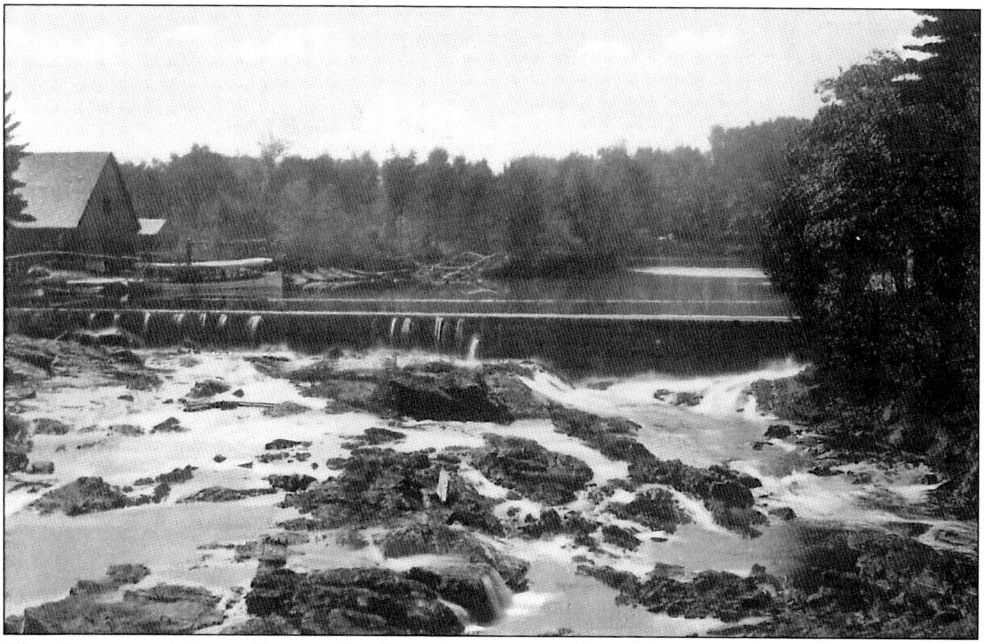

The Contoocook River Dam with a launch getting ready to leave the landing at the River Park boat house, early 1900s.

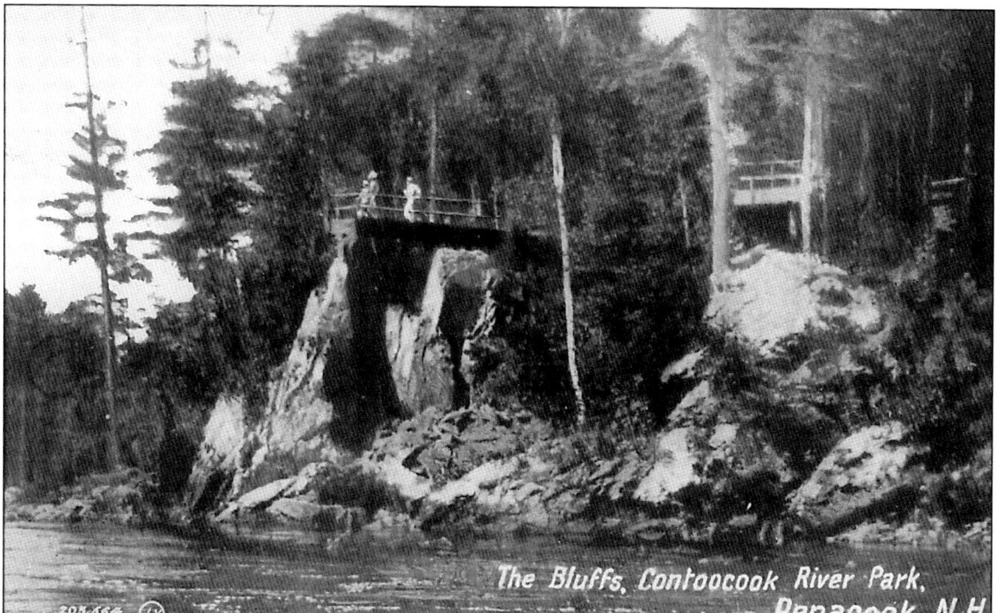

Lookout Point at the Bluff from the river bend just below the Contoocook River Park Dam, early 1900s.

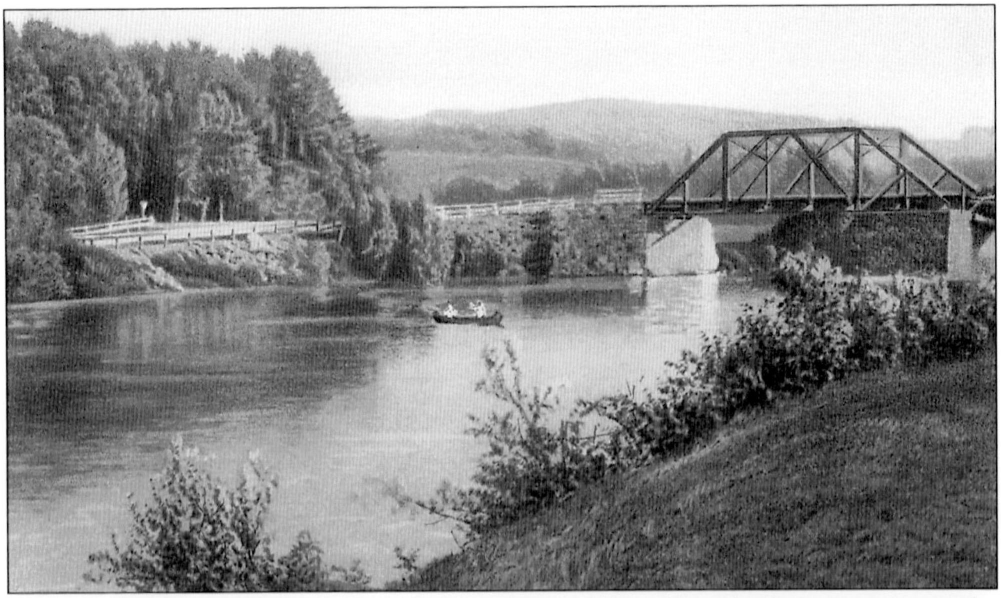

The River Hill Road Bridge over the Contoocook River above the park. The intersection to the left of the bridge included the River Road, Bog Road, and Carter Hill Road.

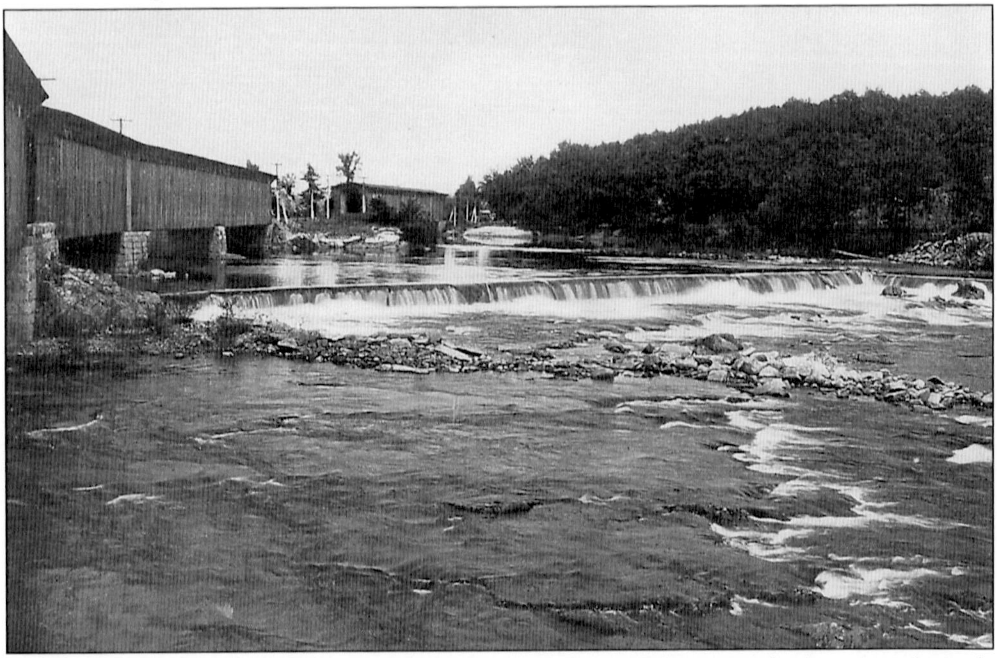

Merrimack River, Hooksett Falls, N.H. The Merrimack River Valley was indeed an artery for trade and provided a thoroughfare over which the pod-teams, the ancestors of the modern vehicles, hauled loads of cheeses, apples, tubs of butter, turkey, chicken, and all the other products of northern N.H. for the markets at Salem, Newburyport, and Boston. They returned with loads of goods needed for the country stores.

Then came the day in the river's industrial life when the Middlesex canal opened in 1803. Dams and locks were put in the river and short canals built round the falls. Later there were short side canals with locks built where the Nashua and Piscataquog Rivers join the larger river.

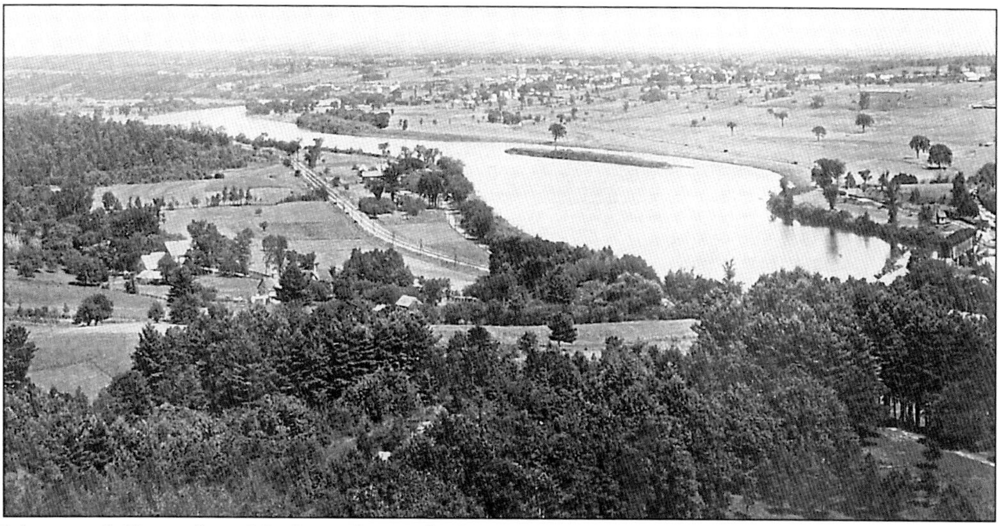

Merrimack River from Hooksett Pinnacle, N.H., 1899. From Concord, the northwesterly arm of the Boston and Lowell, is the Northern Railroad of New Hampshire, which follows the valley of the Merrimack as far as Franklin, and then winds in and out among hills, ponds, and lakes, working up some heavy grades to the summit at Canaan. To this point it had ascended about 778 feet since leaving Concord. Then following the water course of the Mascoma River, skirting the fine lake of the same name, it proceeds down a steep grade from Enfield to West Lebanon, where the Connecticut River is crossed, and the connection made at White River Junction with the Central Vermont Railroad and the Passumpsic Railroad for the north.

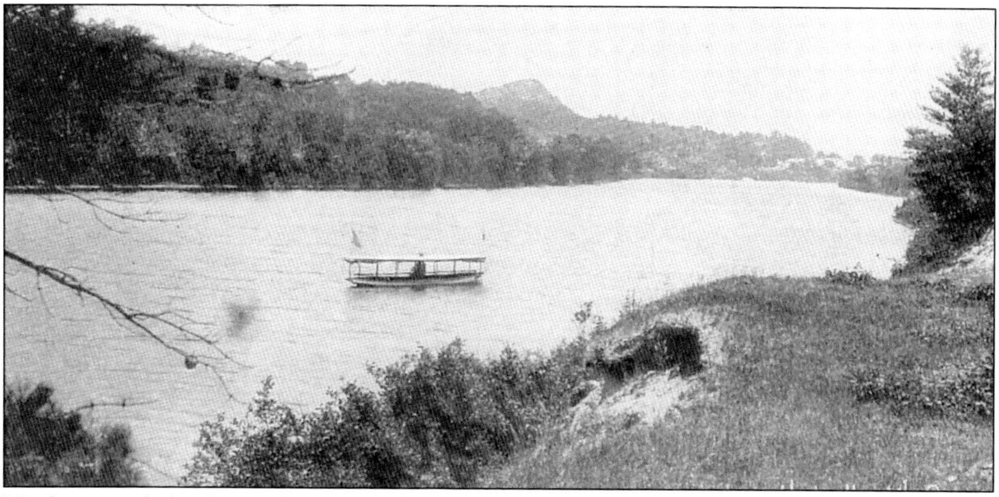

Hooksett and the Pinnacle, 1899. The Penacook Indians are known to have lived in this vicinity. In October 1719, about eighty persons from Hampton and Portsmouth associated for the purpose of obtaining a grant of a township in the "Chestnut Country." The first settlement made in the territory, that now comprises the town, was probably made sometime shortly after this, as there is record of a man being killed near Head's Tavern in 1745 by the Penacooks. The town was detached from Chester on the east side of the Merrimack, and Goffstown and Dunbarton on the west side, and incorporated as a separate town in 1822.

Left of the village by a bridge is the Pinnacle affording a good view of the Merrimack Valley. According to tradition, Native Americans encamped here, their reason probably being that this was an advantageous observation point.

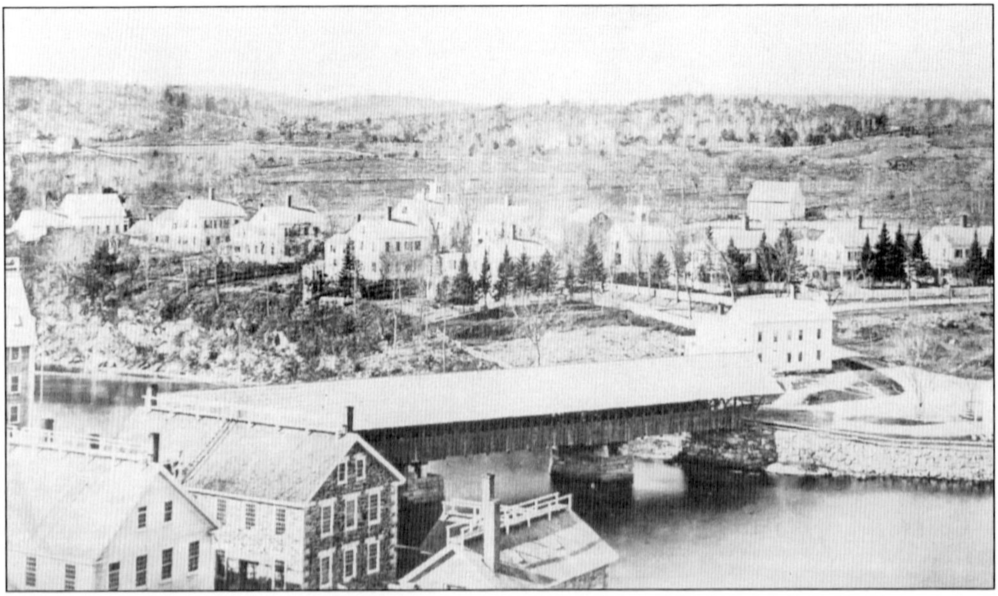

Penacook looking west, Main Street Bridge, 1849–74. During Penacook's early days, it was strongly garrisoned against the Penacooks and was the scene of the skirmishes between them and the white settlers.

The water power of the two rivers gave Penacook an early industrial development which included woolen mills, an electrical instrument shop, and the New England Briar Pipe Co., makers of "Kaywoodie" pipes. The later decline of the cotton industry is evidenced by a vacant mill at the bridge over the Contoocook River.

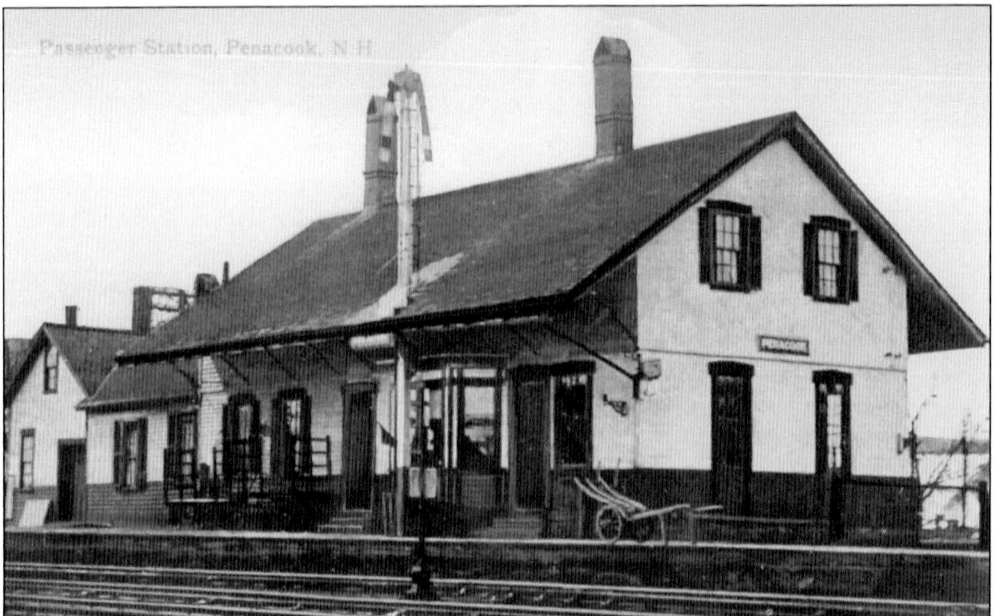

The "Old Northern Railroad" Boston & Maine Railroad. train station looking northeast. This station was located on the Merrimack River side of the railroad tracks just before it was moved to the town side of tracks, *c*. 1850.

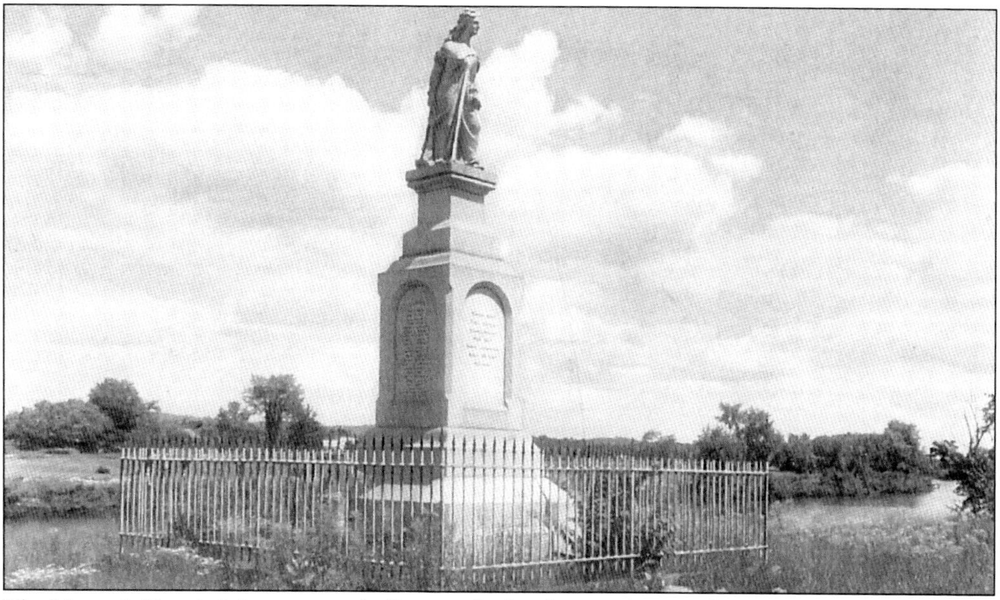

The Hannah Dustin Monument. At Penacook, 7 miles northwest of Concord, the Contoocook River empties into the Merrimack, and at this point of junction in mid-stream is Dustin's Island, on which stands a granite monument to Hannah (Emerson) Dustin, who was captured by Native Americans on March 15, 1697, at Haverhill, Massachusetts, together with a six-week-old infant and a nurse, Mary Niff. The account says that ". . . the child was killed, but the two women were brought by a weary march to a wigwam on this island and left in charge of two men, three women, and seven Indian children, where they also found Samuel Lannardson, a boy captured from Worcester. Mrs. Dustin planned an escape, and, on the early morning of March 31, 1697, awoke her companions, and, with the Indians' own tomahawks dispatched both the men instantly and one woman; the other woman and one Indian boy only escaping."

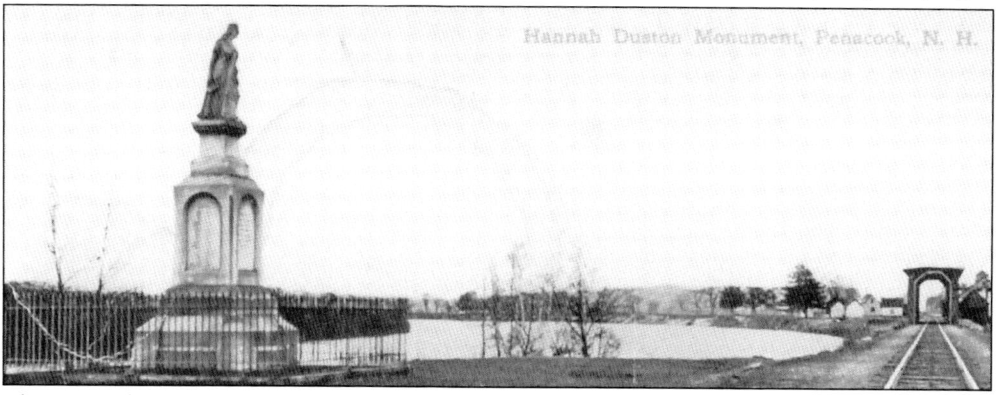

The Hannah Dustin Monument and Merrimack River located on the east side of the Old Northern Railroad tracks at the southern end of Dustin Island, Penacook, N.H. Note the railroad yard at the other end of the bridge.

The account continues: "Taking the sculps as proof, they scuttled all the canoes but one, and then embarked on the then high and turbulent Merrimack for Haverhill, which they safely reached in a few days. She at once became a great heroine, and, being called to Boston, the General Court thanked her and made her a grant of 50 pounds." Fifty years after the Hannah Dustin capture, the white settlers of this region were assailed by Native Americans; some were killed and others carried captive to Canada.

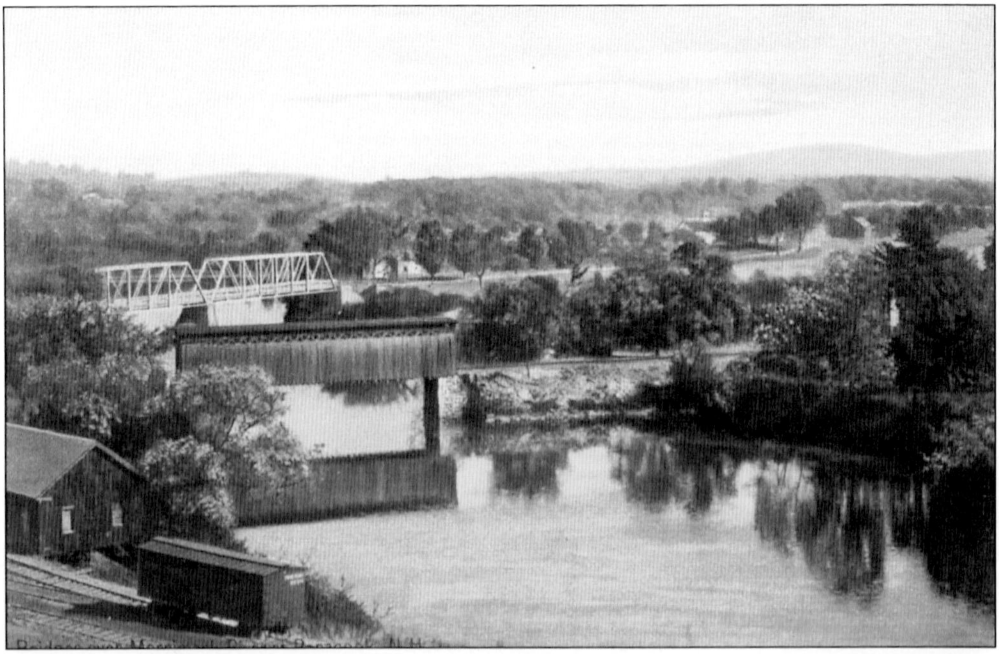

The Contoocook River entering the Merrimack River on the Boscawen side of Dustin Island. Here the wooden railroad bridge of the Old Northern Railroad crosses the Contoocook River. The old steel bridge spans the Merrimack River which Route 3 used to travel.

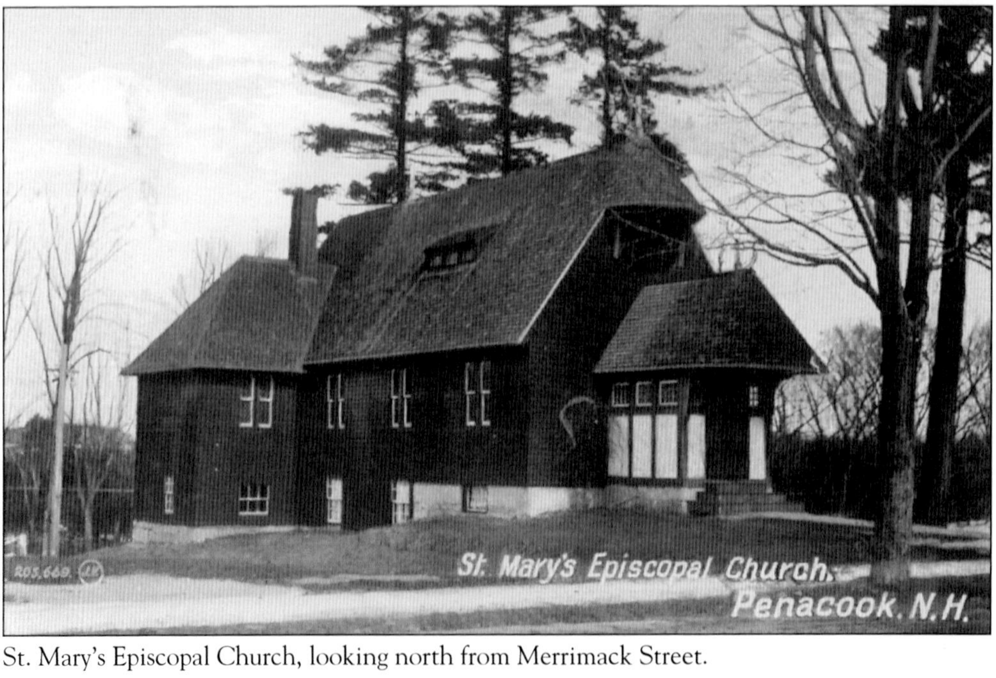

St. Mary's Episcopal Church, looking north from Merrimack Street.

The Baptist church (1858), the United Church of Penacook (1953). This edifice is located on north side of Merrimack Street.

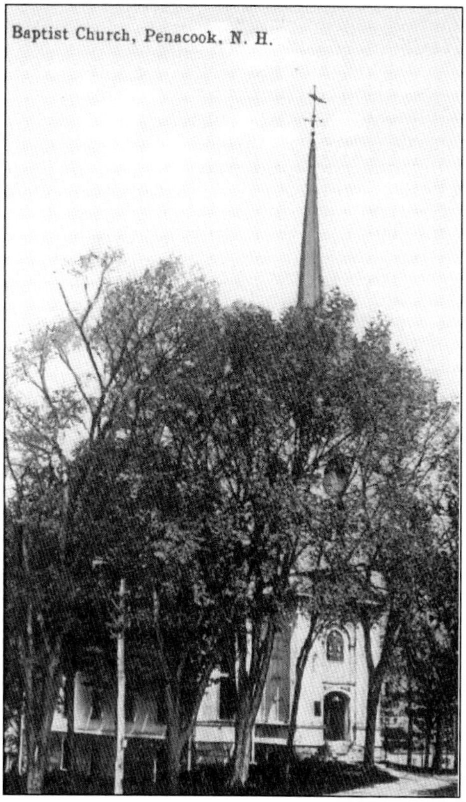

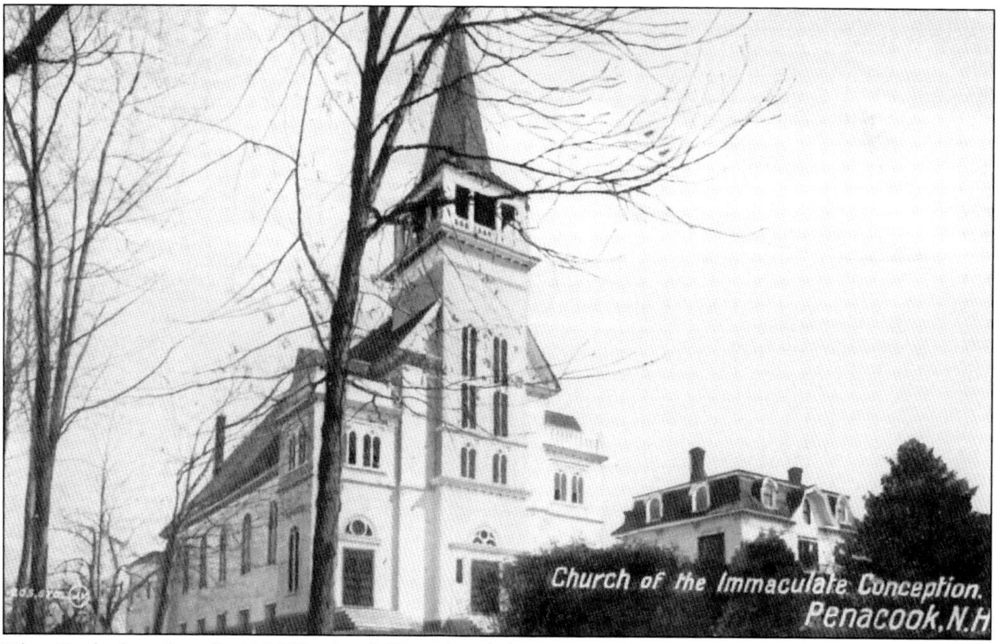

The Catholic church (1898), the "Church of the Immaculate Conception," Pleasant Street, Penacook, N.H.

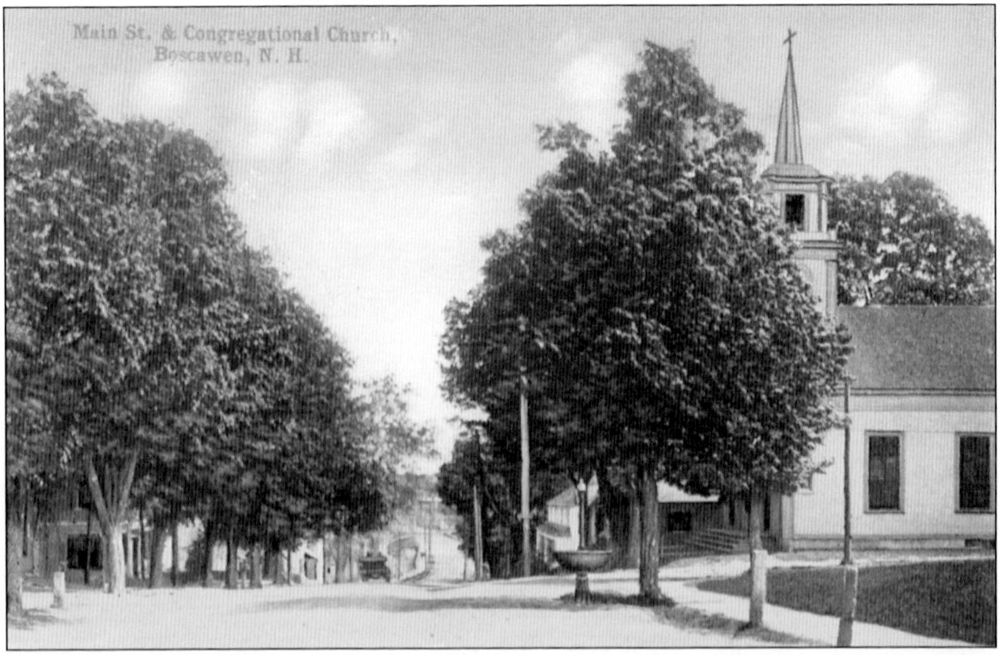

The First Congregational Church and Main Street Boscawen, N.H., looking south toward Penacook, N.H., *c.* 1900.

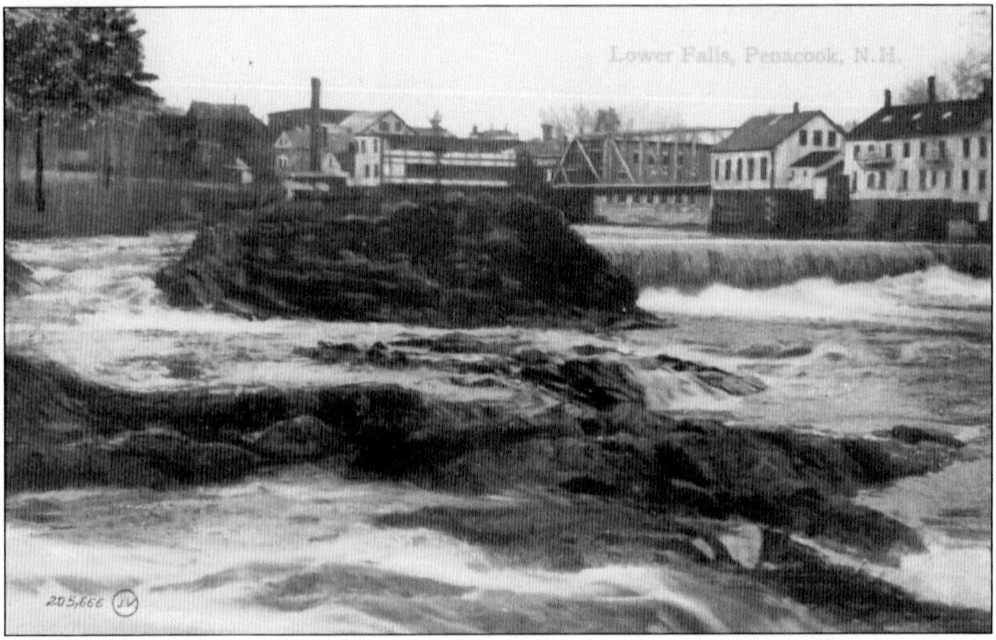

The Contoocook River looking southwest from Lower Falls Dam toward the village of Penacook, early 1900s. In 1733, the General Court of Massachusetts granted a track of land on the west side of the Merrimack, 7 miles square and designated as "the Plantation of Contoocook" to John Coffin and others.

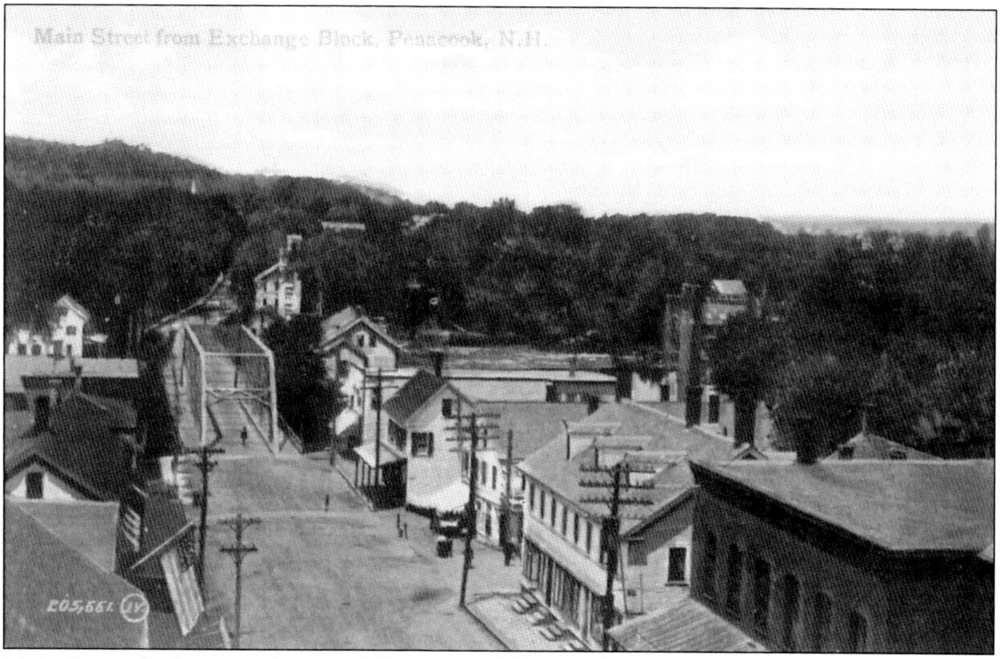

Main Street looking north toward Boscawen, N.H., and east to the Contoocook River. The picture was taken from the Exchange Block, Penacook, 1874–98.

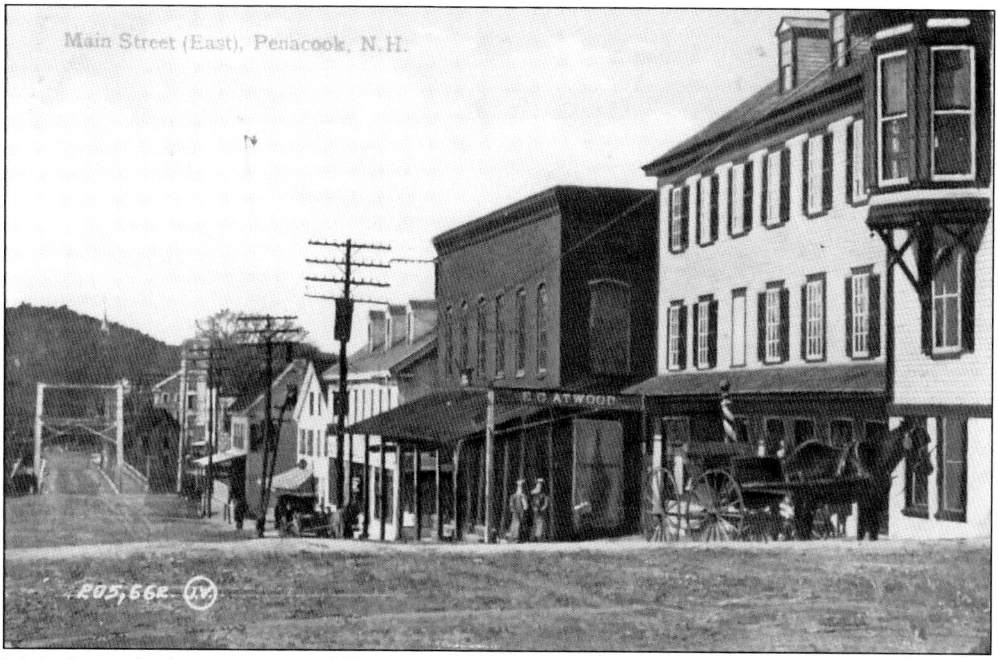

Main Street looking east toward Boscawen, N.H.

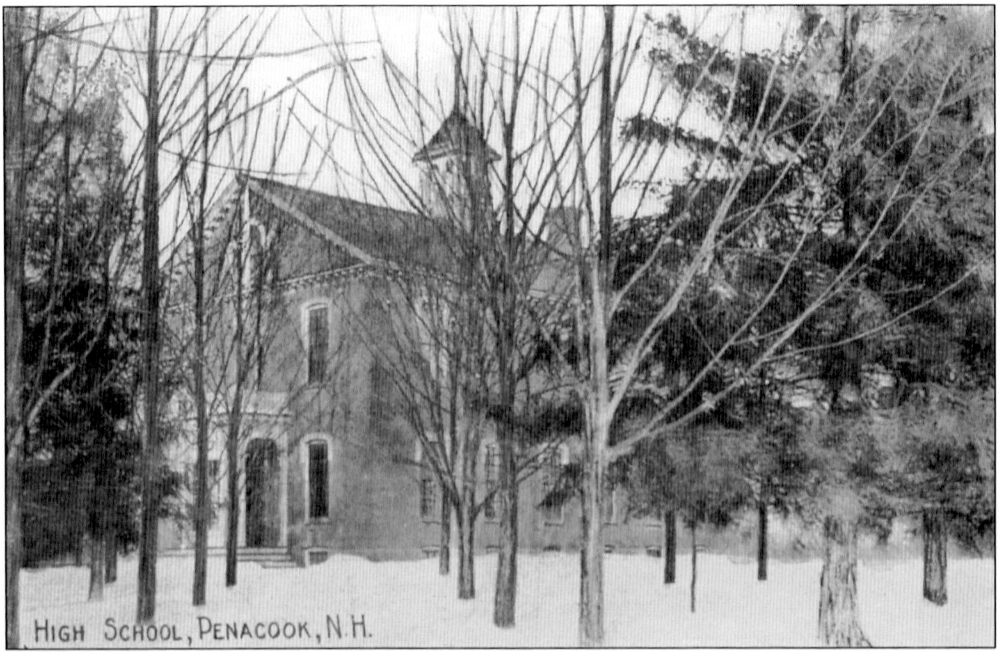

The Old Penacook Academy (1866), Penacook High School (1910–36), and the Boscawen Elementary School (1936).

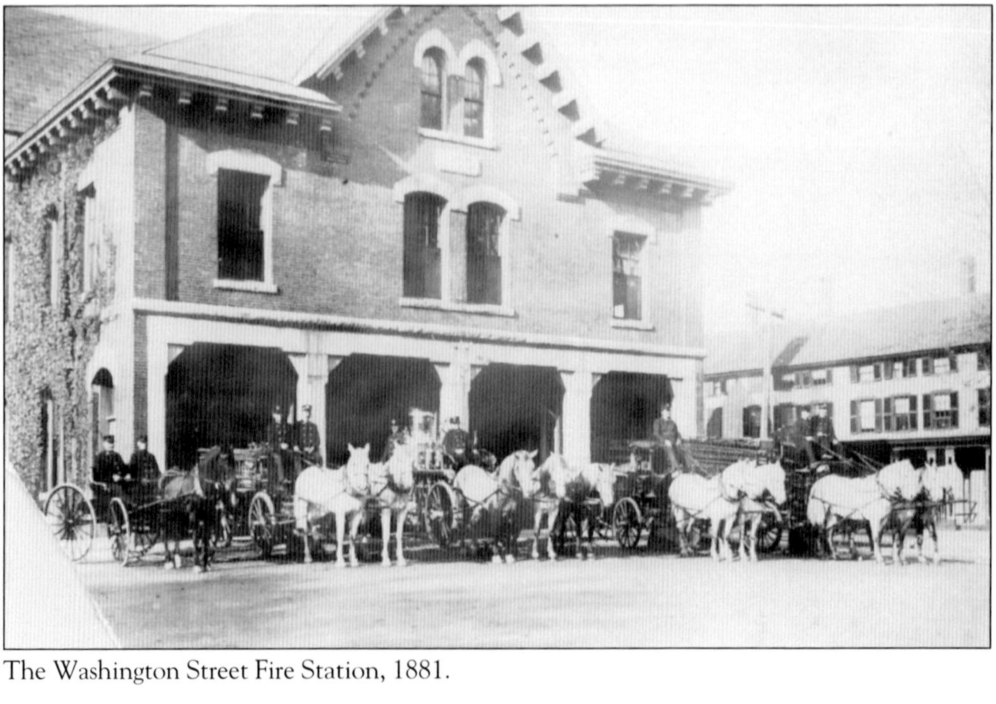

The Washington Street Fire Station, 1881.

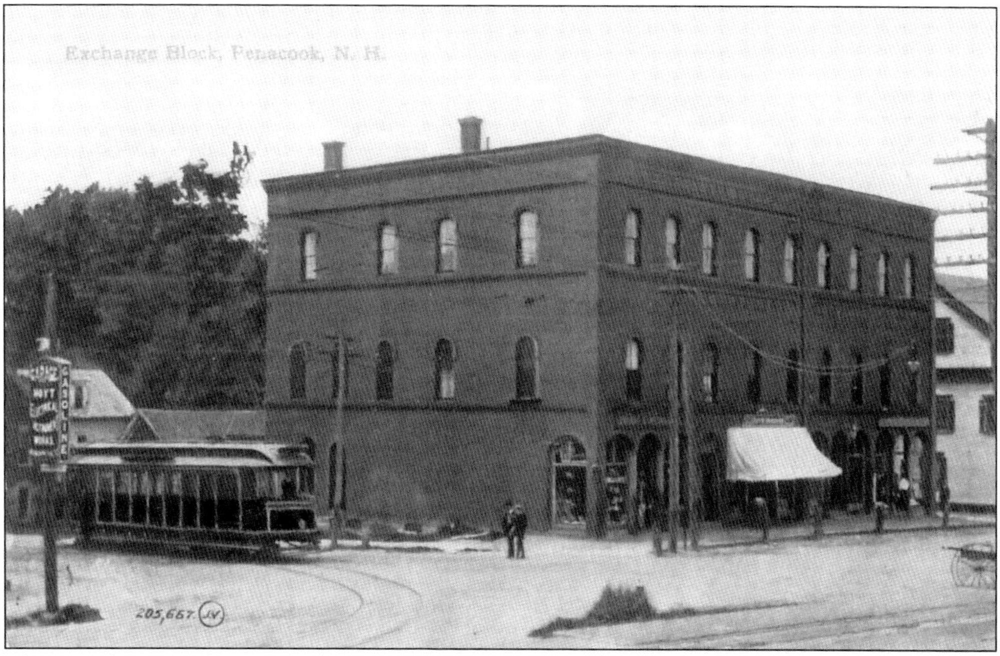

The Merchant Exchange Block and Washington Street, south of the square looking northwest from Main Street, late 1800s.

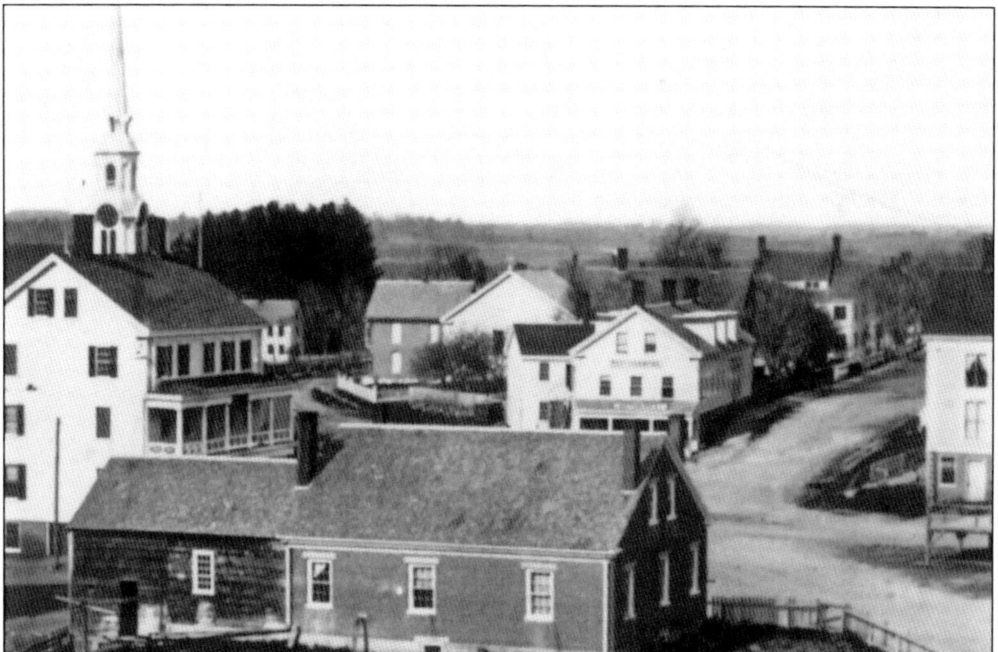

The Captain John Sawyer's House, *c.* 1840. Looking east at the village of Penacook we see the Captain John Sawyer's House before it was moved to Washington Street in 1870, when the Merchant Exchange Block was built on Main Street, late 1800s.

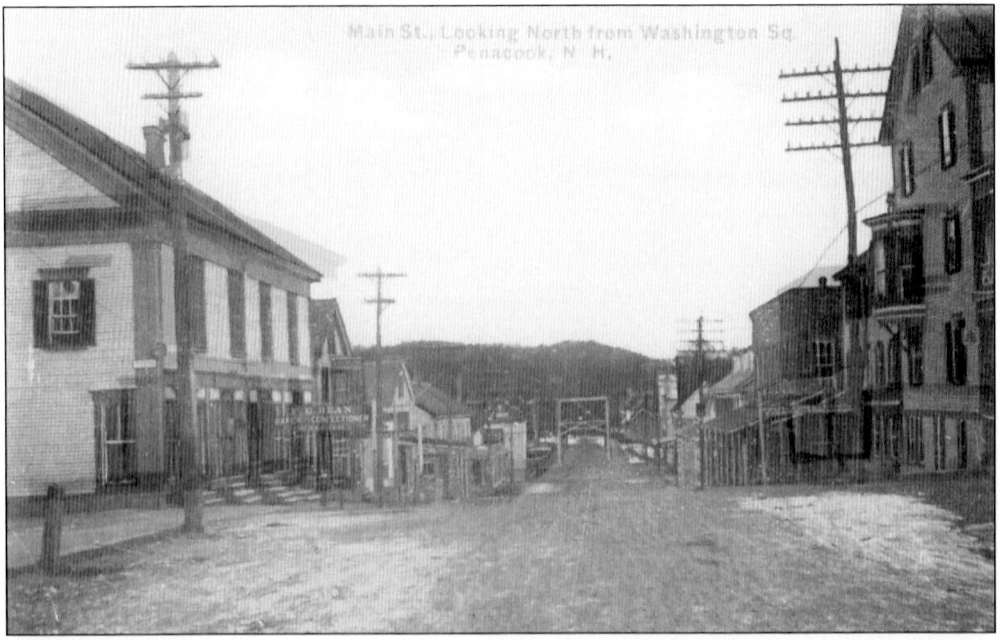

Main Street looking north toward Boscawen, N.H., from Washington Square, Penacook, late 1800s.

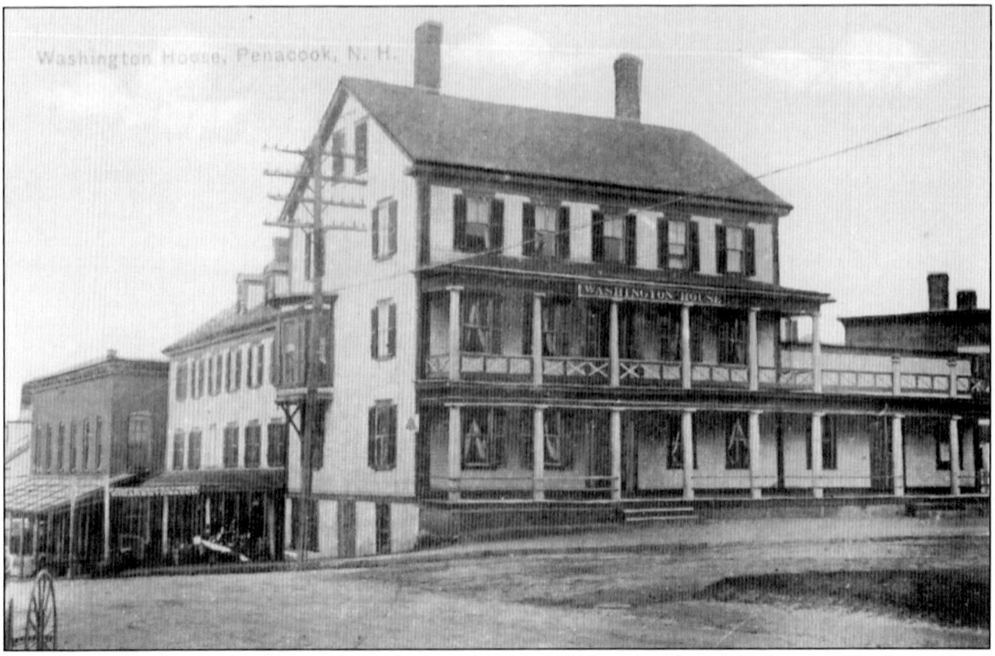

The Washington House as seen from the northeast and the Merchant Exchange Block on Main Street, late 1800s.

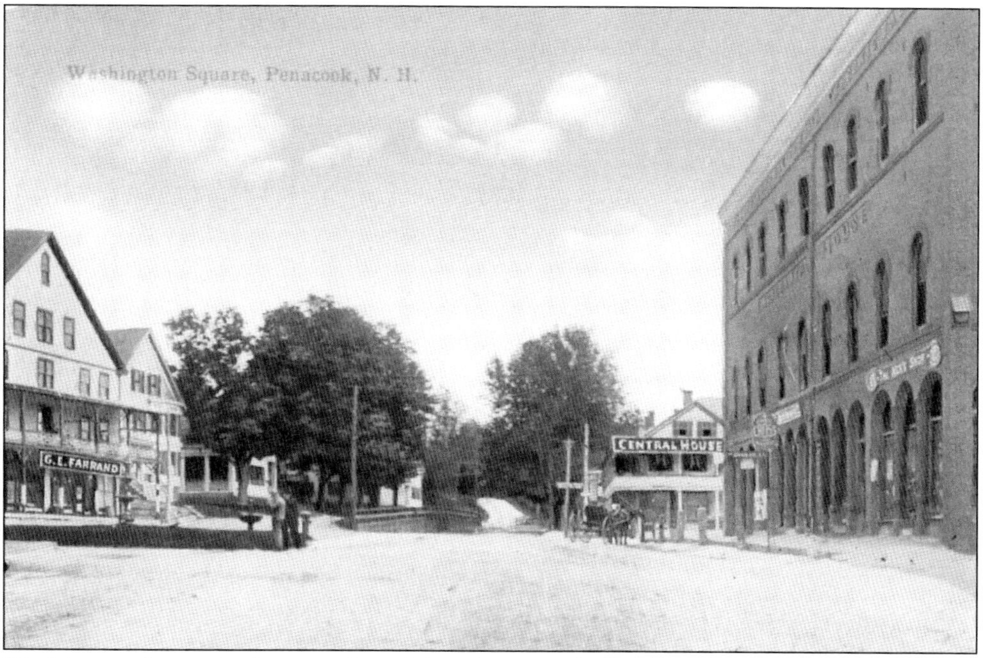

Washington Square looking south on Main Street with the Central House and the Exchange Block to the right and the G.E. Farrand Building to the left, c. 1800.

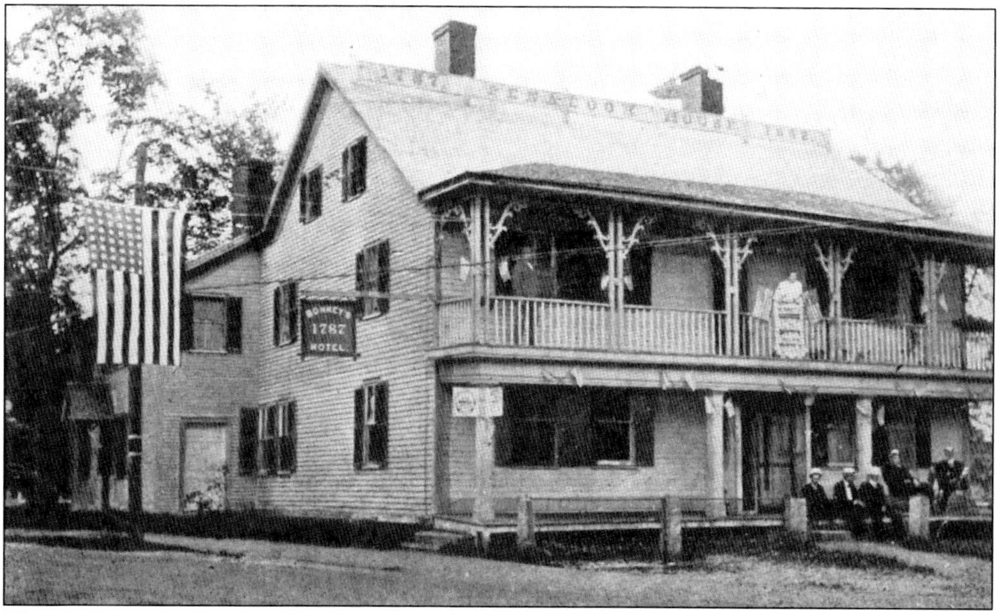

The intersection of Main and Eel Street. The Bonney Tavern (1862–1937) was originally called the Penacook House (1787–1862). The building was later moved to New London, N.H., where it eventually burned.

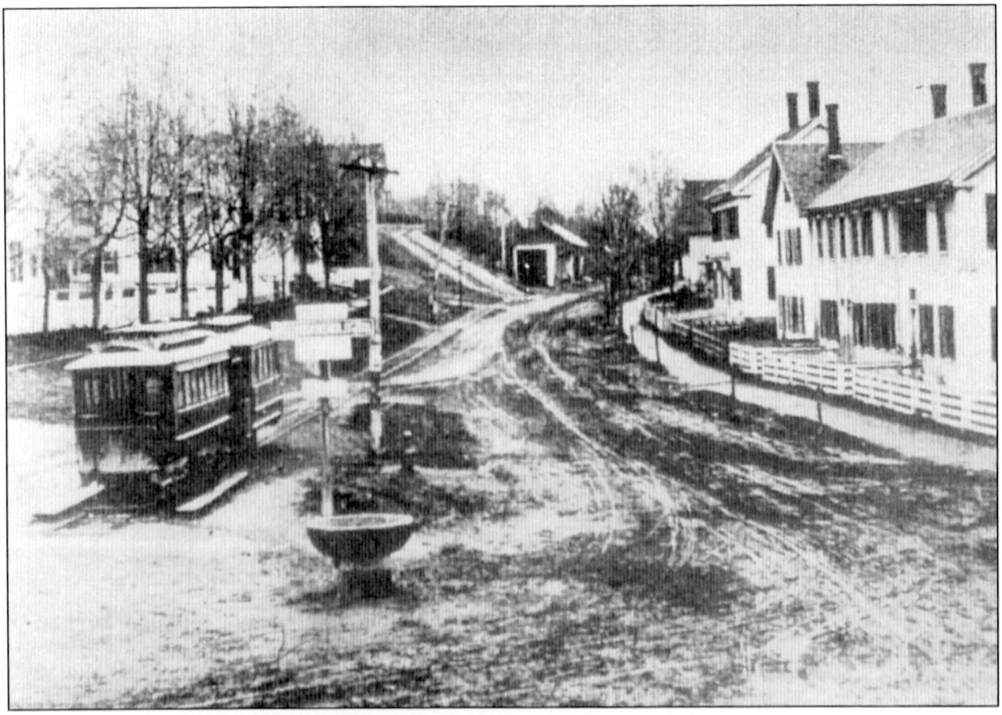

Looking south at the square, *c.* 1882.

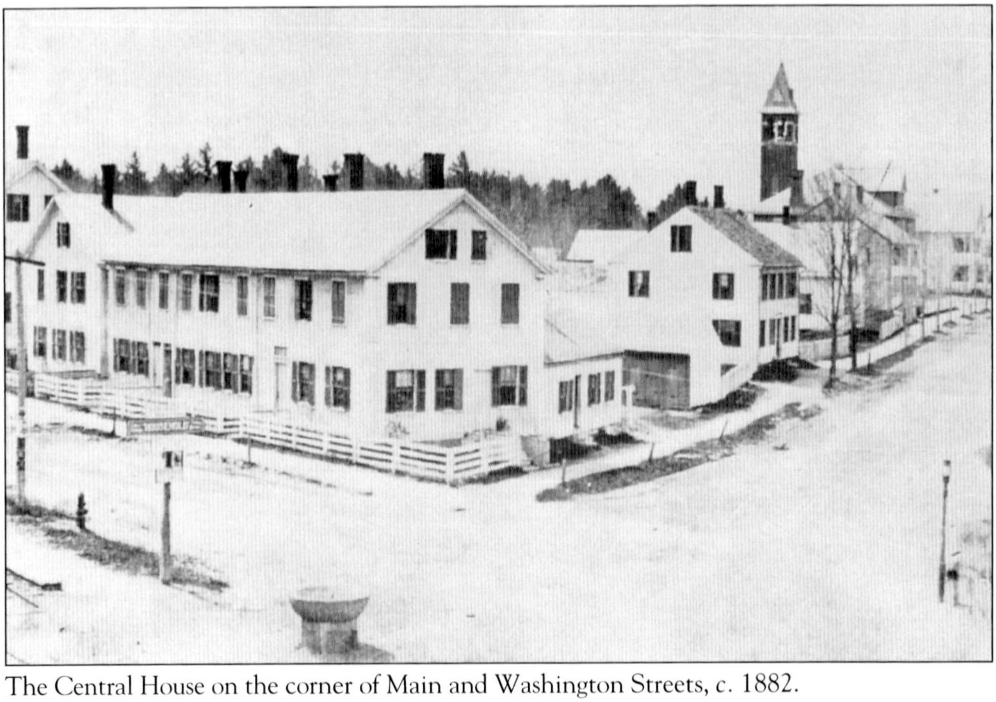

The Central House on the corner of Main and Washington Streets, *c.* 1882.

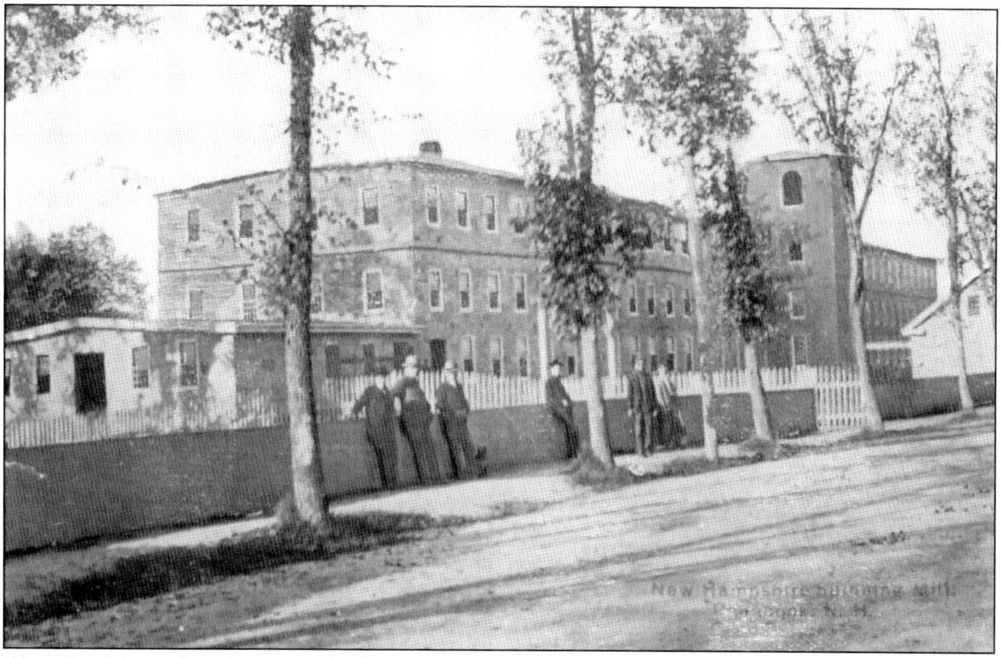

The New Hampshire Spinning Mill, 1899. In 1942, it became the Brezner Tannery Co. In 1953 it was known as the Allied Kid Co., and finally in 1972, the Allied Leather Co.

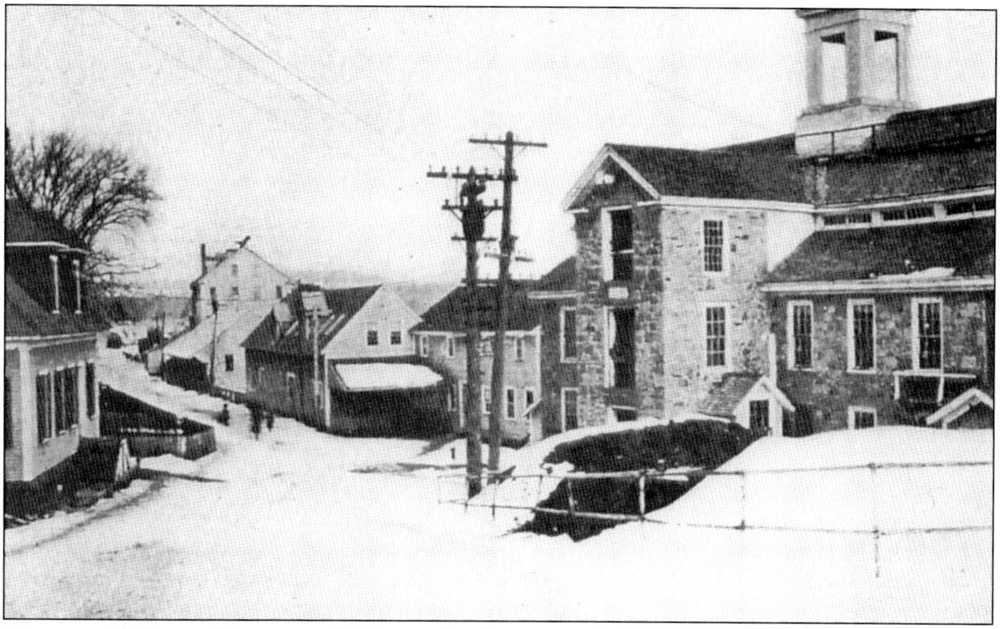

Commercial Street, Boscawen, N.H., at the Contoocook River Mill complex, 1903. You can see the Harris Woolen Mill (1847); the Swenson Granite Polishing Shop (1899); the Fisher Villa Saw Company (1846); and the Stratton Flour and Corn Mill (1857). The flour and corn mill was formerly a sawmill which was remodeled in 1883.

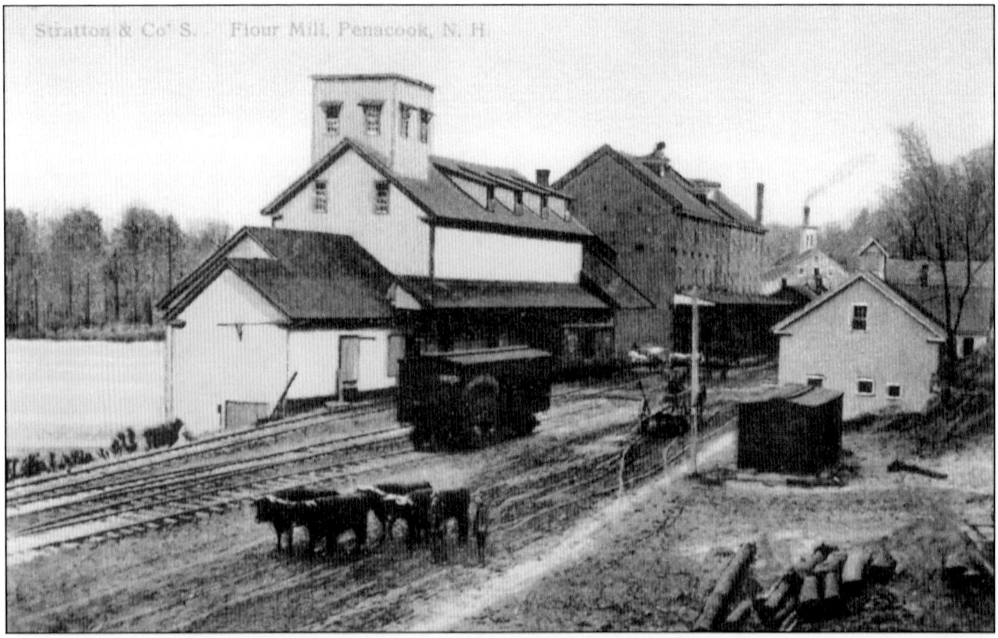

The Stratton Flour Mill in the Dustin Mill complex by the Contoocook River on Commercial Street, 1857. To the right of the village, at the point where the Contoocook empties into the Merrimack River, stood this mill. It was on this site that a sawmill was built in 1789 and later a gristmill of Isaac and Jeremiah Chandler. This flour mill was erected on the site in 1858 by John H. Pearson and Co. Better than 5,000 bushels of corn and several hundred barrels of flour were produced daily. Note the team of oxen that were used to move the freight cars along the mill yard.

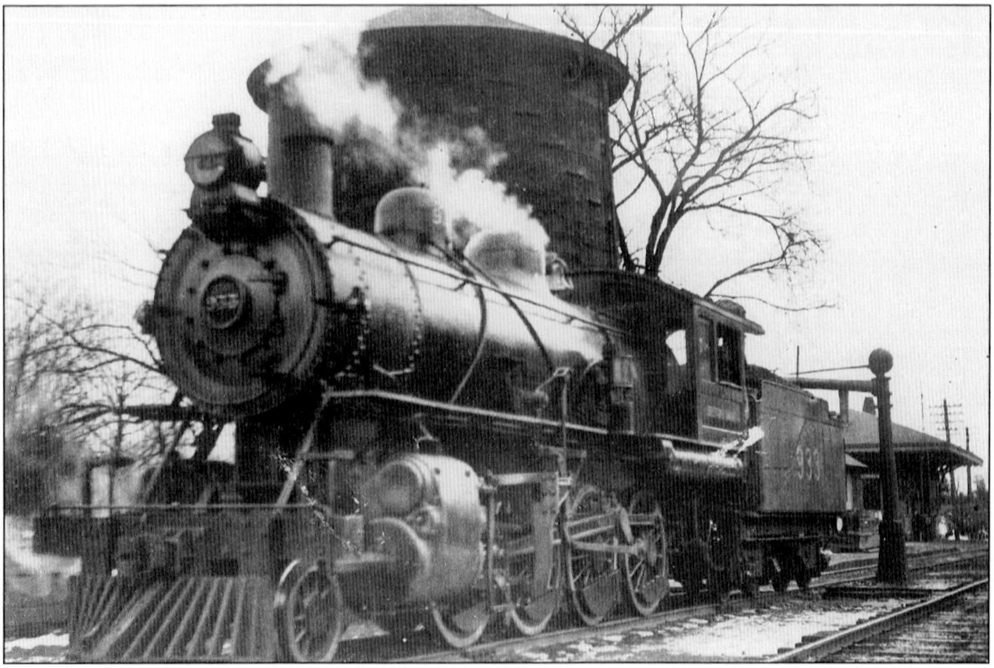

Boston & Maine engine #933 at a water tower en route to Franklin, N.H., early 1900s.

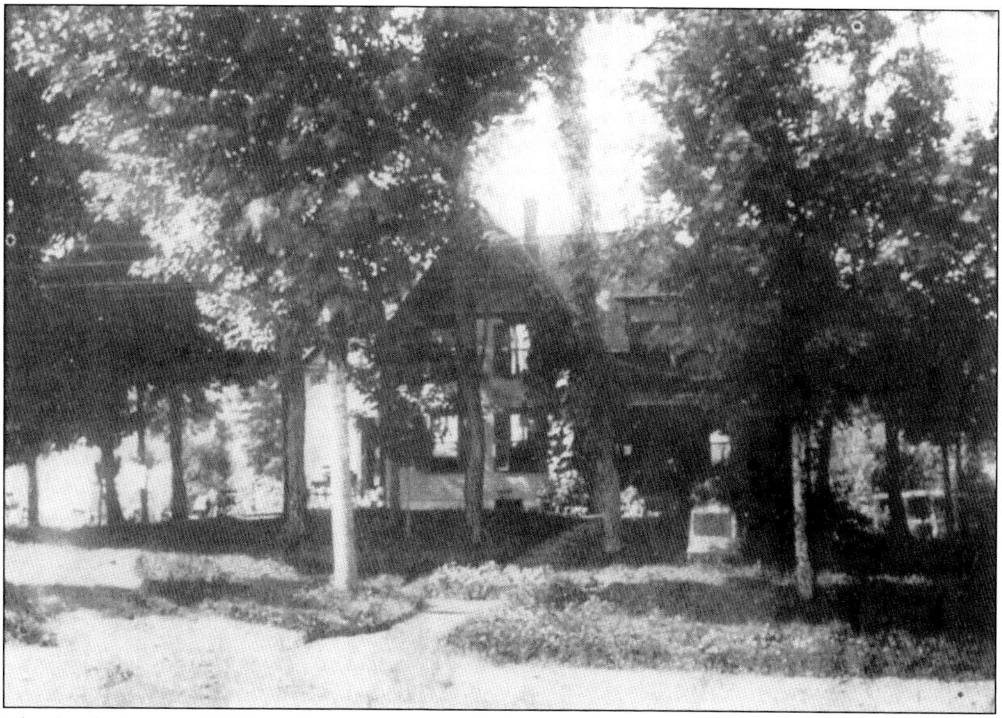

The birthplace of William Pitt Fessenden (1806–1869), a senator from Maine (1854–1864) and secretary of the treasury in Lincoln's cabinet (1864–1865). This house is a large, two-story frame structure with a wide paneled door surrounded by top and side lights. It is located on the east side of King Street, Boscawen, N.H.

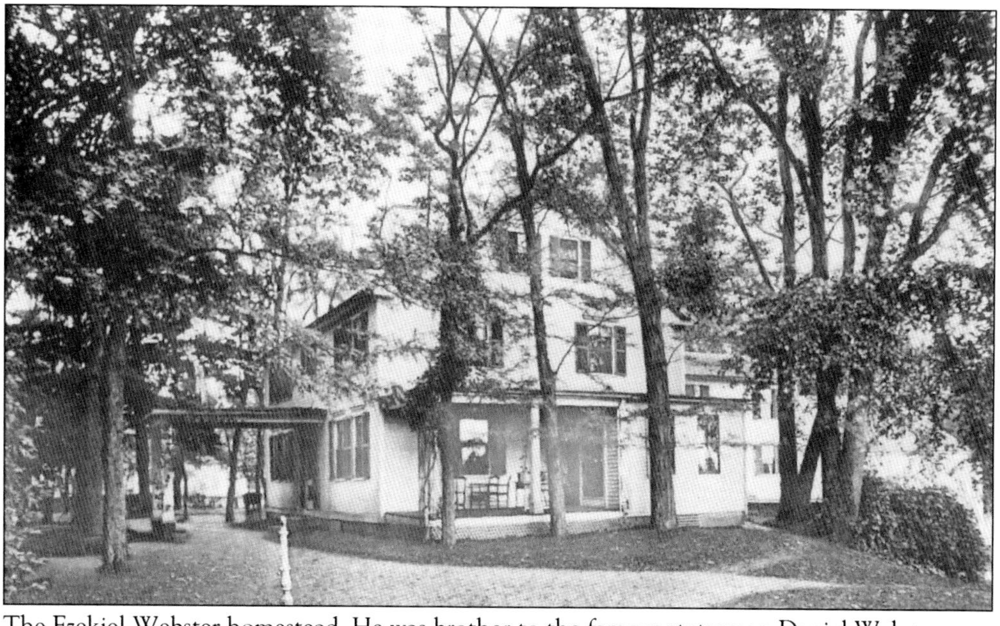

The Ezekiel Webster homestead. He was brother to the famous statesman Daniel Webster.

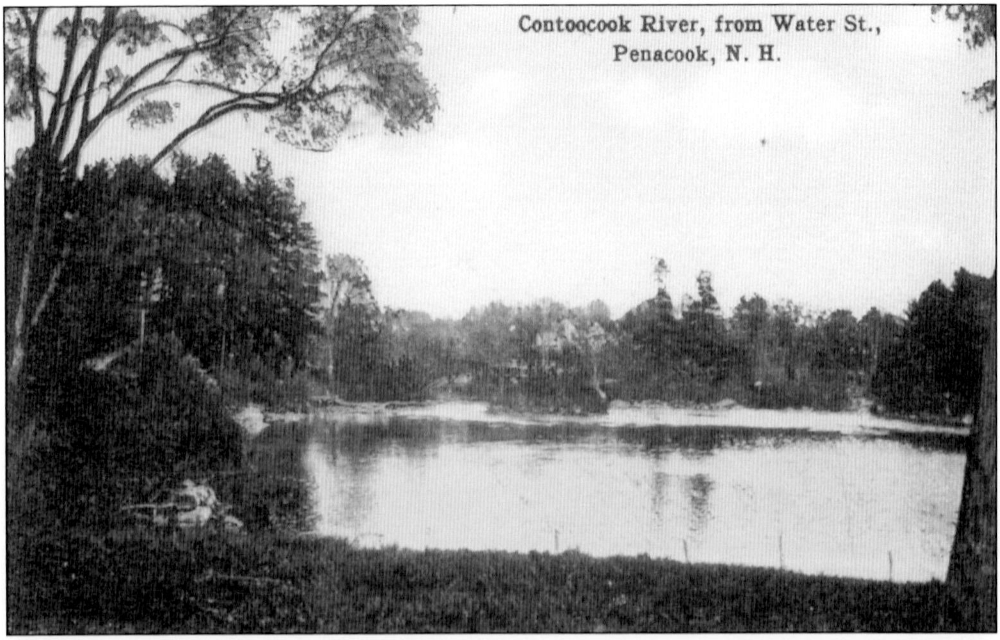

The three islands in the Contoocook River as seen from the bottom of the hill and Eel Street coming from Main Street, Boscawen, N.H., 1914. In 1760, the town was incorporated and named in honor of Admiral Boscawen, a British commander who assisted at the siege of Louisburg in 1758. A century later the section of Boscawen, west of the Blackwater River, was set off and incorporated as the town of Webster. The old town is the birthplace of Gen. Dix, Pitt Fessenden, and Charles G. Greene. The home of Ezekiel Webster, and the law office of his famous brother Daniel, were located here.

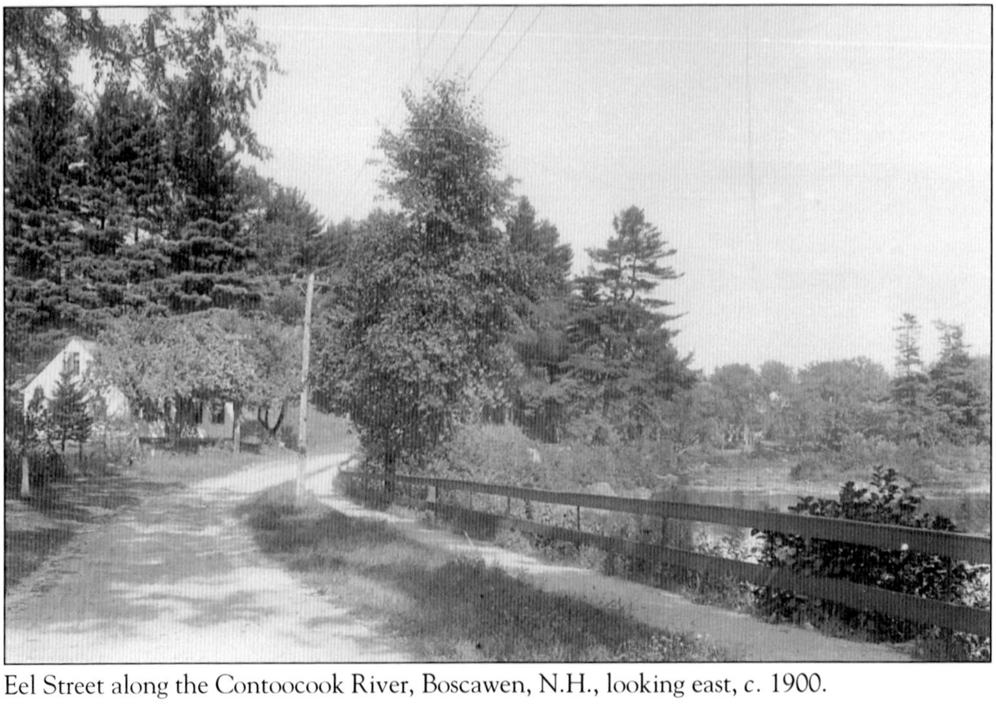

Eel Street along the Contoocook River, Boscawen, N.H., looking east, *c.* 1900.

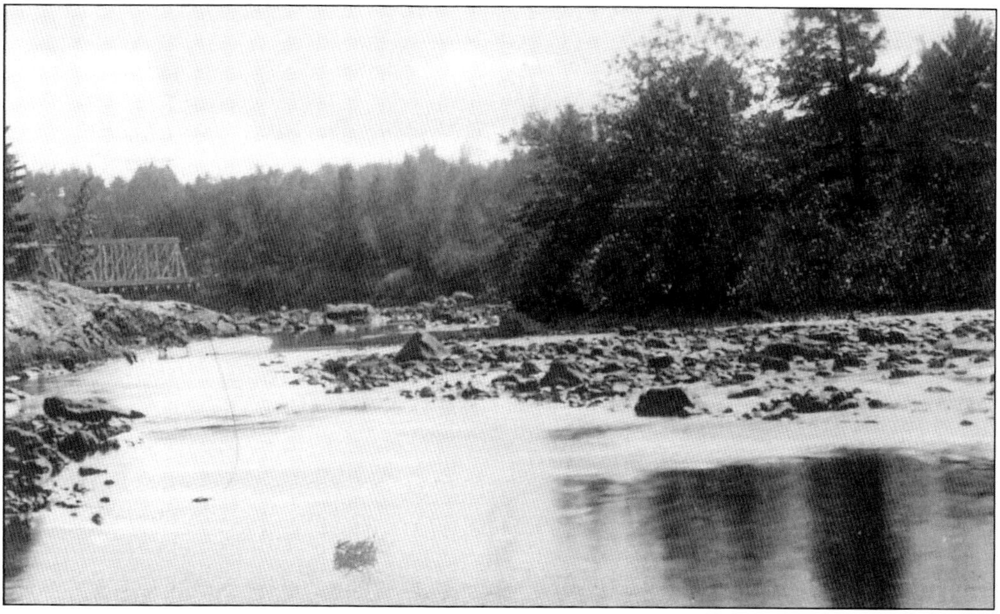

The Penacook and Boscawen twin bridges.

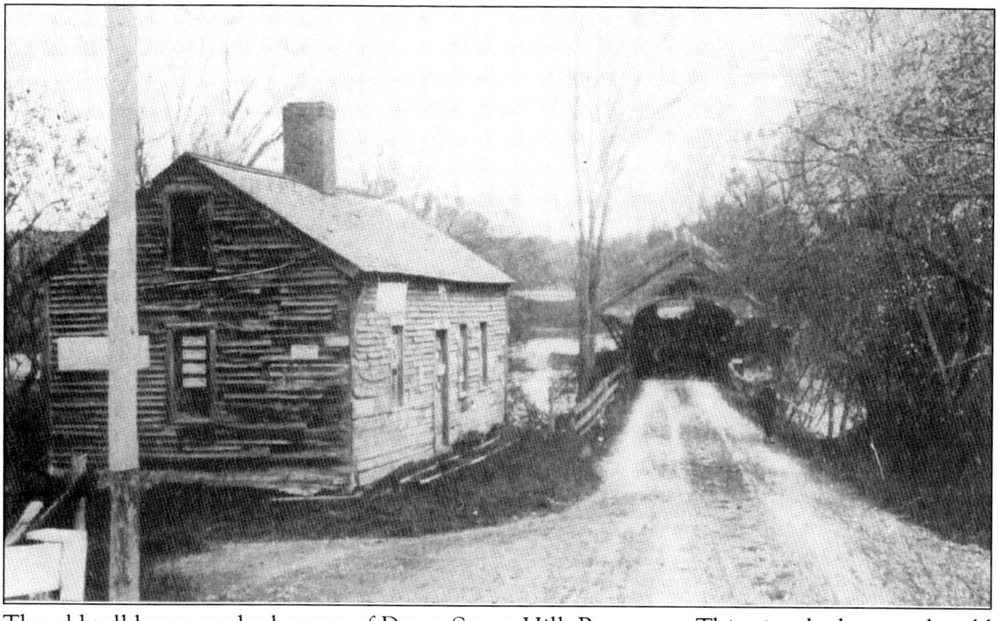

The old toll house at the bottom of Depot Street Hill, Boscawen. This view looks over the old Rainbow Bridge which spanned the Merrimack River to Canterbury, N.H., from 1857 to 1907.

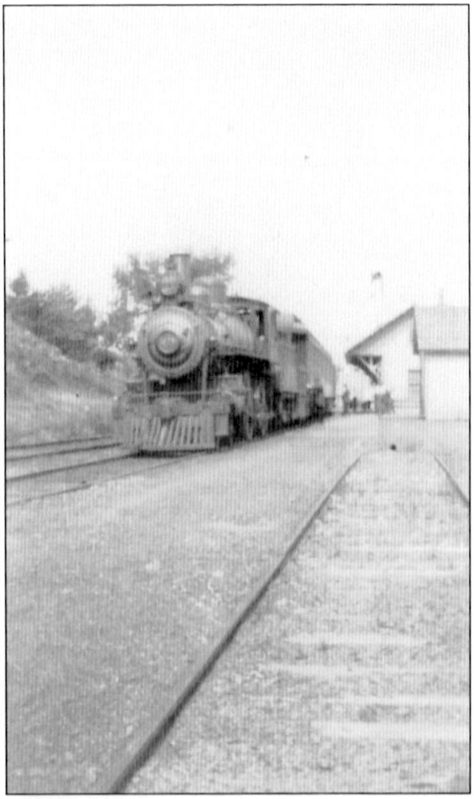

A Boston & Maine train at the Boscawen railroad station.

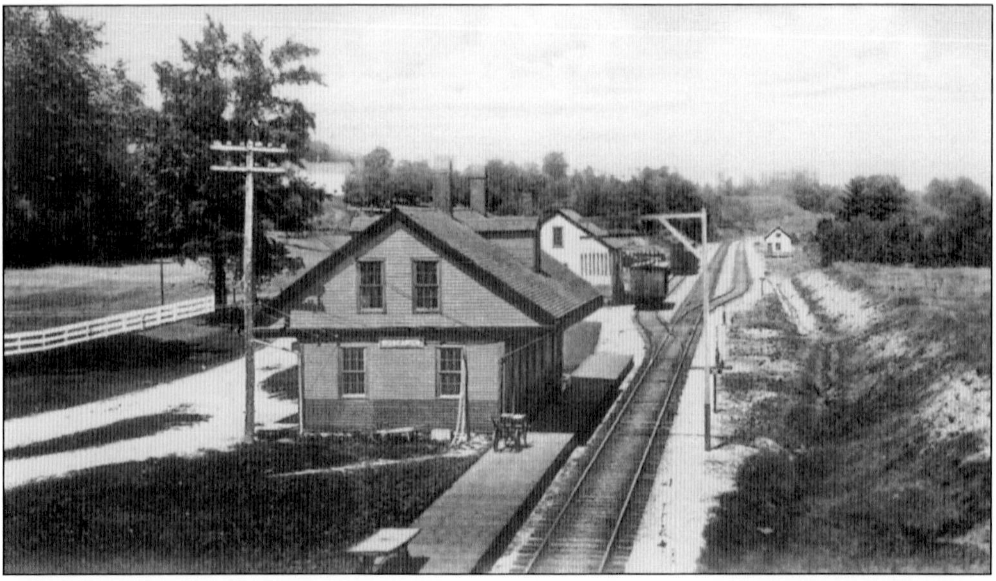

The old Northern Railroad (Boston & Maine) looking north up the tracks from an old overpass at Boscawen. The railroad station and freight building are on the left. Further up the track to the right is the crew work shed. Boscawen station was later moved to N.H. Route 4, just north of Flander's Mill Pond on the left side of Route 4, Boscawen.

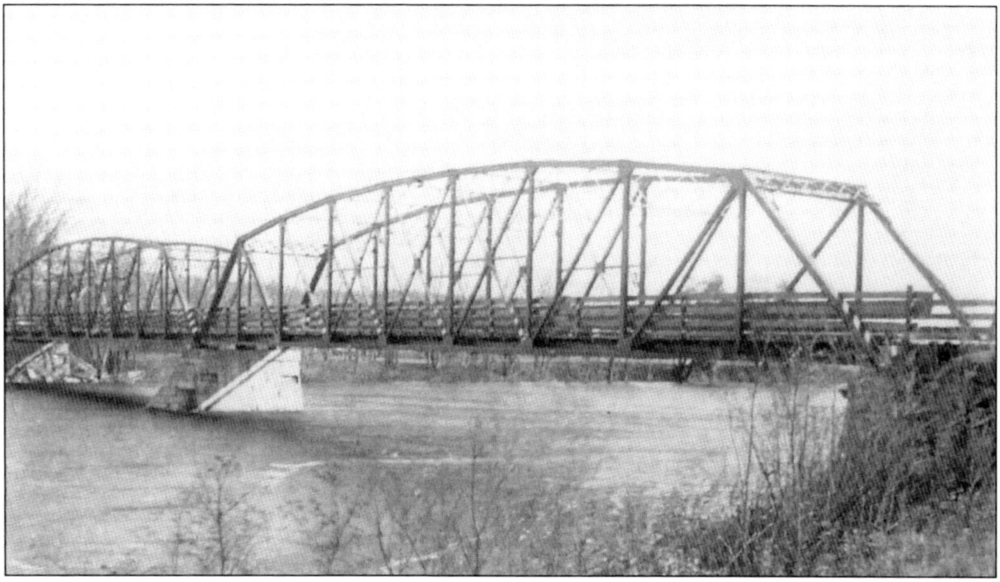

The steel replacement bridge for the old wooden Rainbow Bridge between Boscawen and Canterbury, N.H. Mr. John W. Storrs was the consulting engineer.

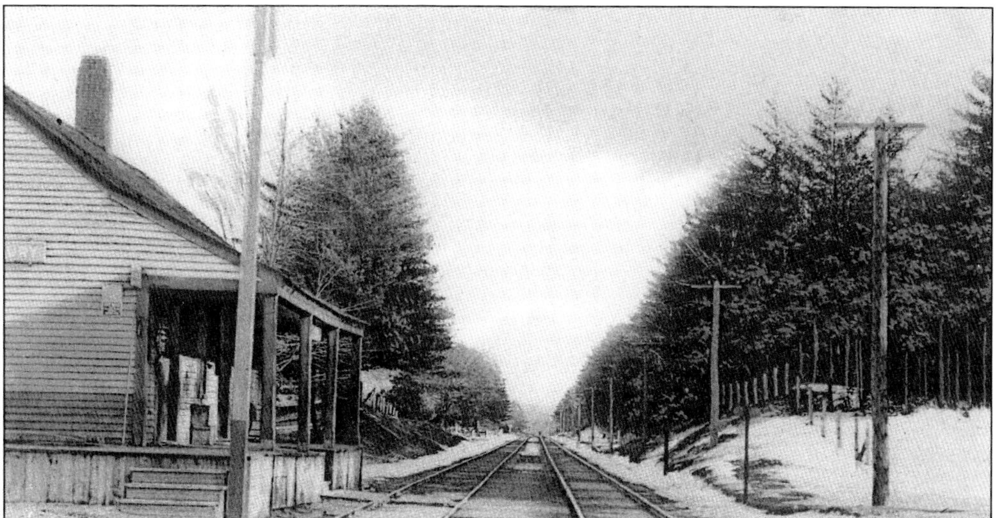

The Canterbury Depot looking south. This is the east side of the main line to Concord, N.H.; the right track is the siding at Canterbury, N.H., 1908.

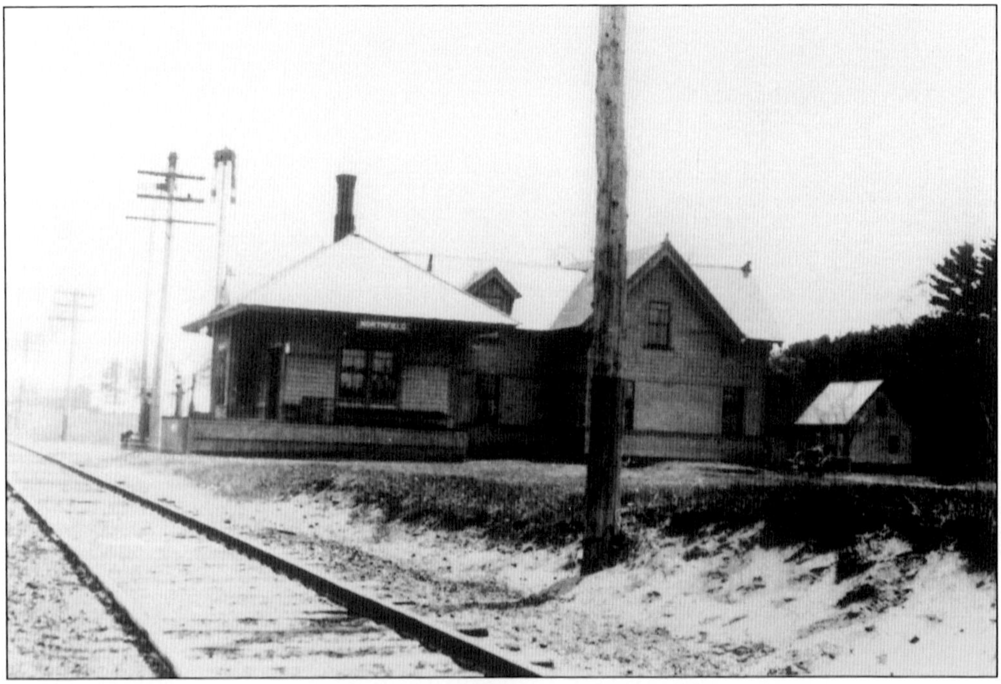

The Northfield Station, "Sandoggedy" Pond Road, Northfield, N.H., early 1900s.

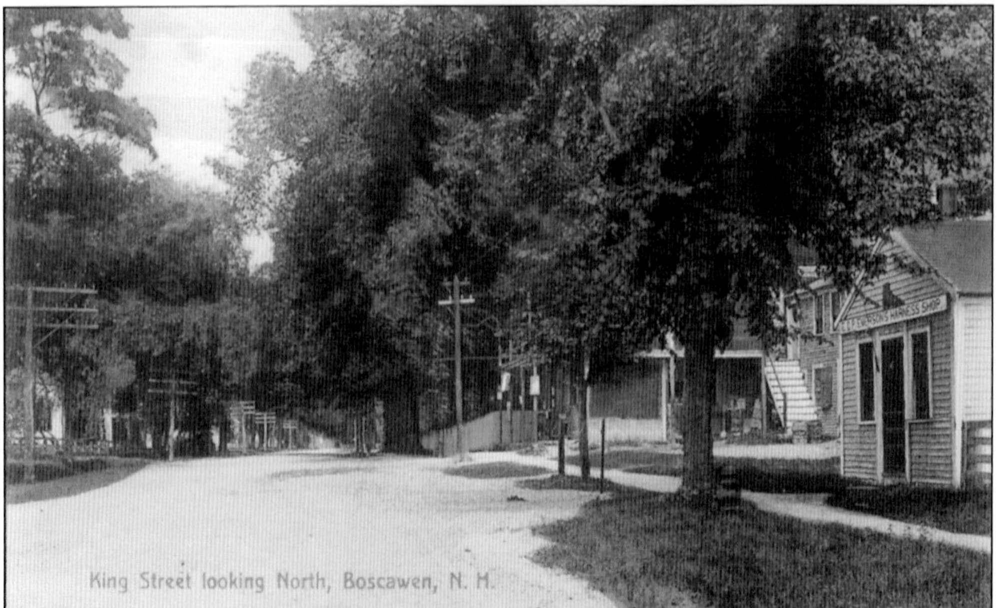

King Street, Boscawen, looking north from the southern end of village. The small wooden building to the right was once E.C.P. Everson's harness shop. The brick building (built 1818–20) was where the famous Boscawen stamp was issued in 1846.

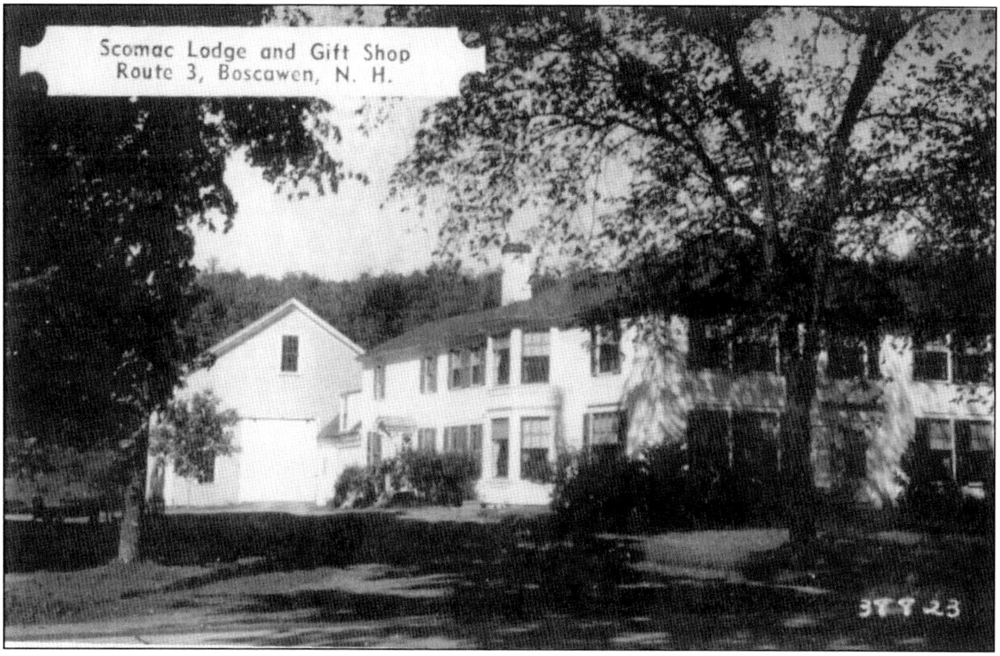

The Scomac Lodge and Gift shop, also known as the Homestead or Carters Tavern, 1765. Today it is known as the Kettle and Crane, Boscawen.

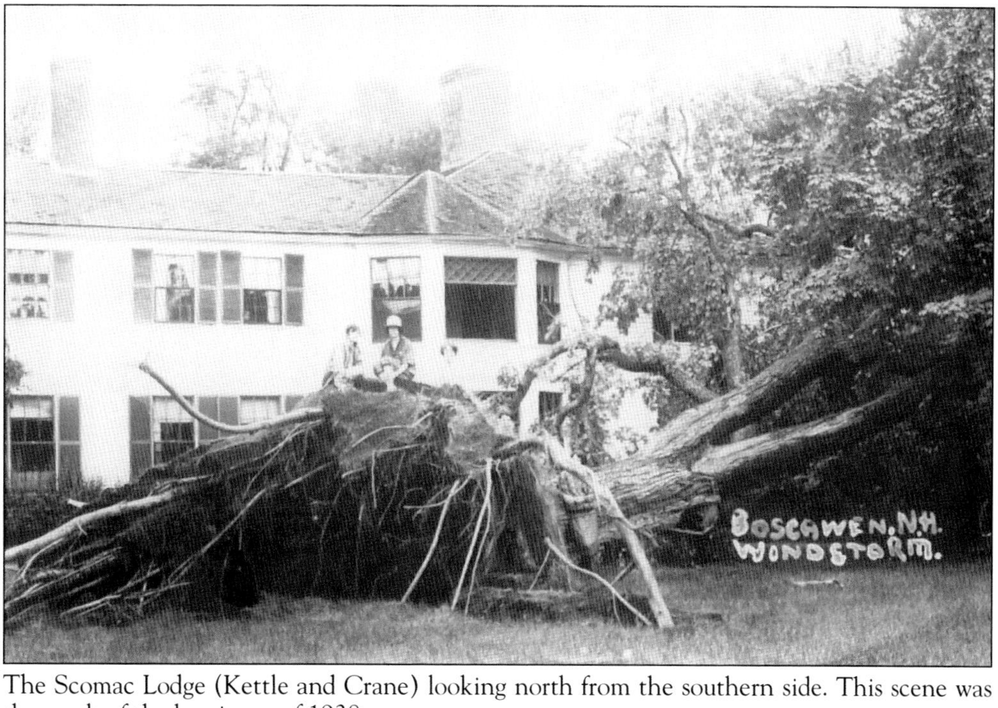

The Scomac Lodge (Kettle and Crane) looking north from the southern side. This scene was the result of the hurricane of 1938.

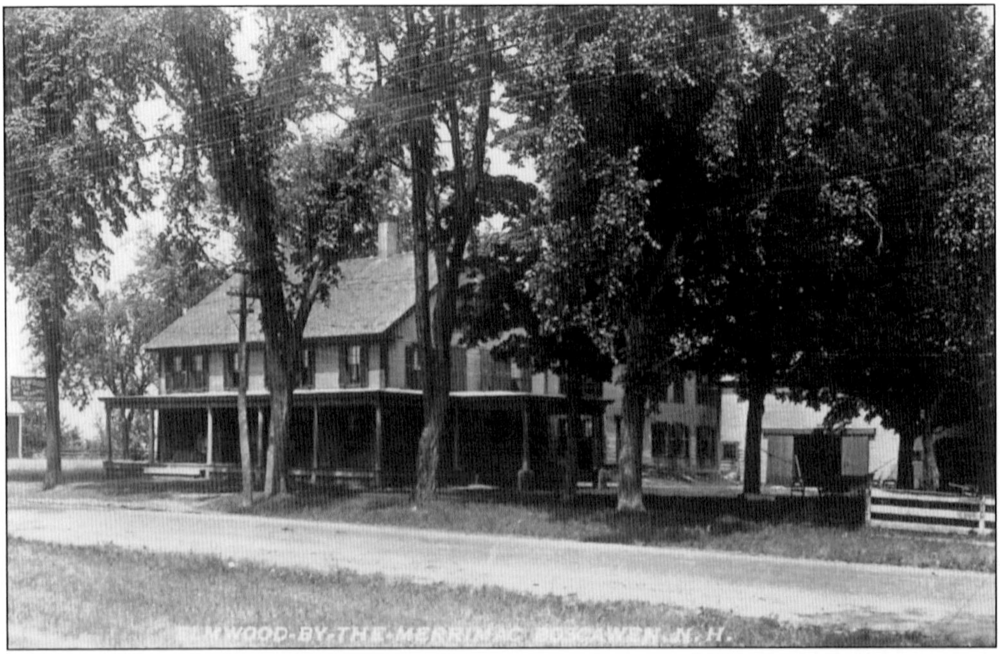

Elmwood by the Merrimack, Boscawen. In 1930 it burned, but soon after it was rebuilt as a diner and motor lodge. It is still called the Elmwood.

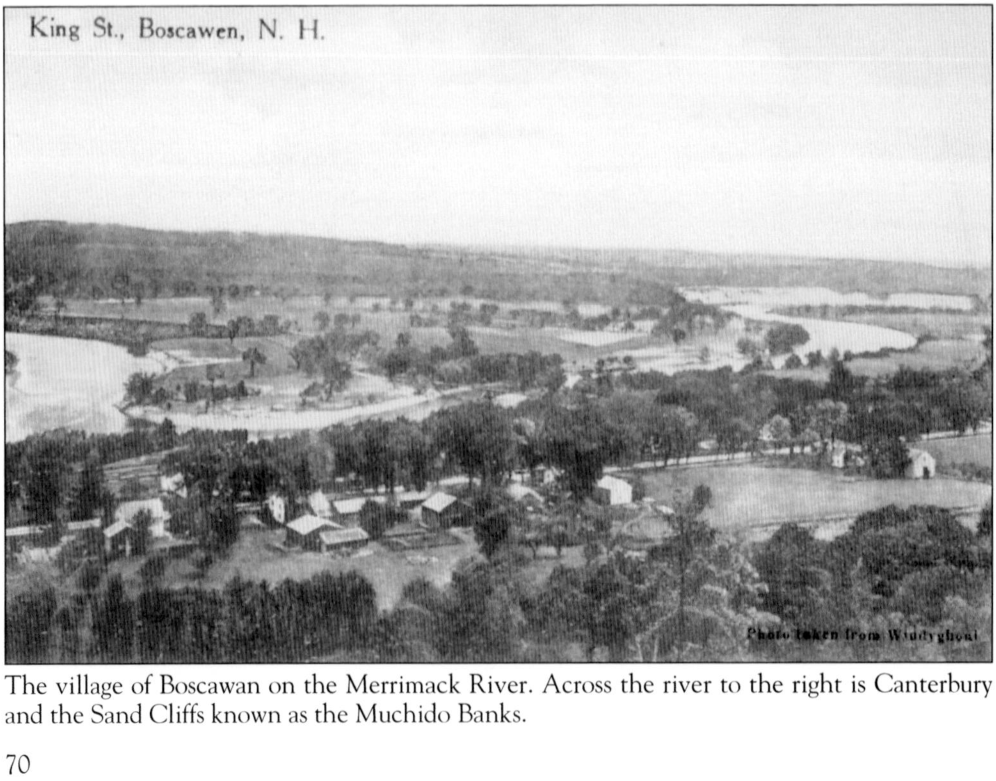

The village of Boscawan on the Merrimack River. Across the river to the right is Canterbury and the Sand Cliffs known as the Muchido Banks.

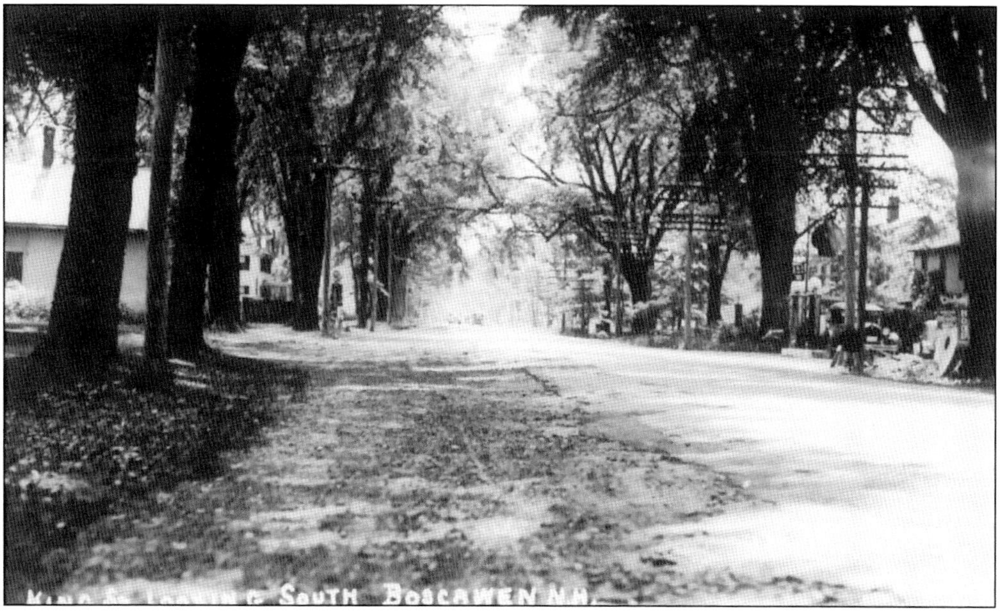

King Street, early 1930s. Here we are looking south by the Grist Store Wheel Garage, Boscawen.

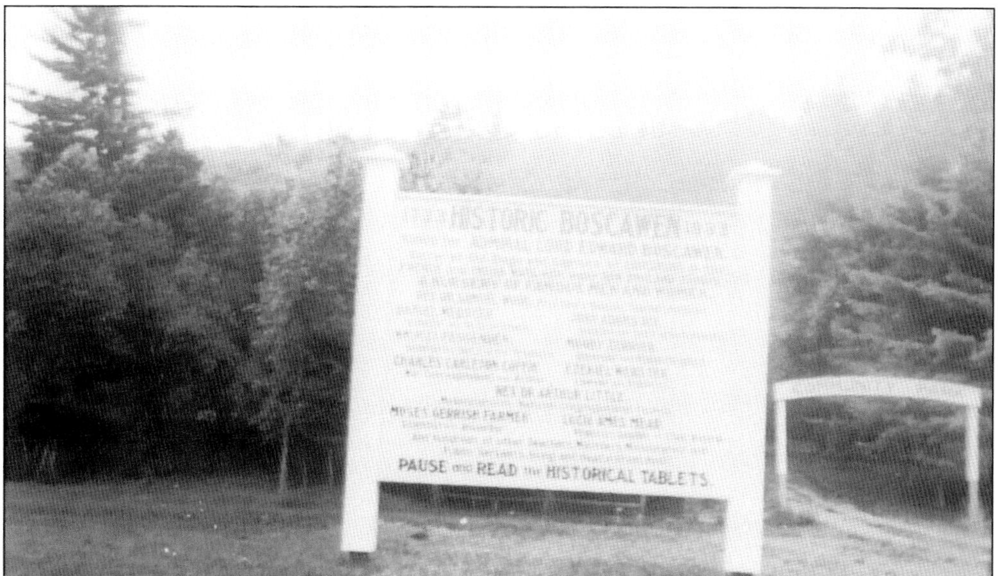

The historical tablet which graces the south side of the entrance to the community park in Boscawen, named for Admiral Lord Edward Boscawen.

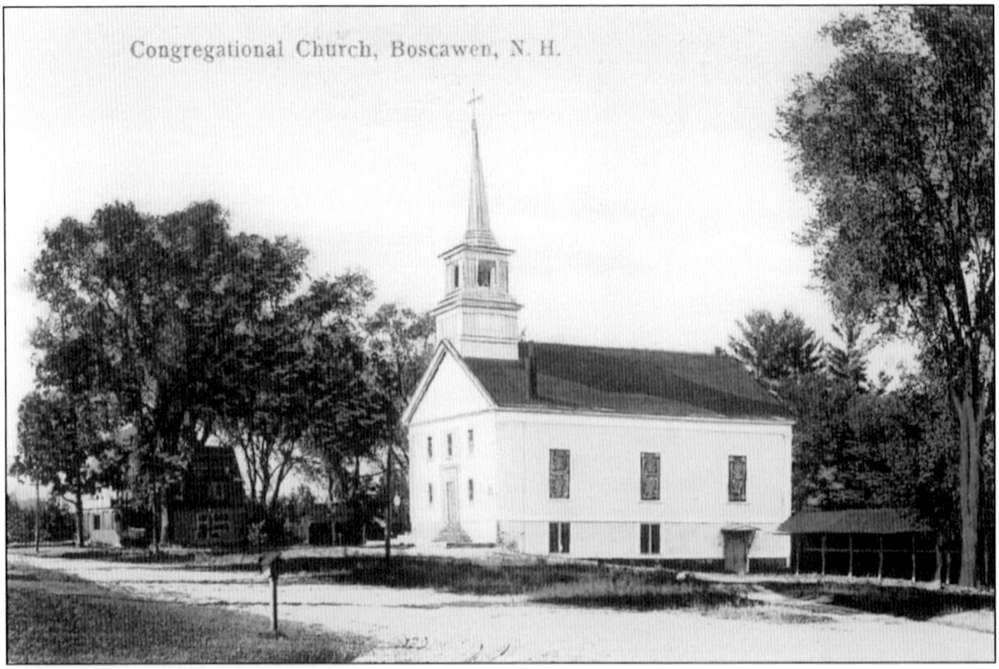

The Boscawen Congregational Church, 1799, facing west onto King Street, after it was turned in 1840 from facing north. In 1940 the church was turned once more to face the south, the direction she faces today.

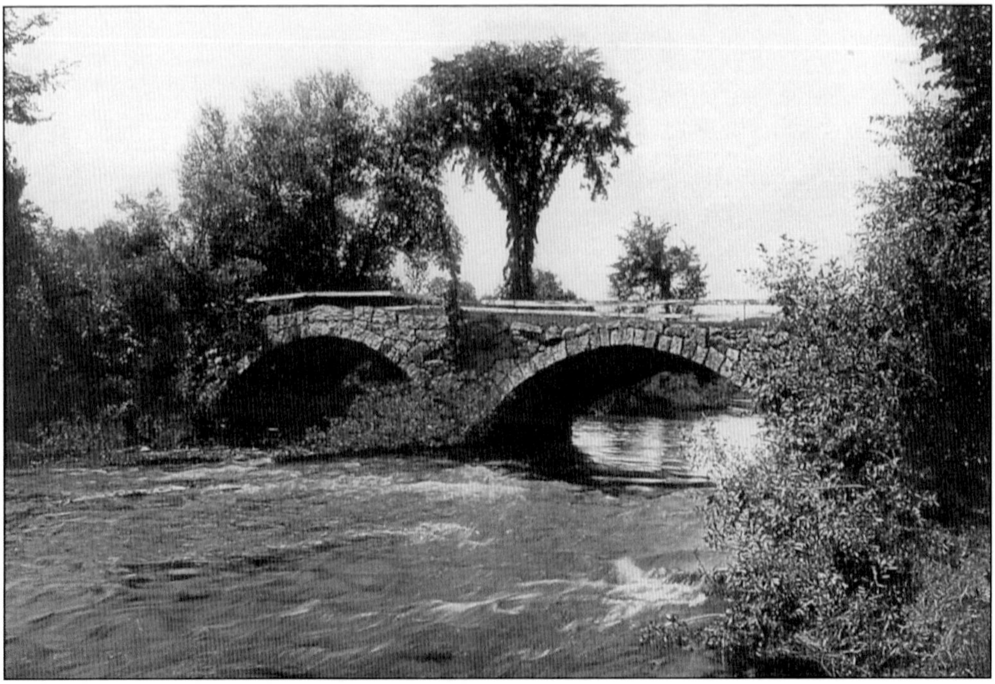

The Contoocook River above Hillsboro, 1899.

Three

The Meeting of the Waters
Franklin, New Hampshire

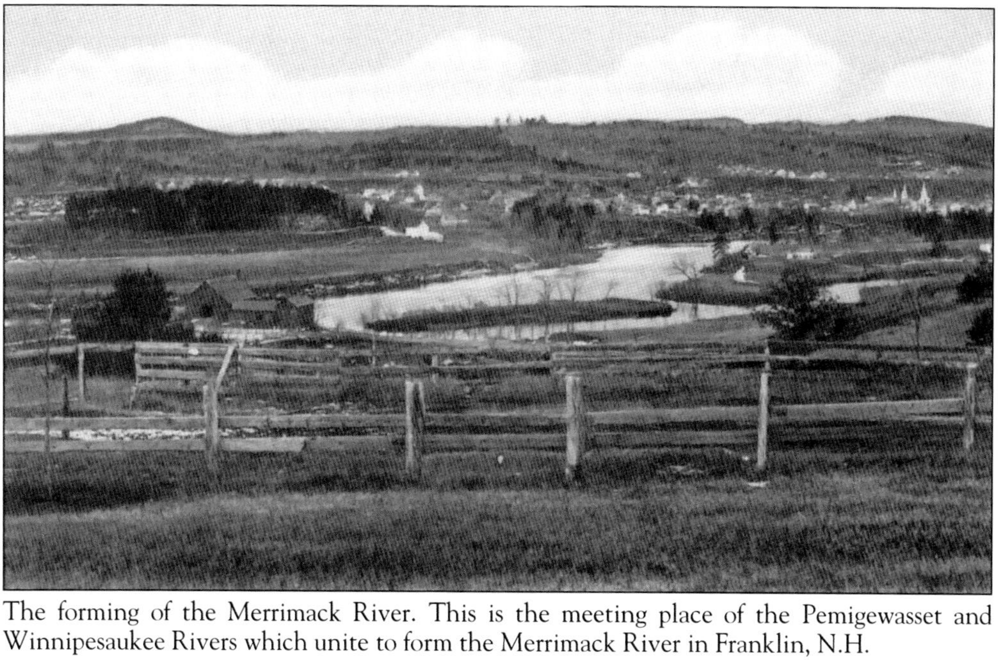

The forming of the Merrimack River. This is the meeting place of the Pemigewasset and Winnipesaukee Rivers which unite to form the Merrimack River in Franklin, N.H.

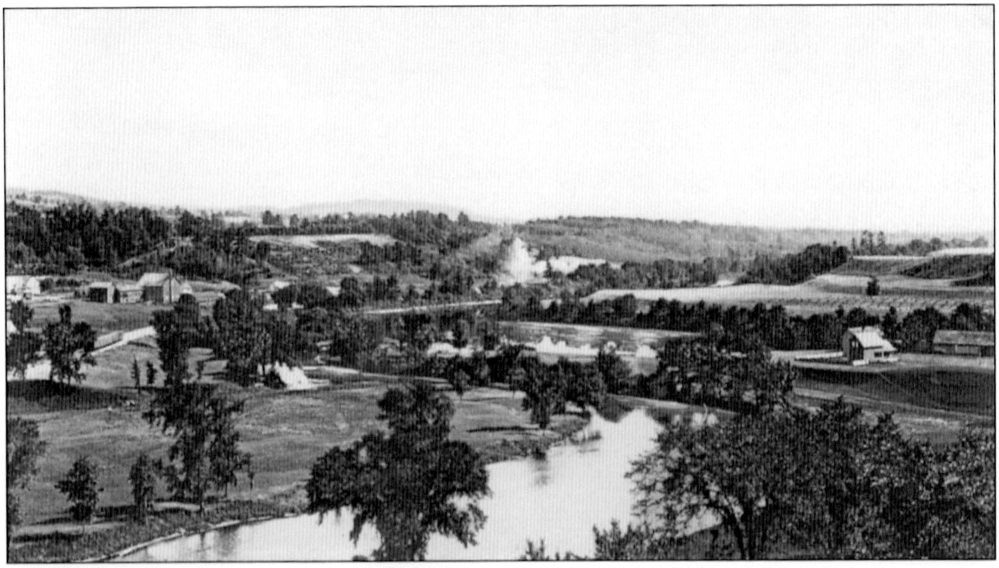

The head of the Merrimack, Franklin Falls, 1900s. From here the Bristol Branch diverges, running to Bristol. The thrifty manufacturing community is 30 miles from this point, on the shore of Newfound Lake, which is mountain-environed, full of fish, and popular with summer campers and farmhouse boarders.

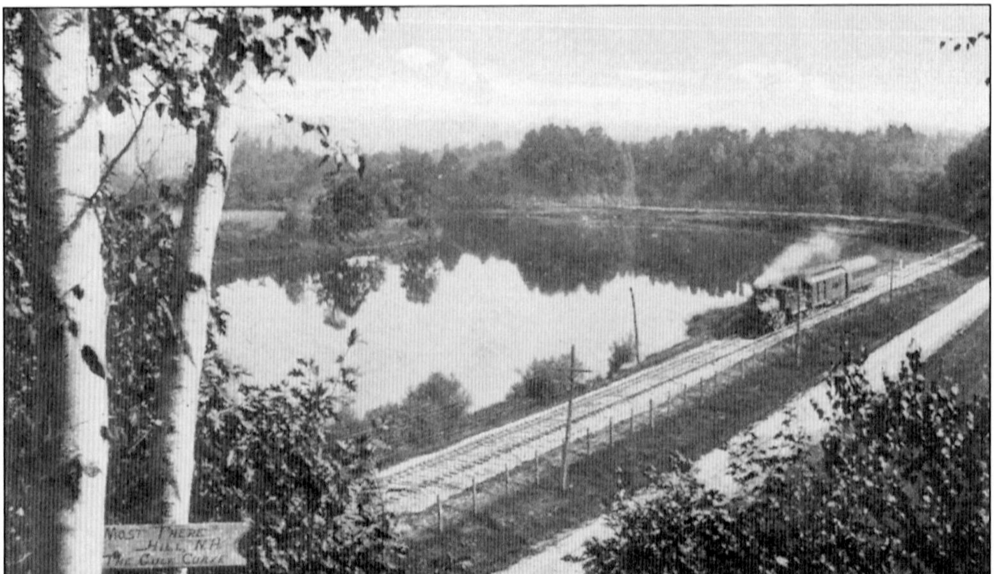

The Gulf Curve, Hill, N.H. Here we are looking down the Pemigewasset River to the old Bristol and Franklin Branch of the B&M Railroad.

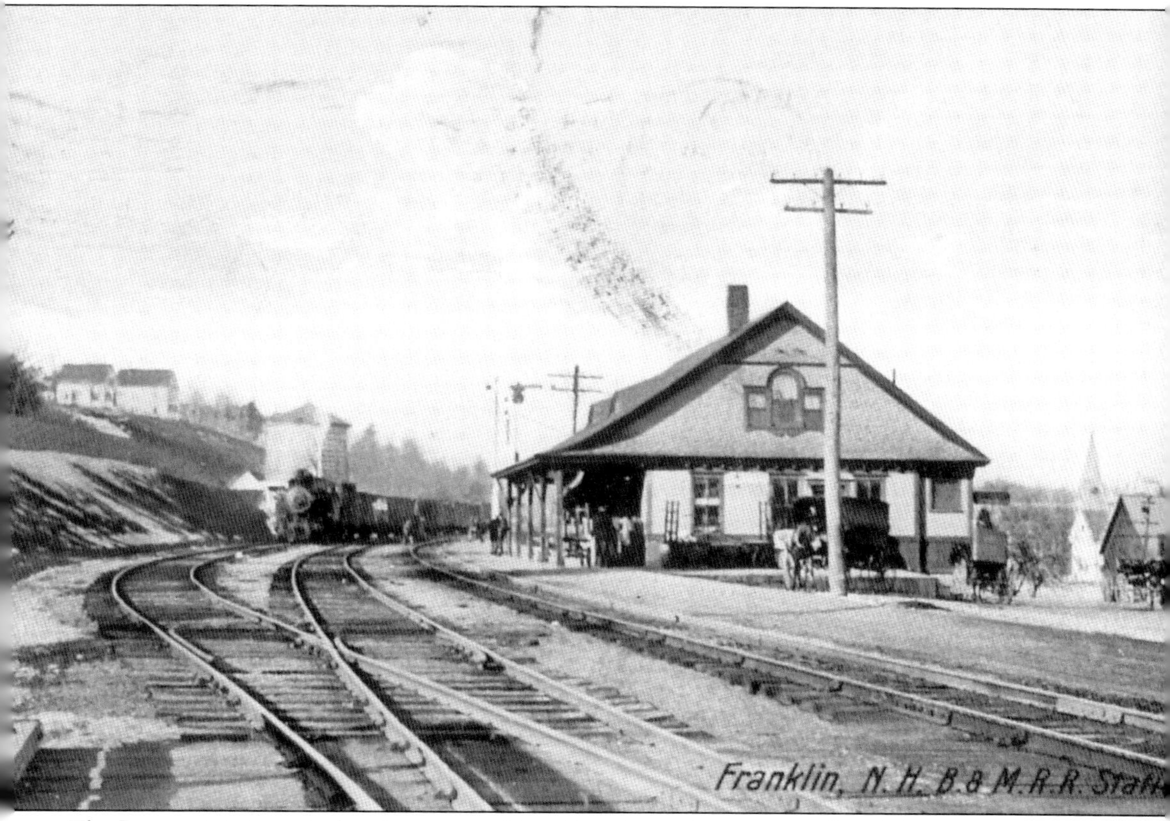

The Boston & Maine Railroad station in West Franklin looking north, 1910. This is where the Pemigewasset and Winnipesaukee Rivers unite to form the Merrimack, from whence some say it derived its name, signifying in the Algonquin tongue, "the meeting of the waters." The rivers furnished the power for numerous large manufactories.

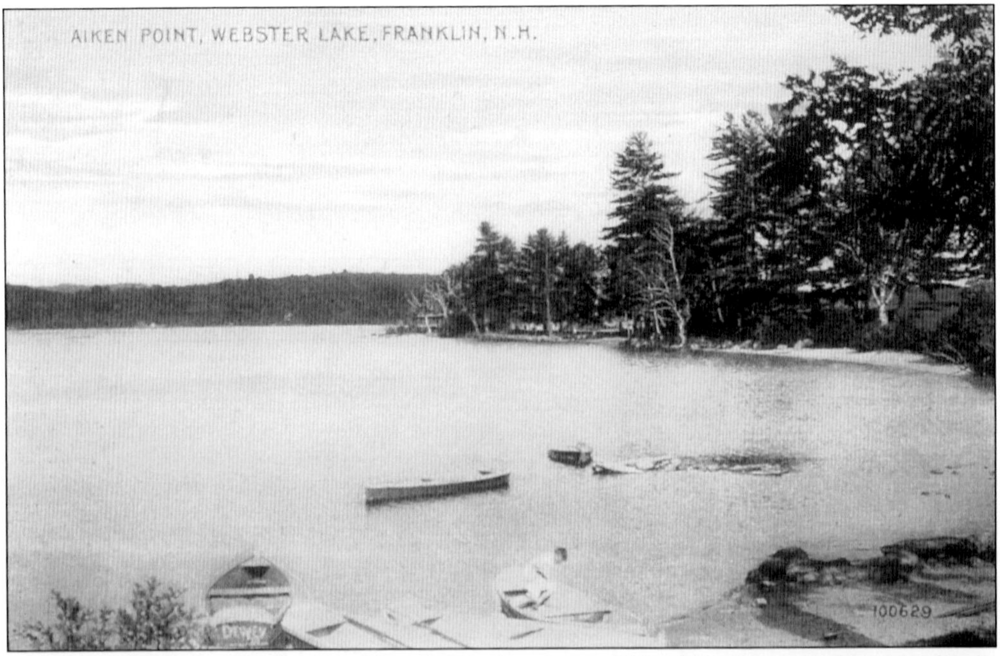

Alken Point, Webster Lake, Franklin, 1900s. Just beyond Franklin the road skirts the banks of Webster Lake, one of the many sheets of water to be seen on this line, and one of the most attractive. It has pleasant camp grounds near the railroad and shoreline.

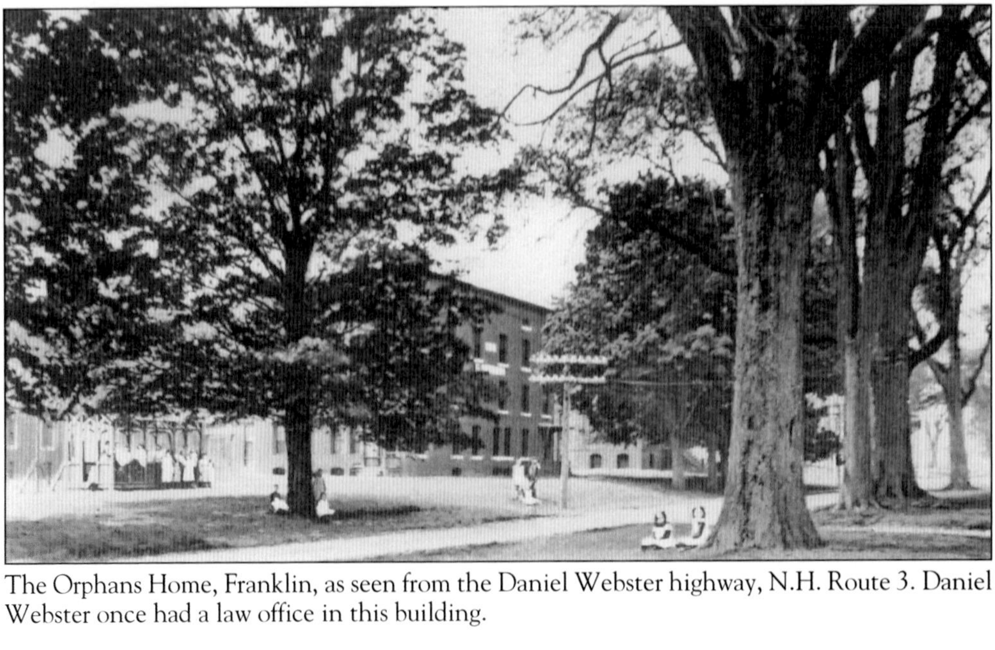

The Orphans Home, Franklin, as seen from the Daniel Webster highway, N.H. Route 3. Daniel Webster once had a law office in this building.

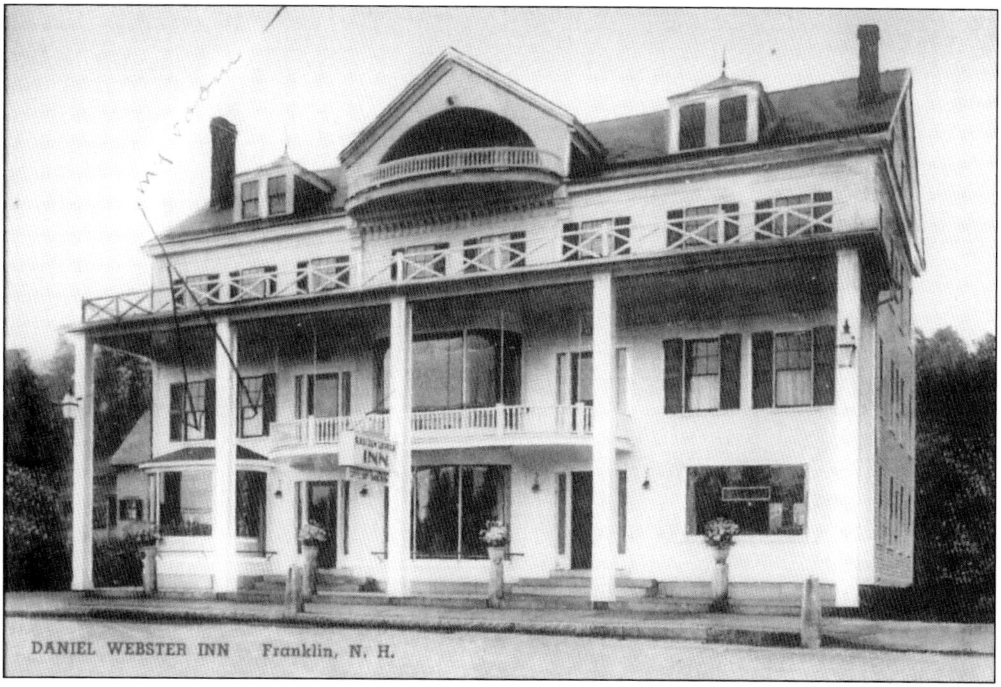

The Daniel Webster Inn, West Franklin, at the intersection of N.H. Route 3 and N.H. Route 3A. This structure was later taken down to make room for the Benson Chevrolet shop.

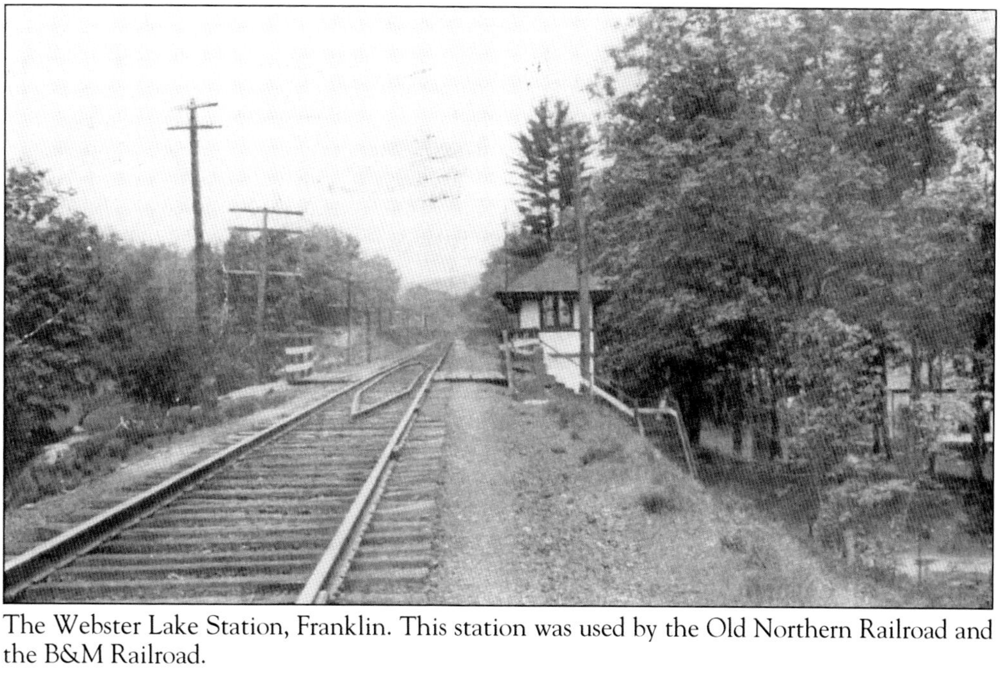

The Webster Lake Station, Franklin. This station was used by the Old Northern Railroad and the B&M Railroad.

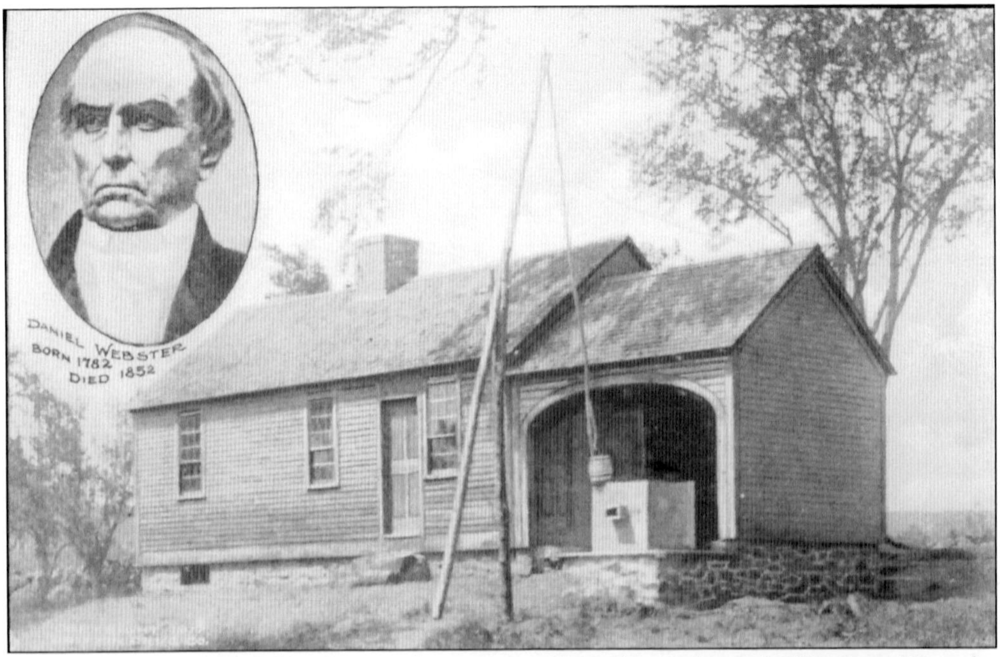

Daniel Webster's birthplace. This small, two-room frame house, located off Route 127, is the spot where the famous statesman and attorney spent his boyhood years. Built about 1780, it was restored in 1913.

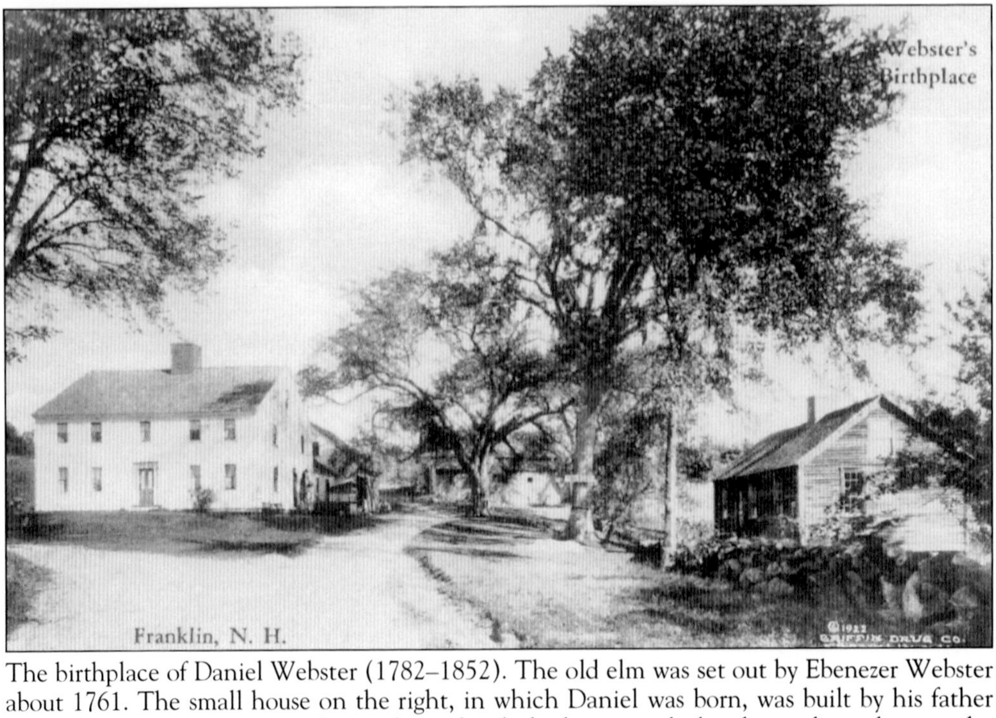

The birthplace of Daniel Webster (1782–1852). The old elm was set out by Ebenezer Webster about 1761. The small house on the right, in which Daniel was born, was built by his father Ebenezer Webster in 1780. The Webster family had previously lived in a log cabin on the opposite side of the road.

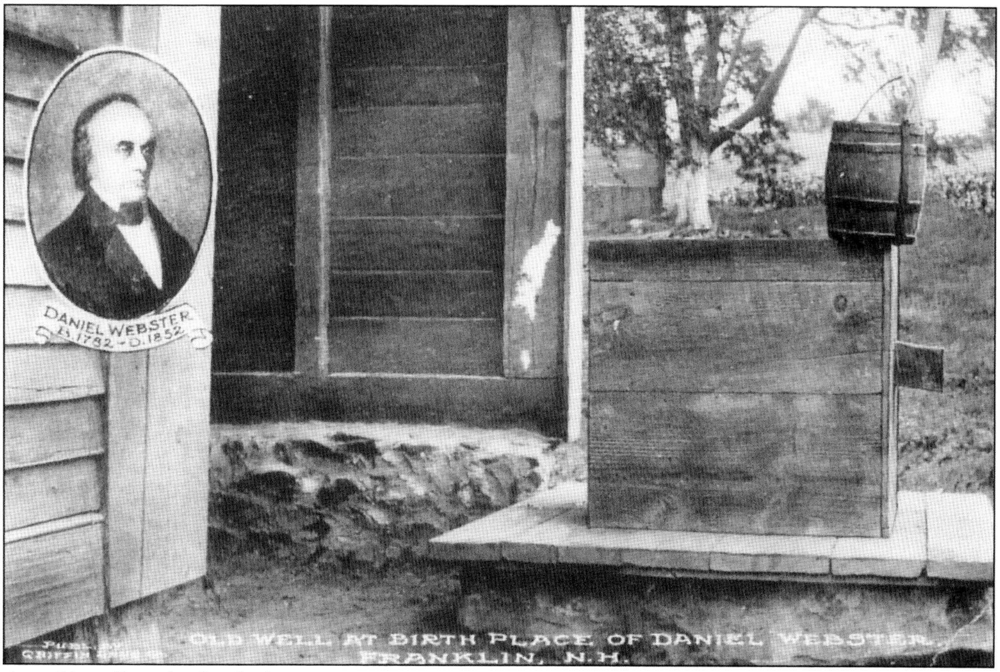

An old well at the birthplace.

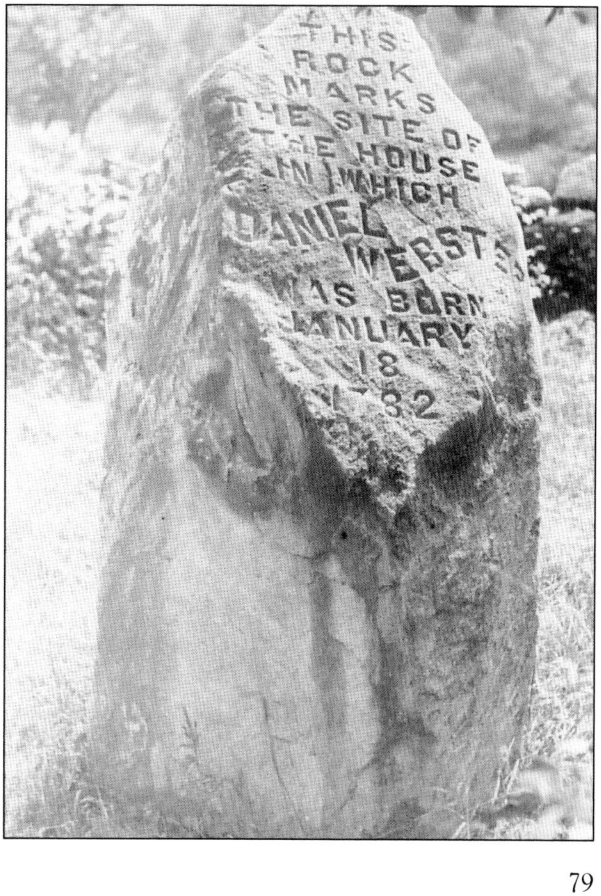

The commemorative rock. The inscription reads as follows: "This rock marks the site of the house in which Daniel Webster was born January 18, 1782."

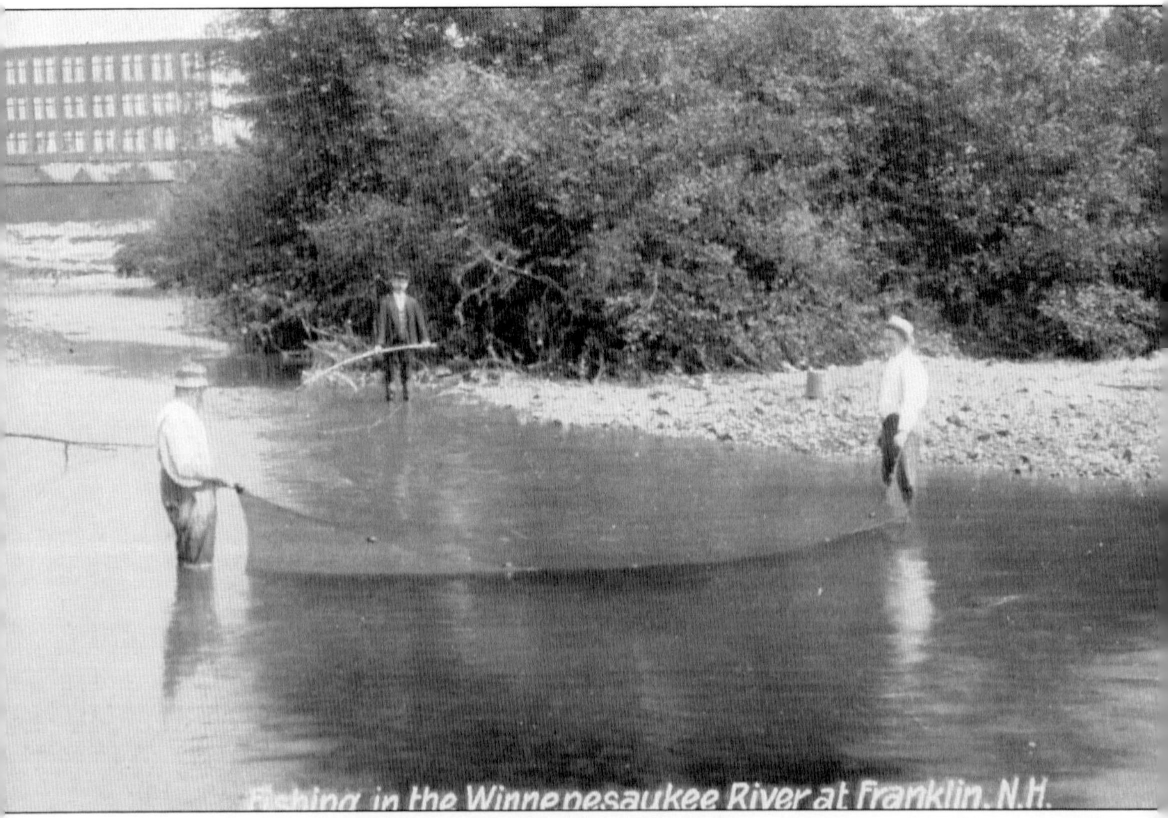

Fishing in the Winnipesaukee River at Franklin, 1908. Fishing was very good in this river, and also provided recreation for the many townspeople in the area.

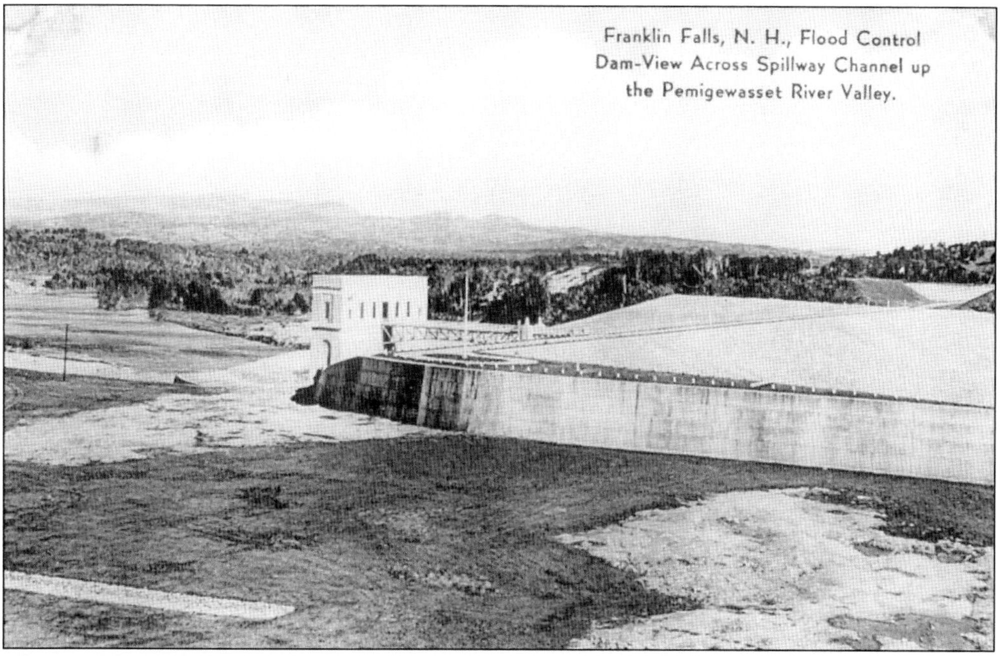

The Franklin Falls Flood Control Dam in a view across Spillway Channel up the Pemigewasset River Valley. This dam, constructed under the supervision of the Boston District, Corps of Engineers, U.S. Army, provides flood control for the Merrimack Valley. Construction of the $4,900,000 dam was commenced in November 1939, and was completed in October 1942.

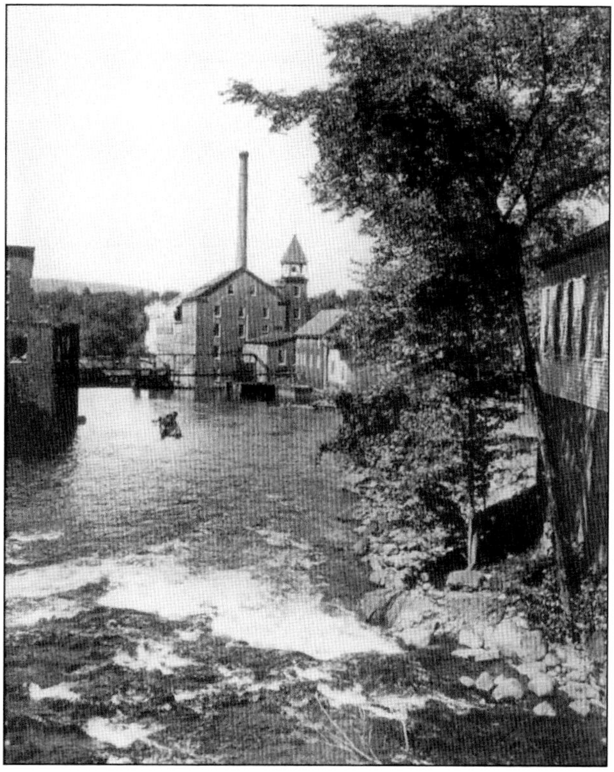

A mill on the Winnipesaukee River. The first planning mill in this section of the country was located in Franklin, but it was destroyed by a freshet in 1824. Another planning mill, built by the Morrisons, burned about 1850, and in 1855 the costly structure known as the Granite Mill was built and later met with a similar fate. The erection of the Franklin Mills in 1863 proved a great benefit to the village. The Upper Dam at Franklin Falls was built about 1852 to create power for a two-story hosiery mill erected at the same time. This mill was built of stone but it was also destroyed by fire.

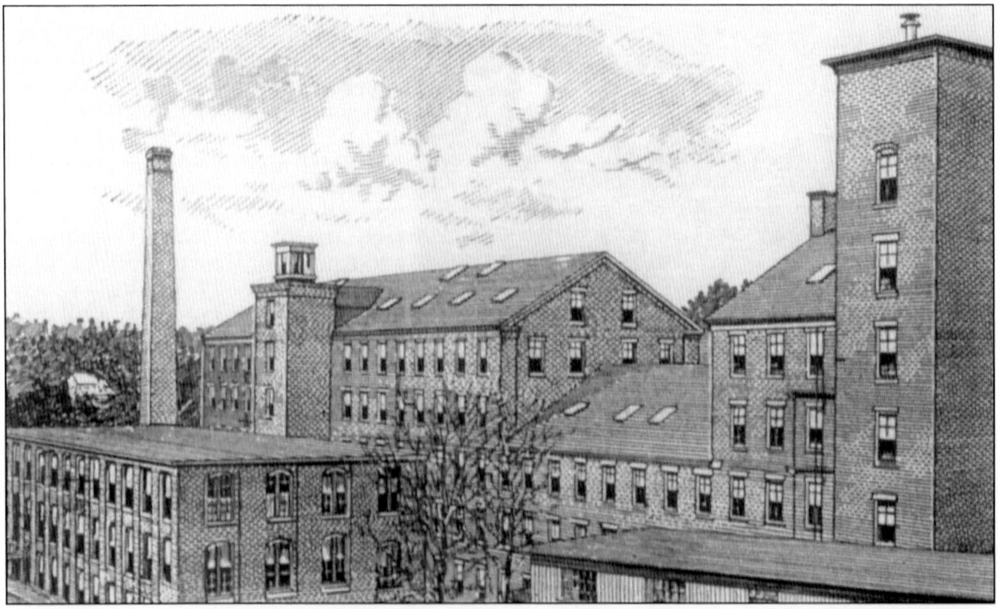

M.T. Stevens & Sons, the proprietors of Franklin Mills at Franklin Falls. The mechanical facilities here included 15 sets of cards and 120 broad looms. Employment was afforded to 250 hands, and, as the demand for ladies dress goods increased, the annual output reached higher figures. M.T. Stevens & Sons' fabrics were handled by the leading dealers throughout the entire United States during the nineteenth century.

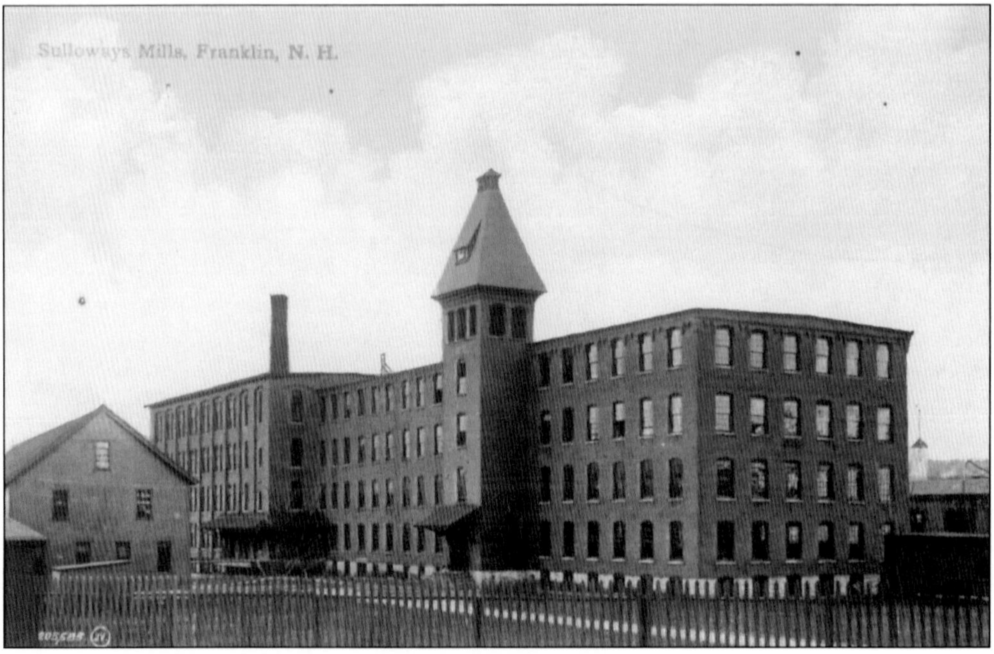

The Sulloway Mills on River Street, Franklin Falls, *c.* 1914.

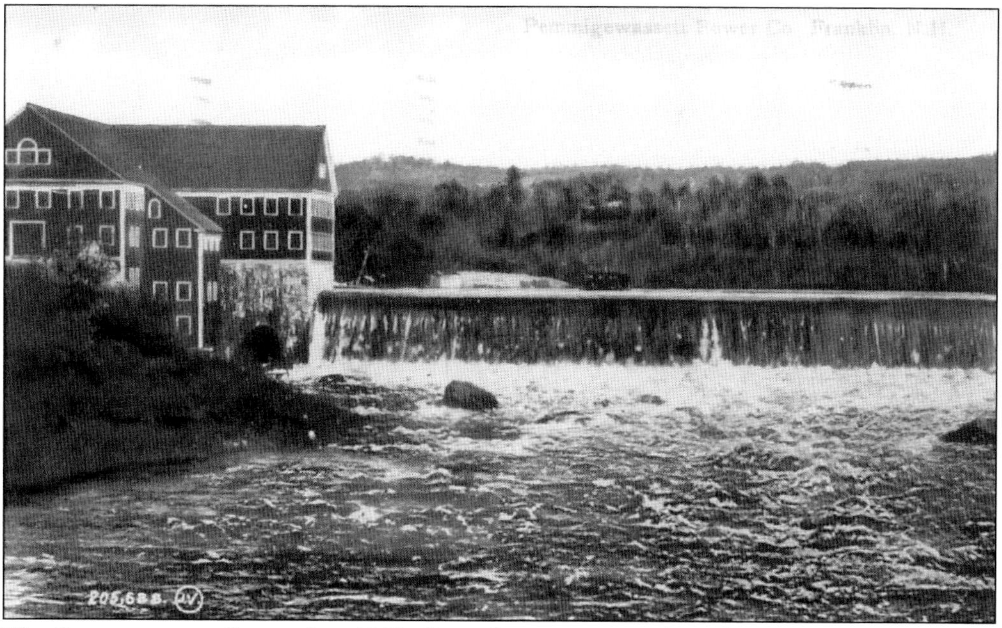

The Pemmigewasset Power Co., 1909. Over the years, a number of mills were started in the Lakes Region, particularly along the banks of the Winnipesaukee and Merrimack Rivers. By 1828, the use of water power for industry had become an established fact. Sawmills and gristmills were followed by paper mills, knitting mills, and factories for making machinery, tools, and textile needles.

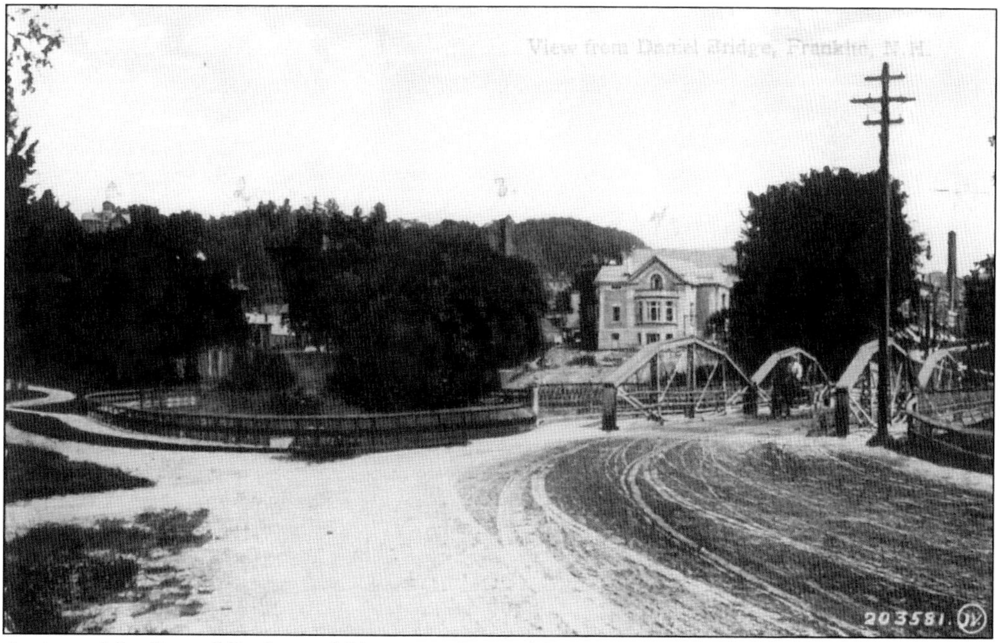

A view of the Daniel Bridge and library on Central Street entering the village of Franklin Falls, c. 1900.

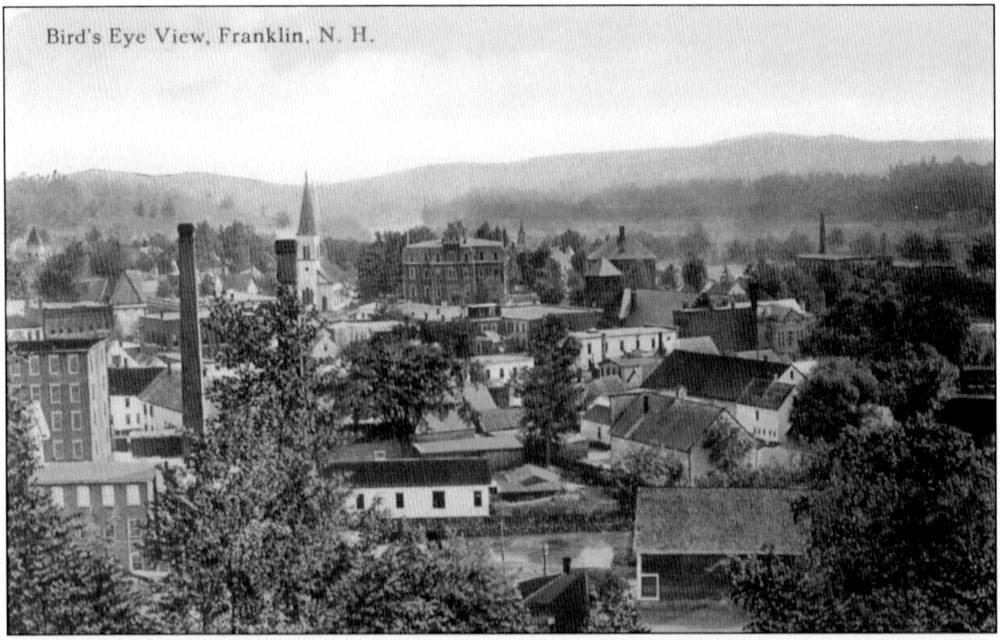

A view of Franklin Falls village, c. 1890. Franklin's history parallels that of Salisbury, since it was part of that town until 1828, when it was incorporated as the town of Franklin, taking its name from Benjamin Franklin. Sanbornton, Northfield, and Boscawen also contributed portions of their township to the new town. It was granted a city charter in 1895.

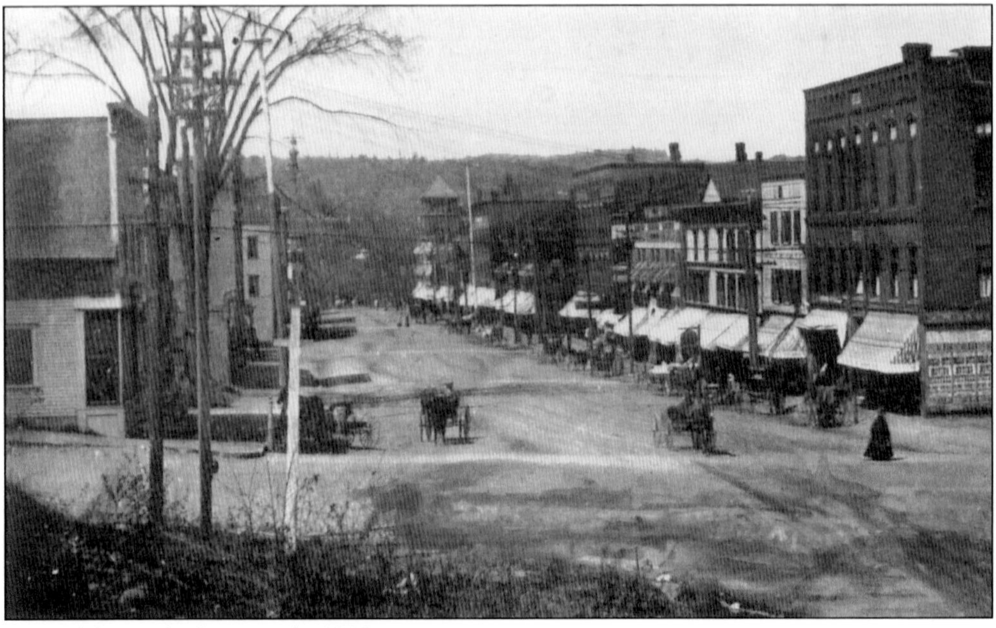

Central Street, looking south, 1900.

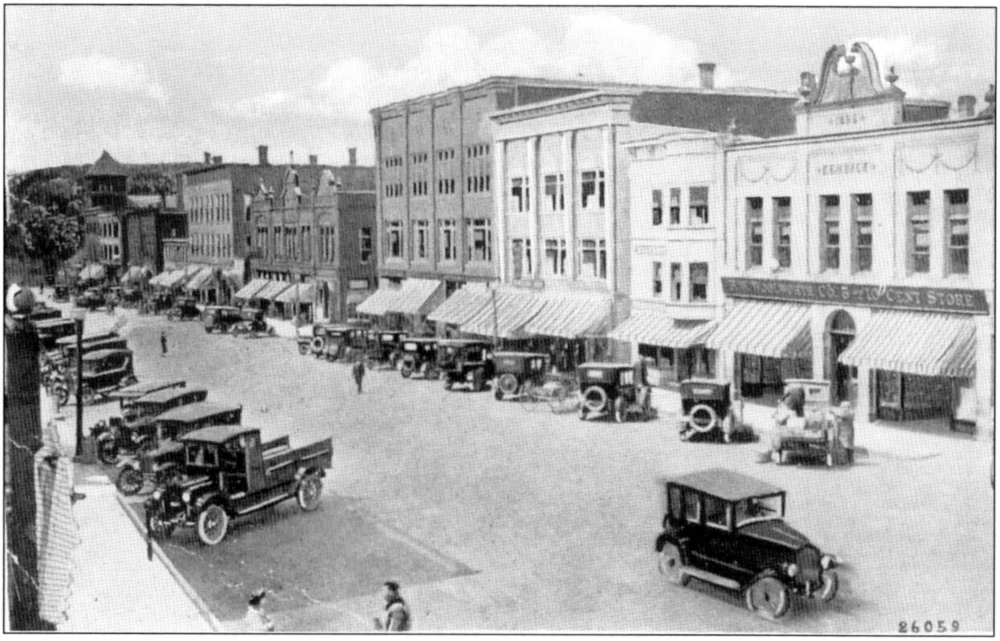

Main Street, looking south during the 1920s.

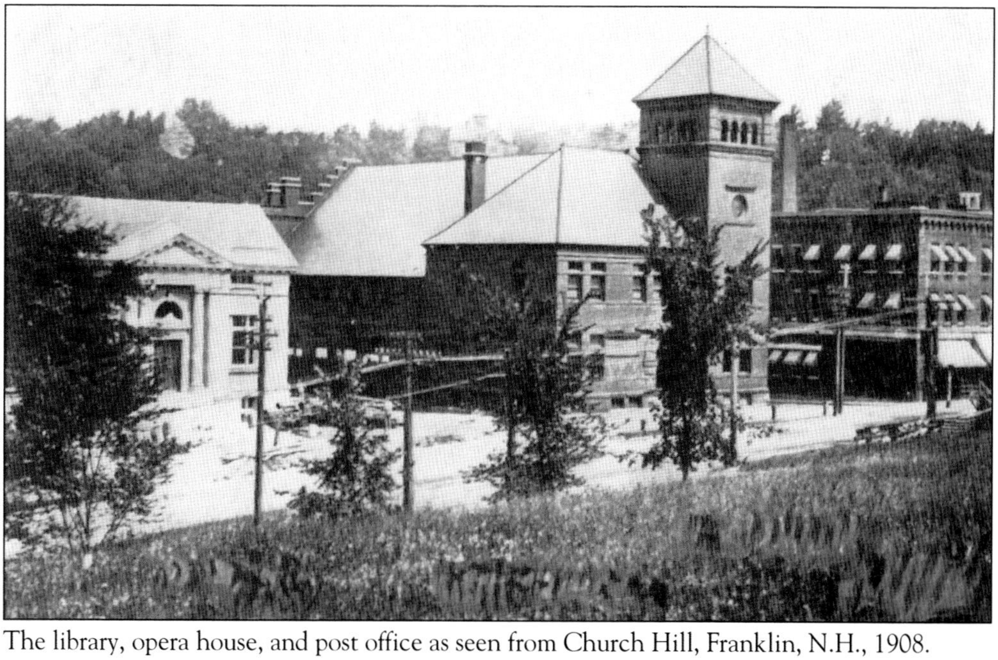

The library, opera house, and post office as seen from Church Hill, Franklin, N.H., 1908.

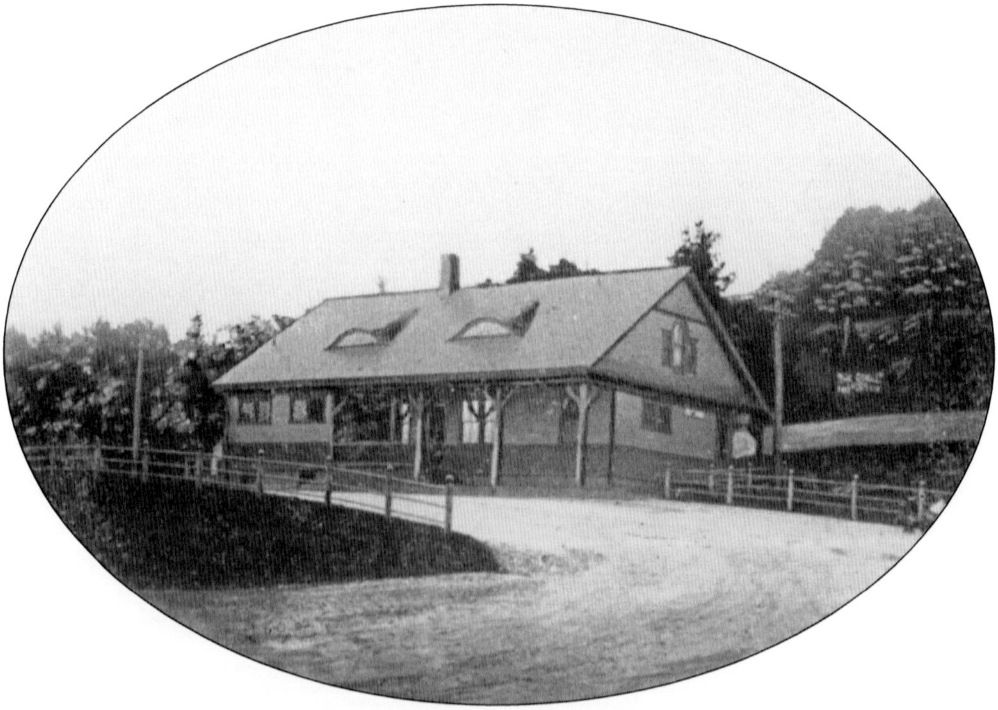

The Boston & Maine Railroad station, Franklin, early 1900s.

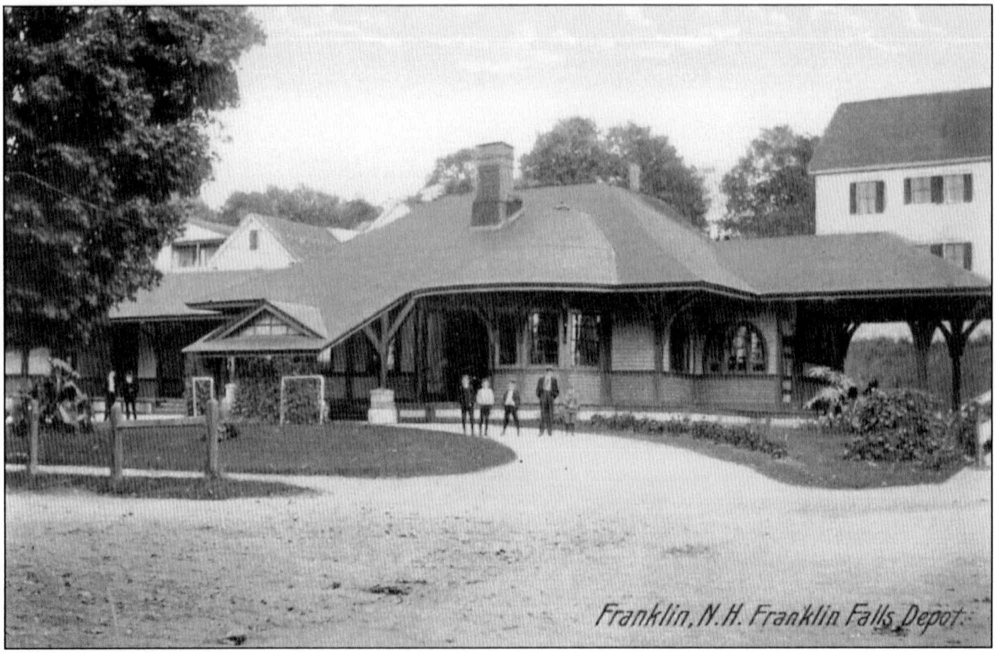

The Franklin Falls Depot. This was originally part of the old Tilton, Franklin & Belmont Railroad, Franklin.

Four

The Winnipesaukee

Tilton, Winnisquam, Belmont, and Laconia, New Hampshire

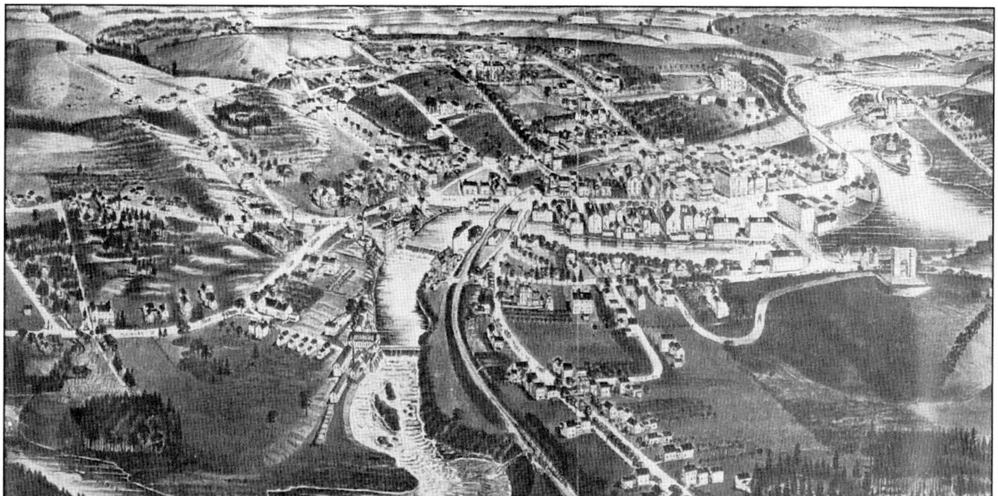

A bird's-eye map of Tilton and Northfield, 1884. Tilton was originally part of Sanbornton, and the first settlement of that town occurred within the limits of what is now Tilton in 1765–66.

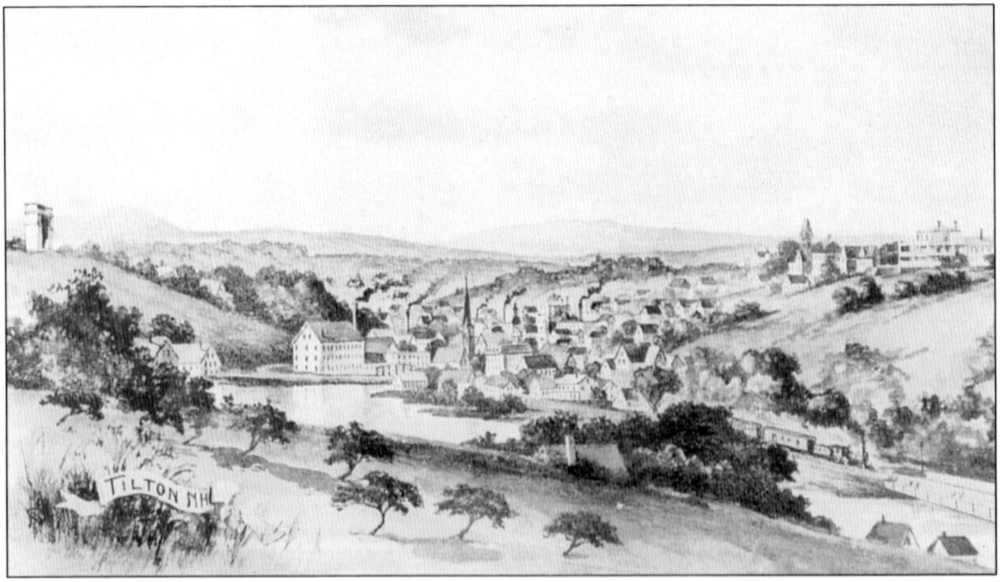

A view of Tilton, 1900. The attempt to form Tilton was made nearly a century later, with a petition presented to the General Court of the State of New Hampshire in 1850. In 1860, the town of Sanbornton held two special meetings to consider the matter, but nothing was accomplished until nearly a decade later. The act incorporating the town of Tilton was finally approved on June 30, 1869.

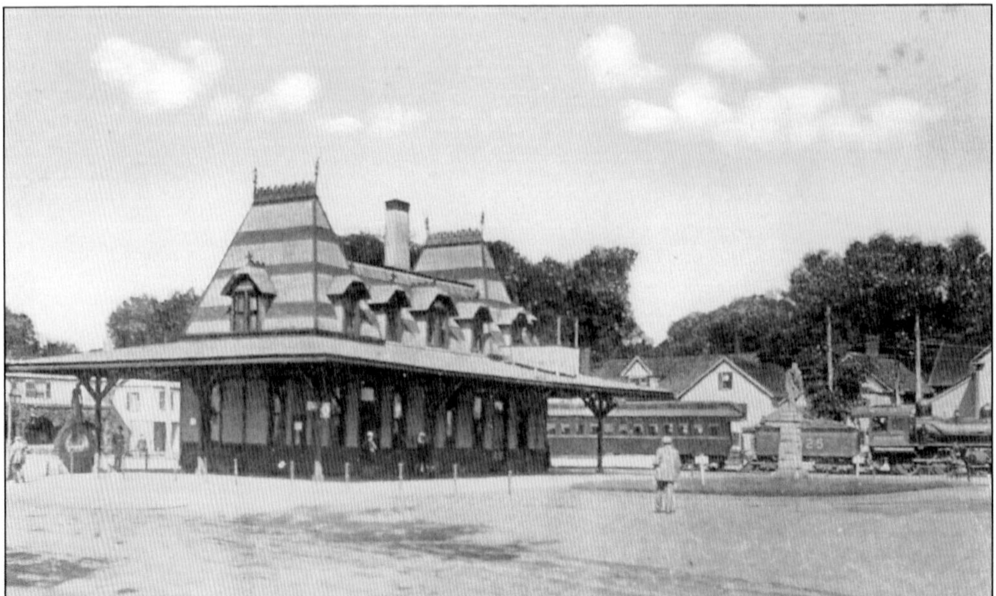

The Boston & Maine Railroad station, Tilton, *c.* 1912. To the right is "Indian Square." The road from Concord to Tilton was completed in 1848.

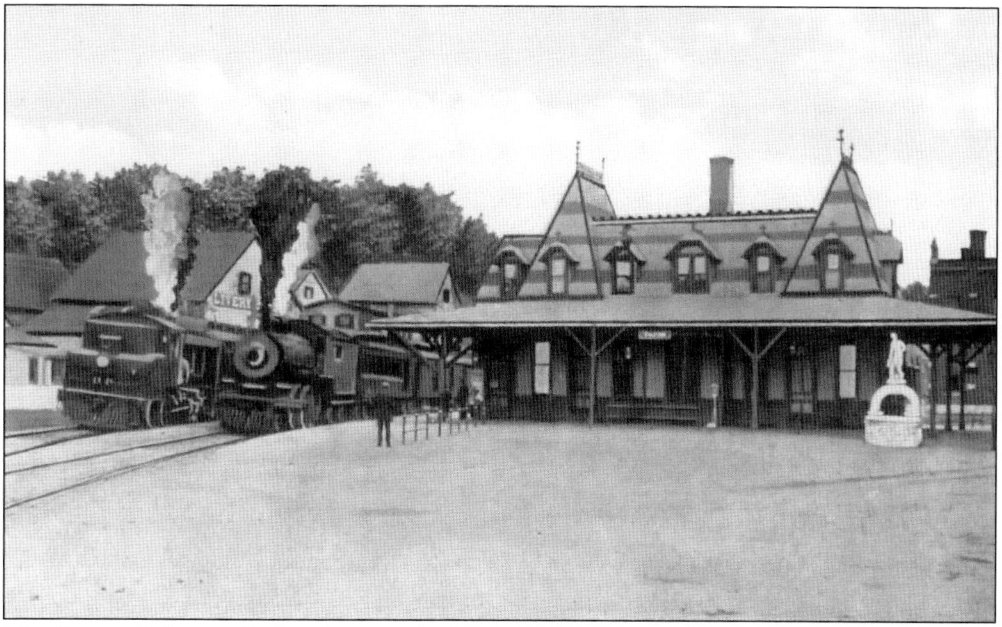

The Boston & Maine Railroad station looking east from Main Street. The train on the left is the Tilton, Franklin & Belmont Branch Line which shows part of the of the B&M main line to Tilton and Belmont Junction from Tilton, *c.* 1912.

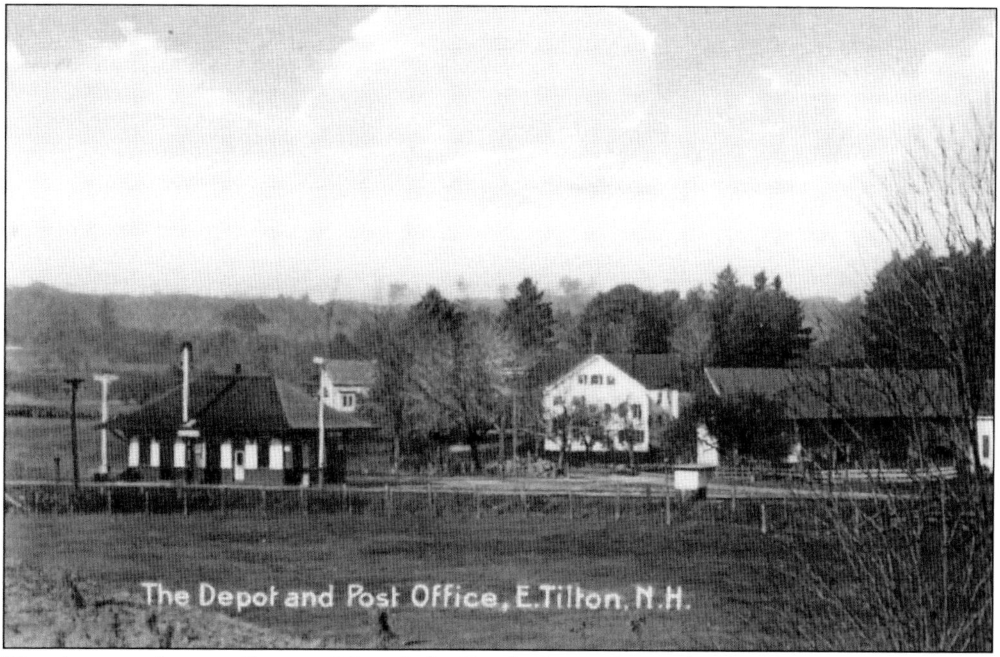

The depot and post office on Silver Lake Road, East Tilton. This building is known as the Mohawk Store.

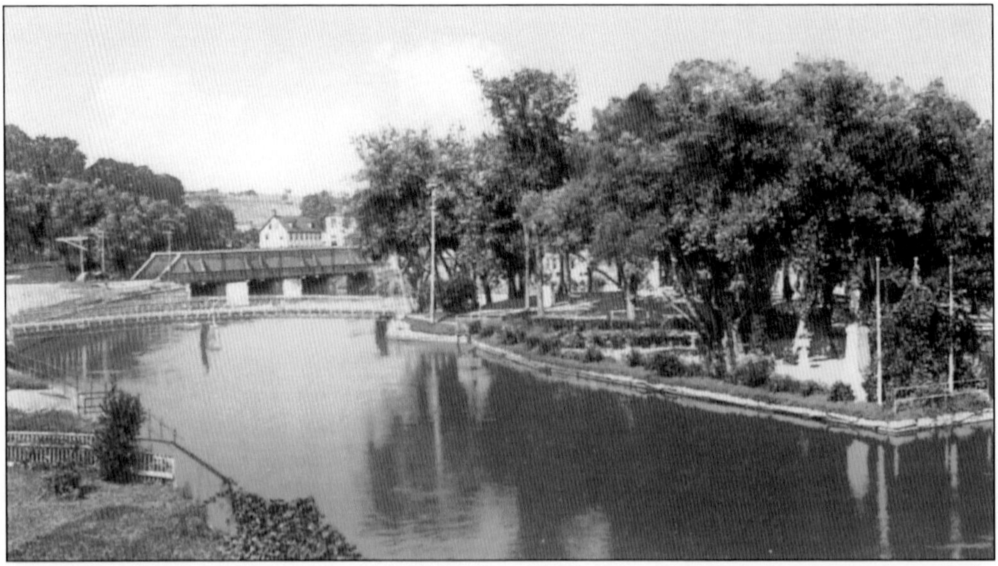

The Winnipesaukee River with a railroad bridge and island, *c.* 1908. This is the junction of the Tilton and Belmont Railroad Branch with the main line of the Concord & Montreal Railroad, later known as the Boston & Maine Railroad.

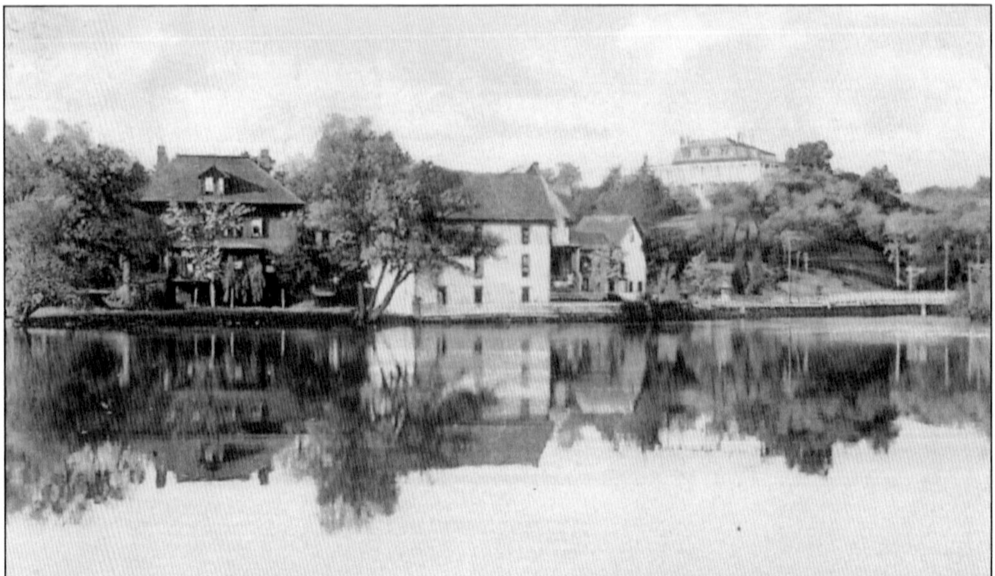

The Winnipesaukee River, Tilton Home, 1911. The Winnipesaukee River flows through Tilton. A short distance above the railroad station, and within the village, is the charming summer house built by Mr. Tilton.

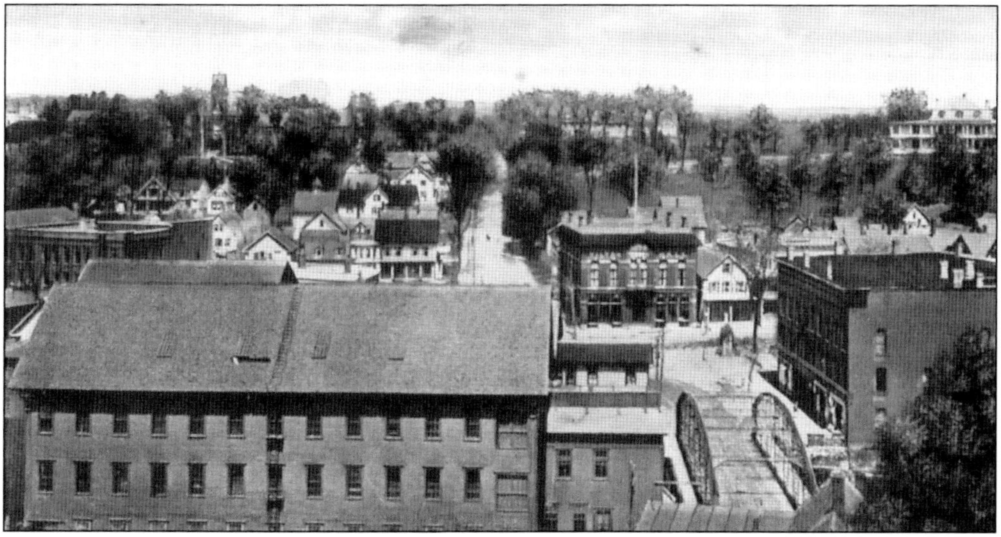

A bird's-eye view from Tilton Arch looking north, 1921. The town of Tilton is 97 miles from Boston, and was one of the important centers north of Concord on the main line of the railroad. Tilton was originally called Sanbornton Bridge; the present name was given from the principal family in the town of that name. The largest Native American fortress in New England, consisting of several lines of entrenchments faced with stone and palisaded, was situated here at the head of Little Bay (Lake Winnisquam).

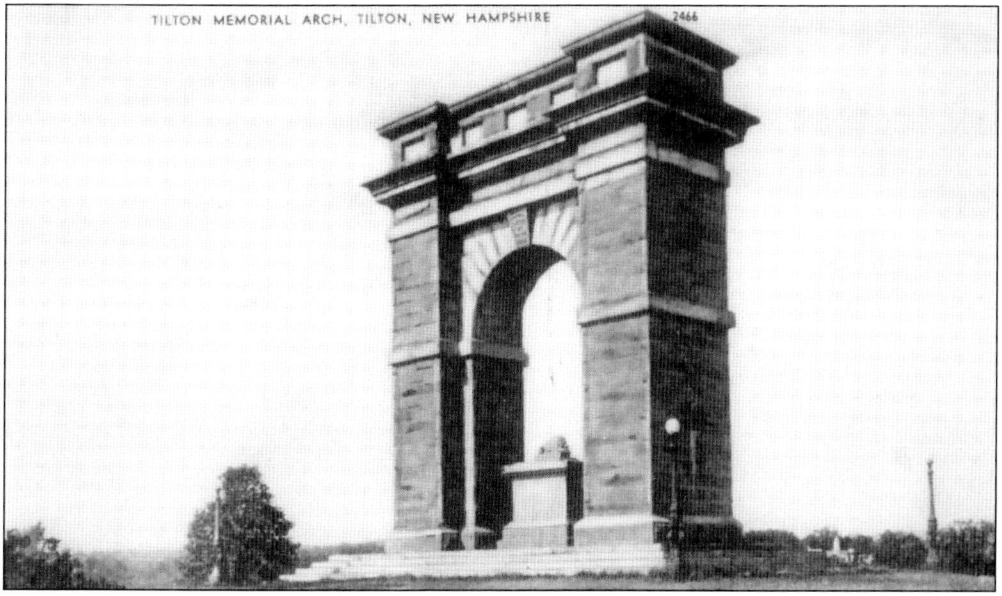

The Tilton Memorial Arch, Northfield. The name of the new town was adopted in honor of the Tilton family, which had been very prominently identified with the settlement and development of Sanbornton since Deacon Nathaniel Tilton settled there between 1768 and 1771. The family name is also commemorated by the Tilton Memorial Arch, a unique structure built of hewn stone with a height of 55 feet and a width of 40 feet. Between the columns of the arch is a device of polished Scotch granite bearing up a Numidian lion. On this device is the inscription "Tilton, 1883," and each end of the keystone bears the legend "Memorial Arch of Tilton, 1882," in raised letters.

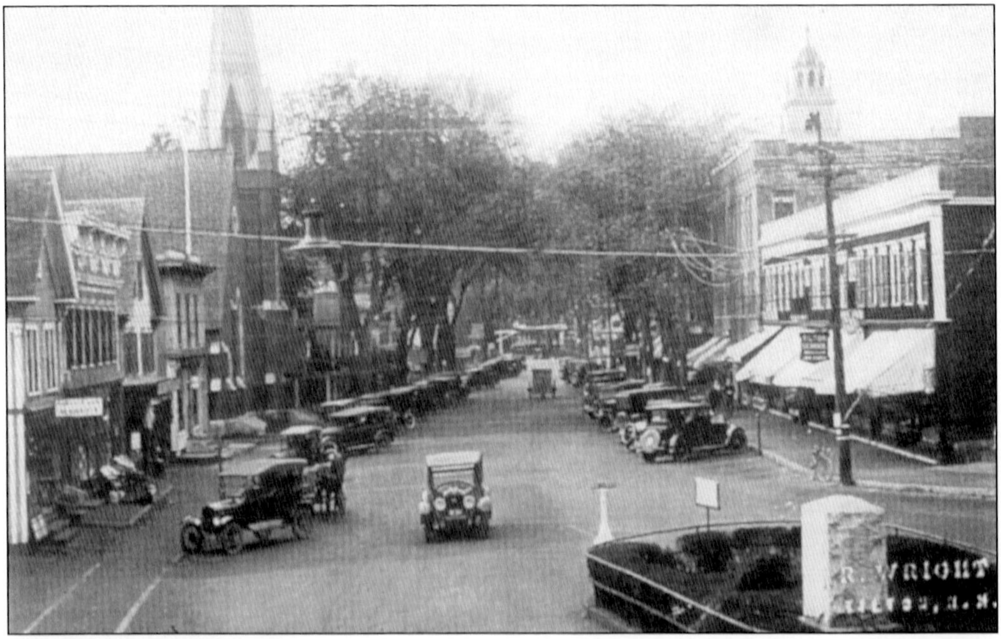

Main Street in Tilton, 1920.

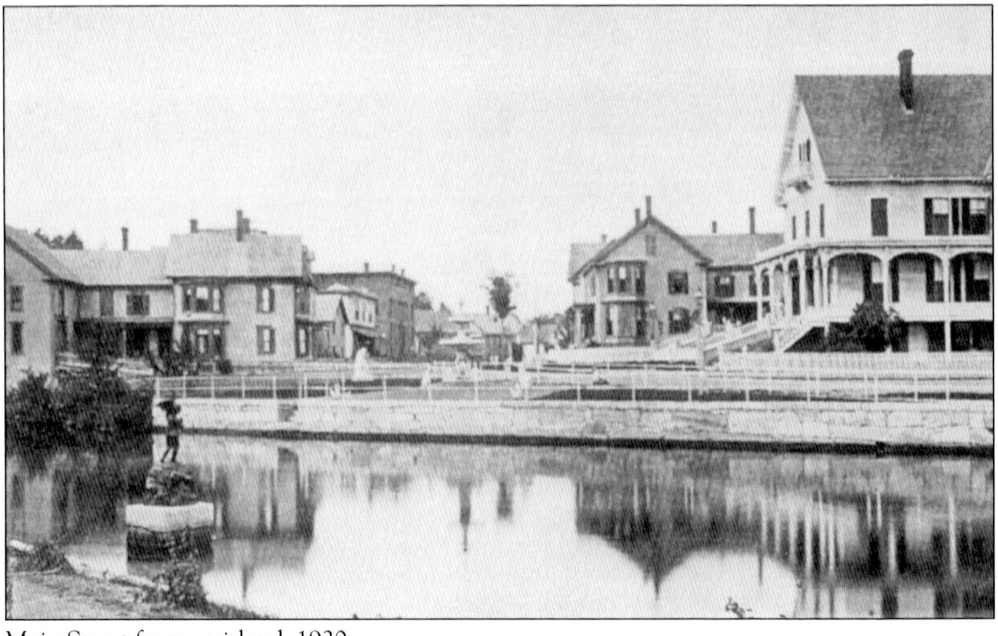
Main Street from an island, 1920.

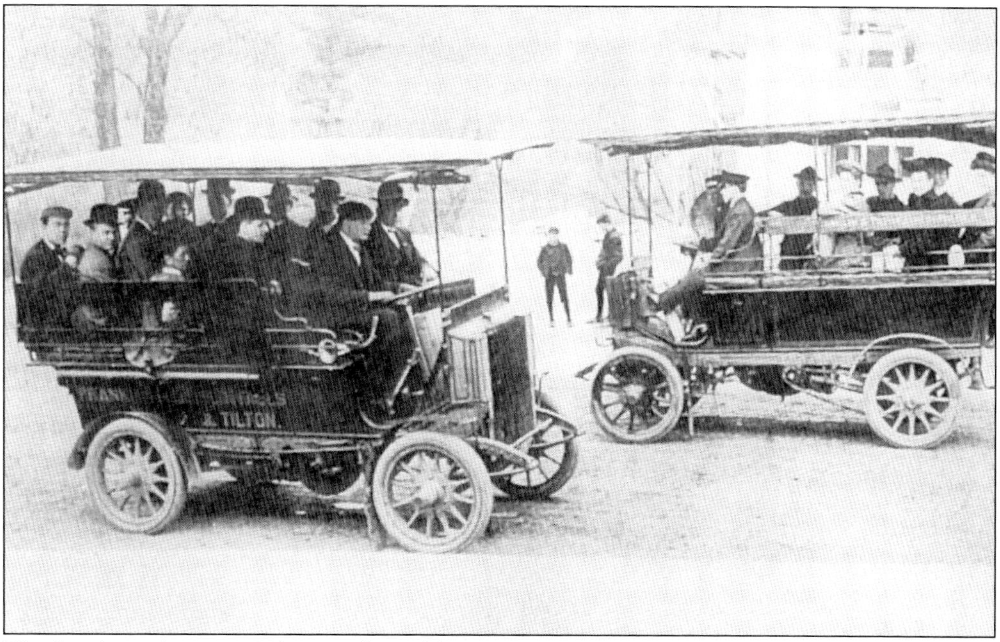

The first buses between Tilton and Franklin, *c.* 1900s.

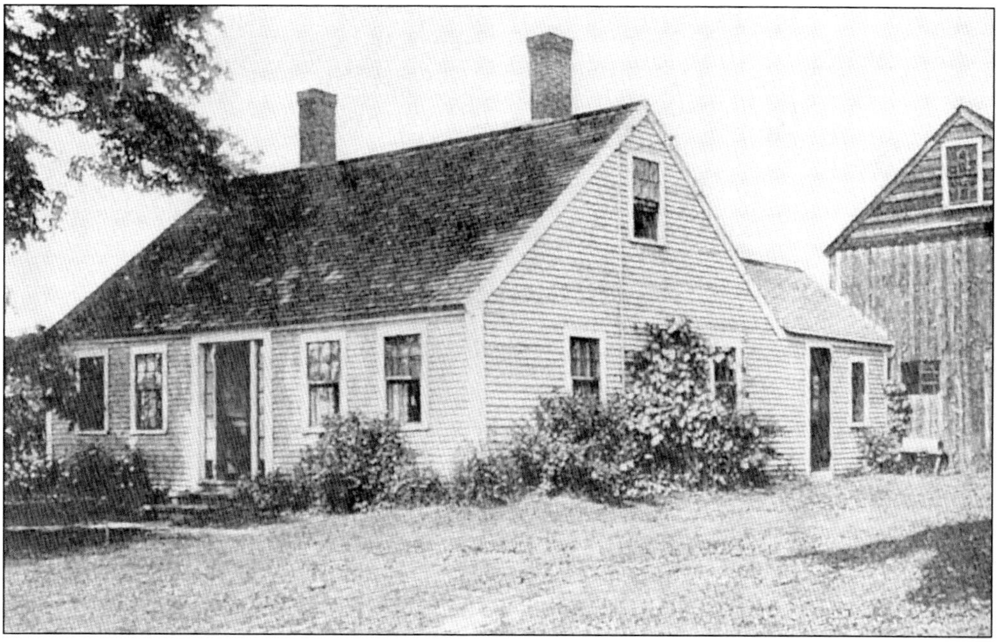

The home at 61 School Street. It was here that Sam Walter Foss, the well-known New England poet, was entertained during his school days at Tilton. It is supposed to be the original "House By The Side Of The Road."

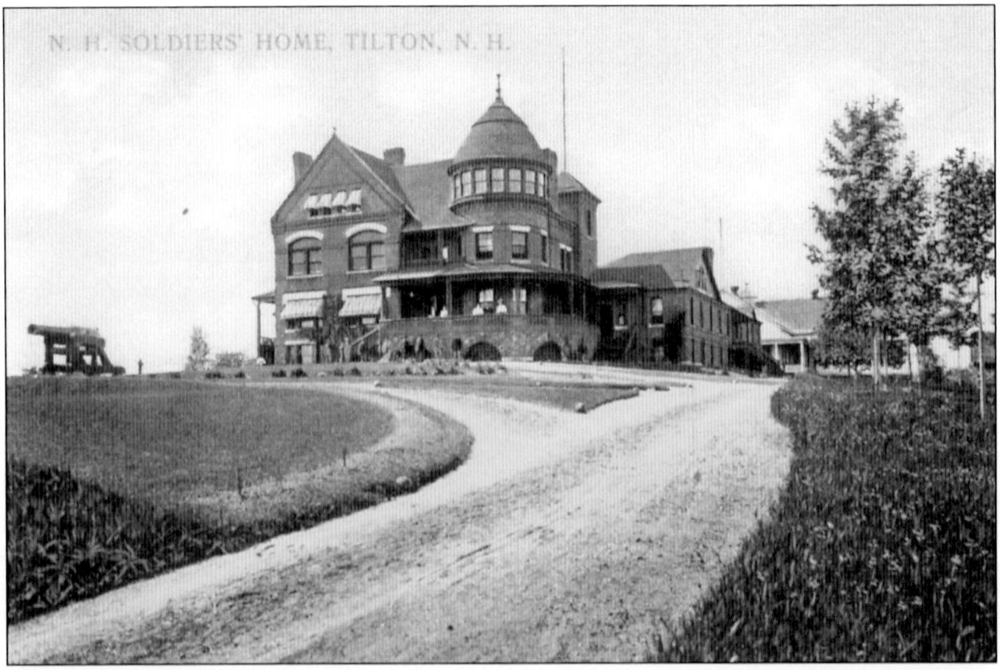

The New Hampshire Soldiers Home, 1913. Here, upon a breezy and beautiful site a few miles of out the village, is located the State Home for Disabled Soldiers. This home was established by the New Hampshire State Legislature for the purpose and care of men who had served in the armed forces of the United States, been honorably discharged and were unable to earn a livelihood by reason of wounds, disease, old age, or infirmity, and had no adequate means of support.

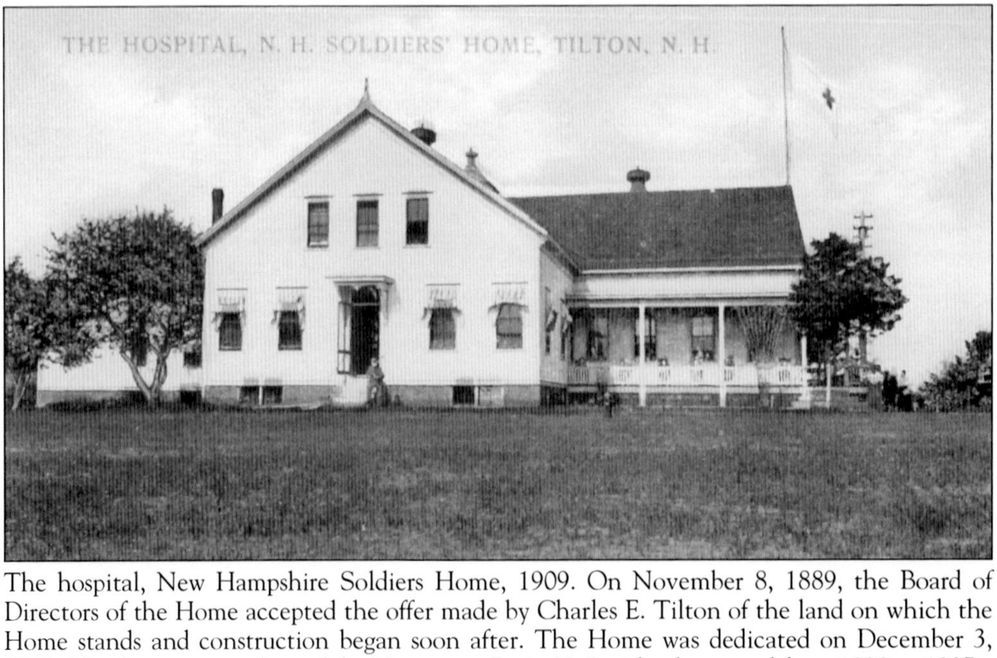

The hospital, New Hampshire Soldiers Home, 1909. On November 8, 1889, the Board of Directors of the Home accepted the offer made by Charles E. Tilton of the land on which the Home stands and construction began soon after. The Home was dedicated on December 3, 1890. The first commandant of the Home was Ervin H. Smith who served from 1890 to 1907.

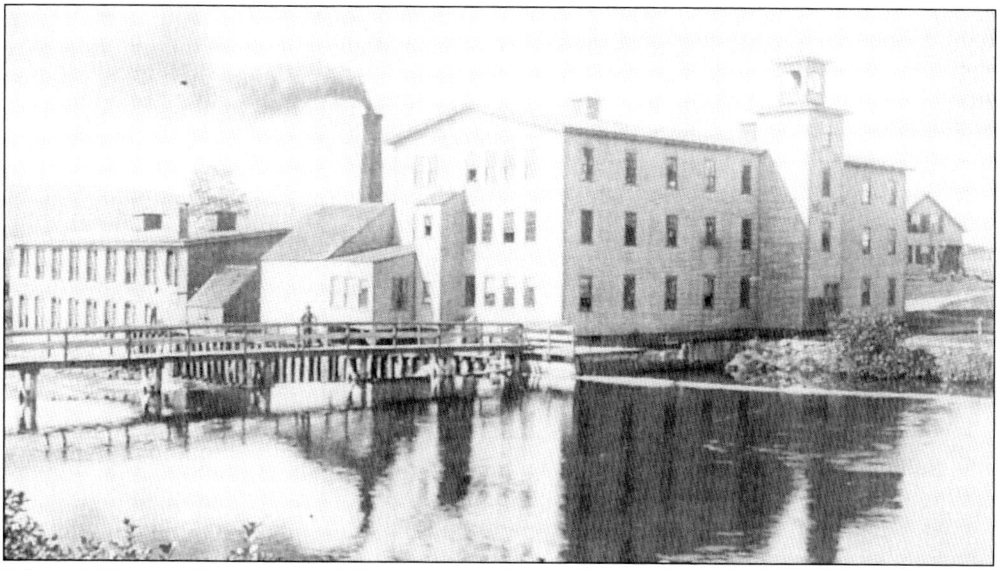

Tilton Mills. In 1828, Nathaniel Holmes moved here from Meredith and built the first cotton mill for making yarn and warp on the site at the foot of Mill Street. In 1859, the Holmes' Mill consisted of the mill building proper and several warehouse structures. It was about this time that Alexander Hamilton Tilton bought the mill, converted from cotton to woolens manufacture, and eventually doubled its size. During the end of its existence, the Tilton Light and Electric Company operated here before the PSC bought them out. The mill was torn down in 1949.

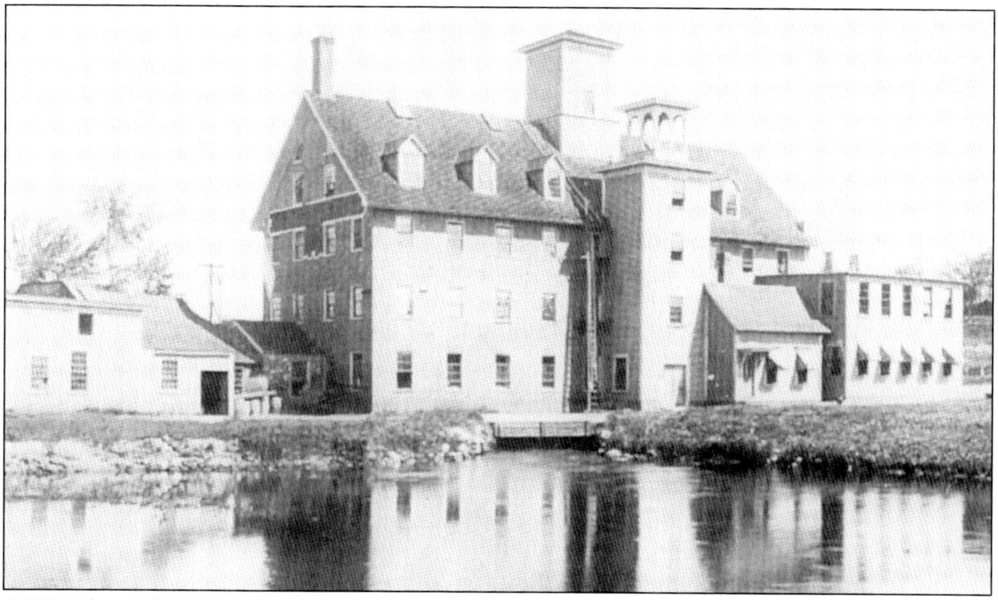

G.H. Tilton's hosiery mill. The Granite Mill and the adjoining mill of Clark and Dodge, with other contiguous property, became, in 1891, the property of G.H. Tilton & Sons of Laconia. In the early 1900s, their production was confined entirely to children's cotton hosiery of many styles. The cotton material was dried on a island which was connected to the mill by a footpath. Also connected to the mill, by a walkway over the dam, was the Box Factory, originally built as a sawmill by A.G. Cook of Laconia.

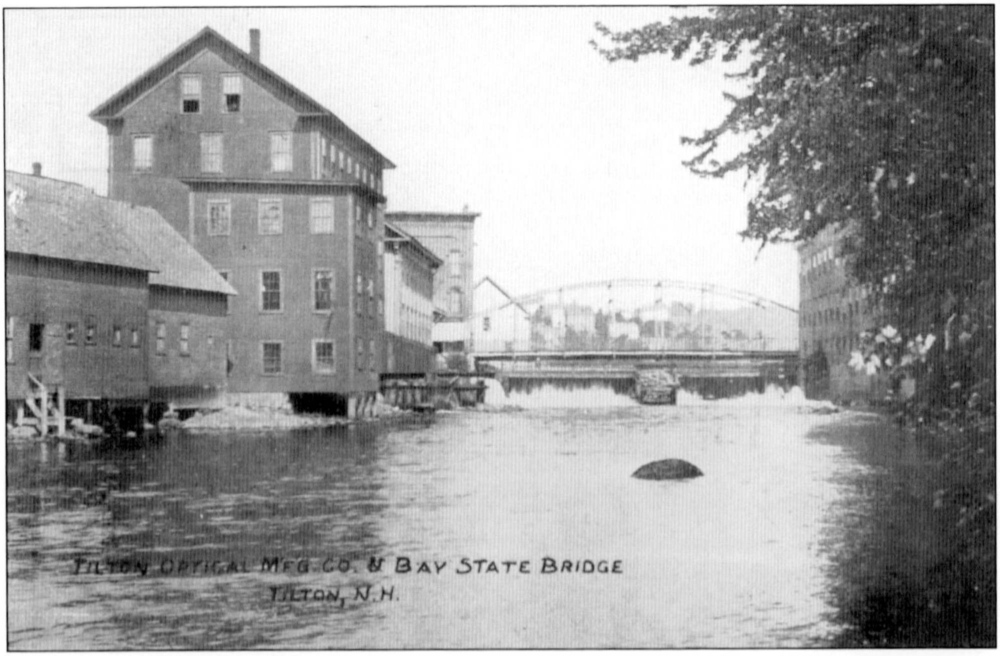

The Tilton Optical Manufacturing Co. and the Bay State Bridge, Tilton, 1908.

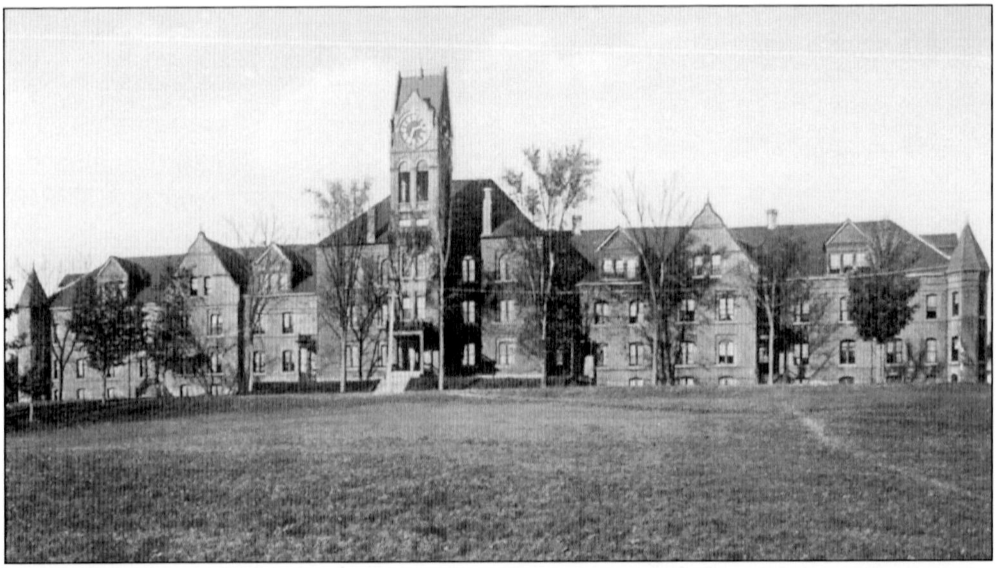

Tilton Seminary, *c.* 1906. This school was established in 1845 under the sponsorship of the Methodist Episcopal Church, and was incorporated in 1852 as the New Hampshire Conference Seminary. In 1923, the present name, Tilton School, was adopted. The school has a general and college preparatory program, offering individual instruction. Today this private school ranks among the finest in the nation.

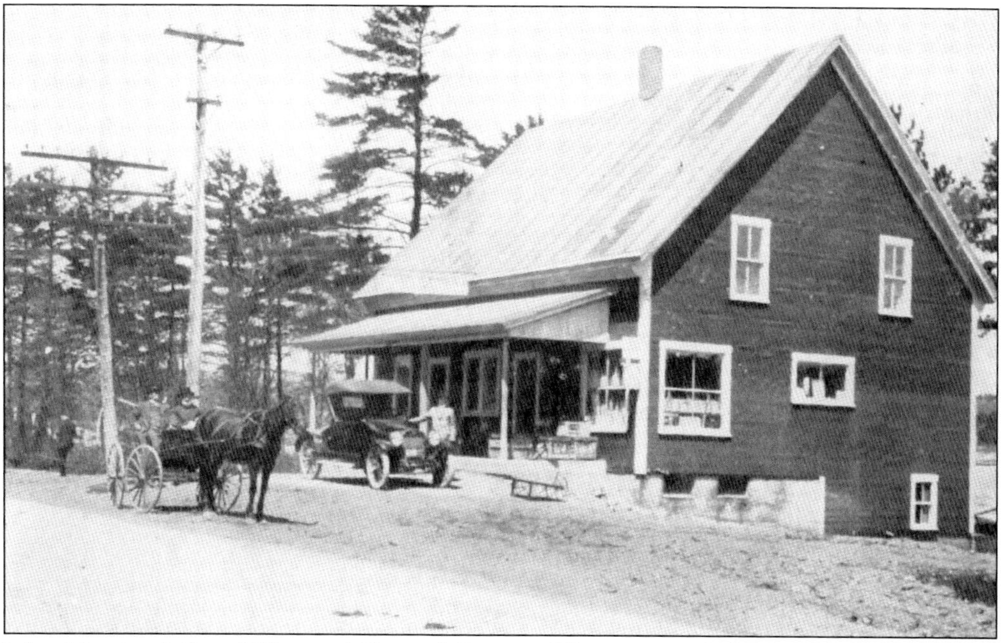

John Morrison's Post Office and General Store in Winnisquam. Lake Winnisquam, and the bridge crossing the lake toward Laconia, can be seen in the back of the store.

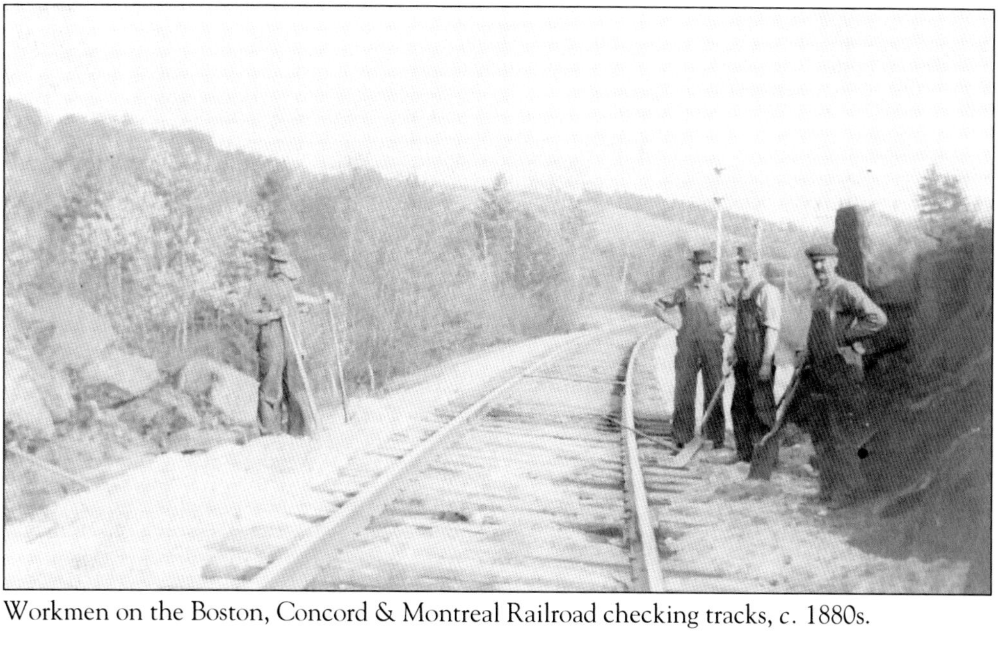

Workmen on the Boston, Concord & Montreal Railroad checking tracks, c. 1880s.

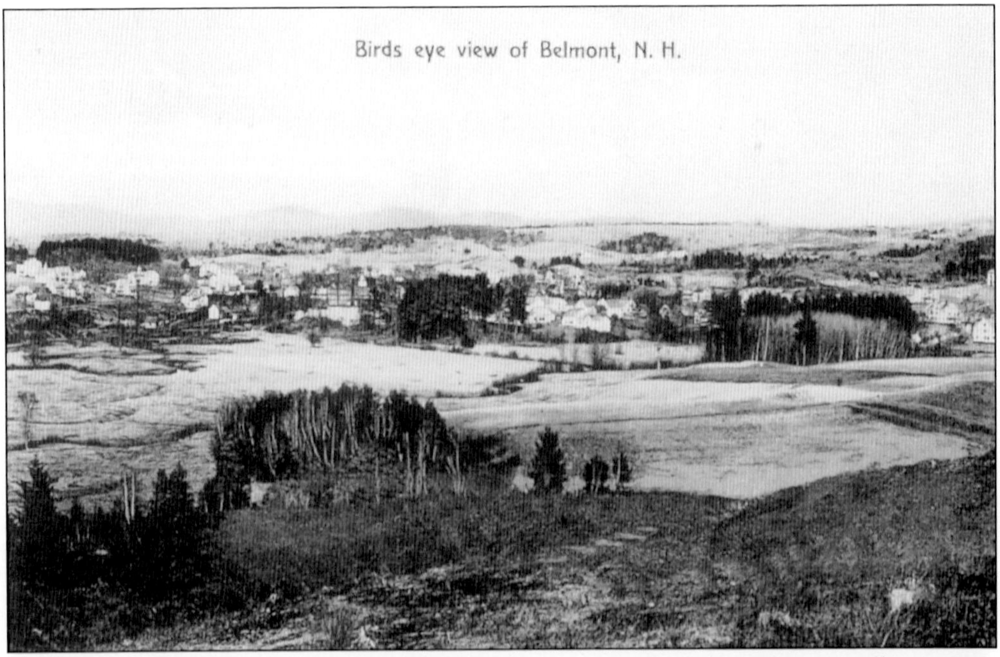

The village of Belmont as seen from the hills southwest behind the Belmont Mills, c. 1848. Originally part of Gilmanton, this area changed its name to Upper Gilmanton in 1859, and to Belmont ten years later. Until 1859, the name Gilmanton applied to the present towns of Gilmanton and Belmont; prior to 1812 it also applied to the town of Gilford.

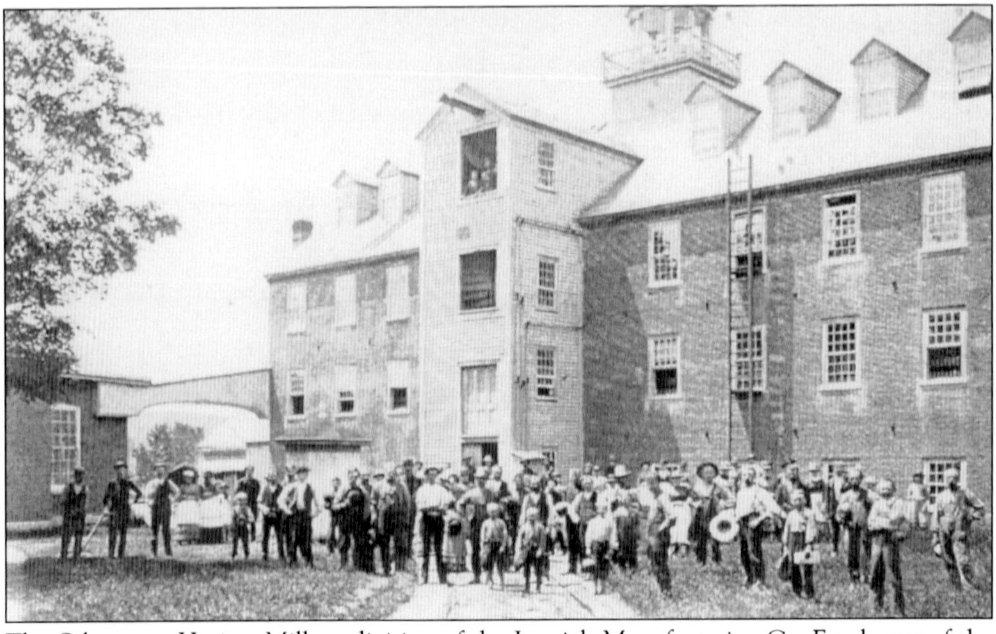

The Gilmanton Hosiery Mills, a division of the Ipswich Manufacturing Co. Employees of the Gilmanton Hosiery Mill in Belmont are shown here during the 1880s. The one-story addition to the original structure can be seen at the left, but the dormer windows had not yet been removed, nor the flat roof installed. Note the number of young employees.

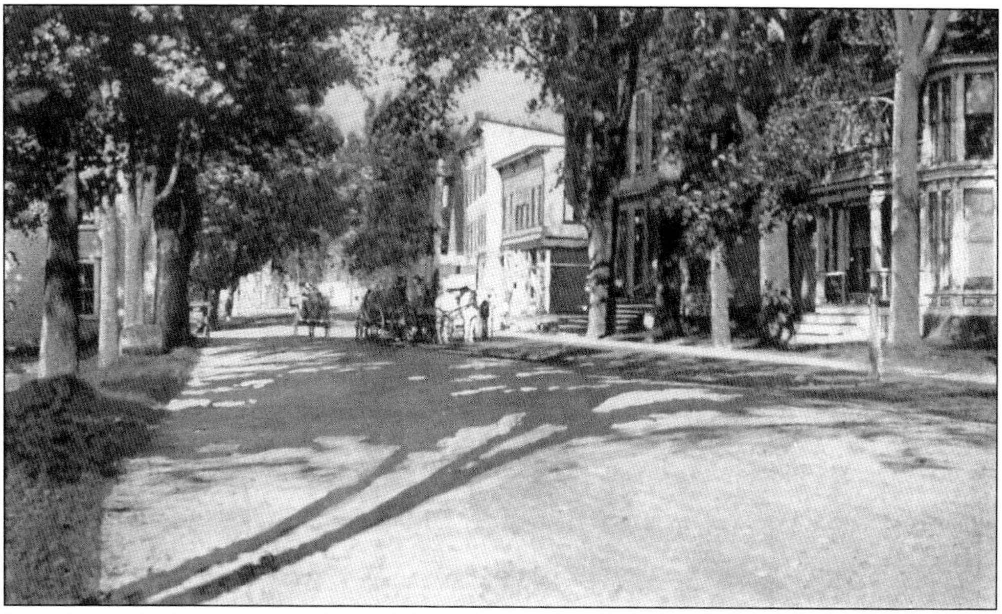

Main Street looking north in front of the village bank in Belmont, *c.* 1900s.

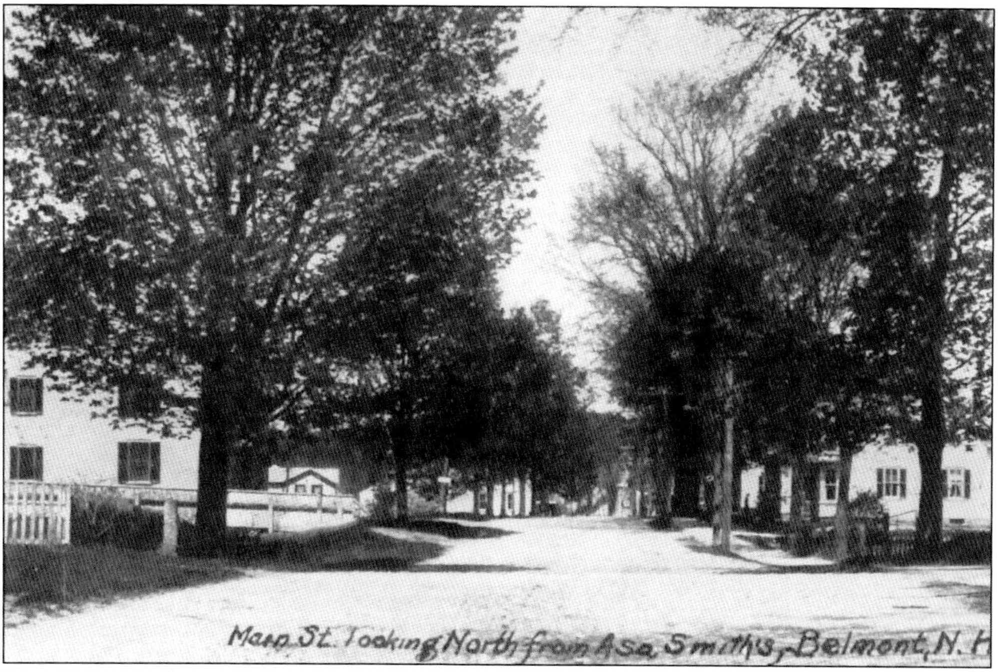

Main Street looking north, just south of Mill Street, 1911.

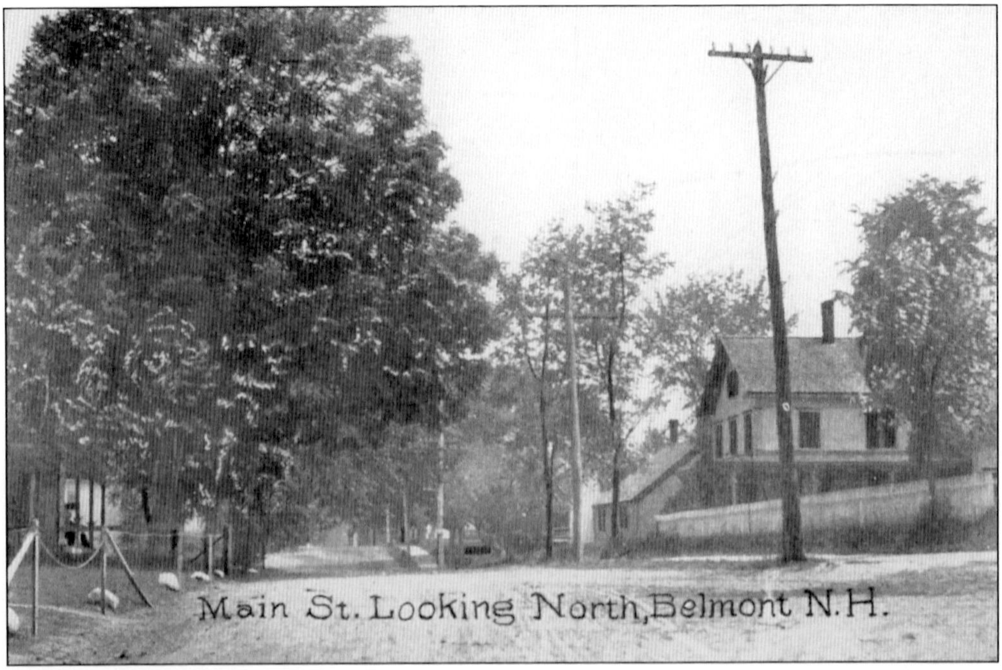

The intersection of Main Street, Shaker Road, and Concord Street looking north, *c.* 1900s.

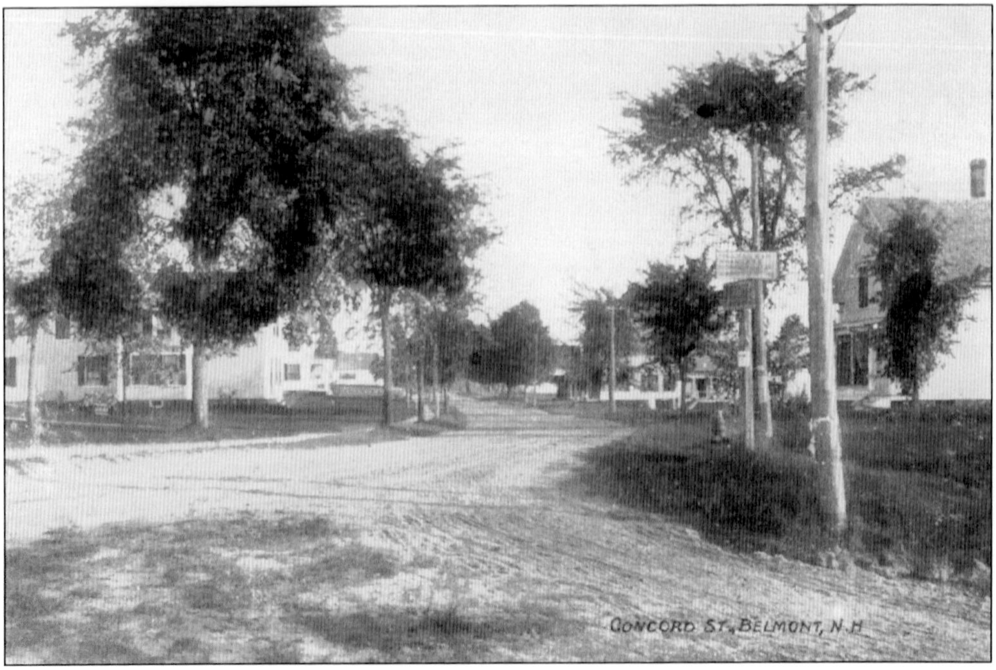

Shaker Road looking east down Concord Street in Belmont, 1908.

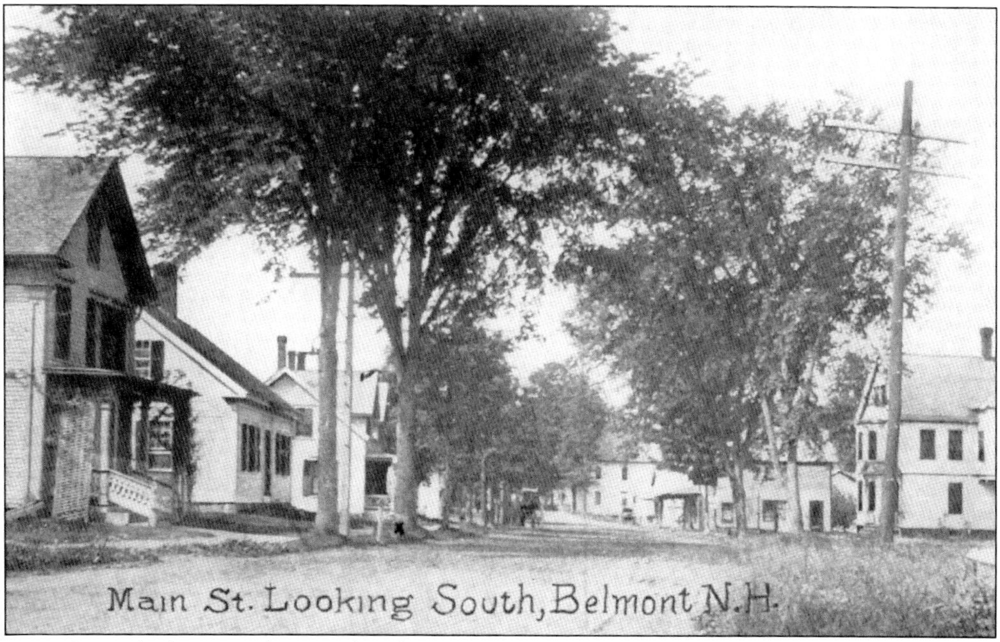

Main Street looking south toward Gale Street.

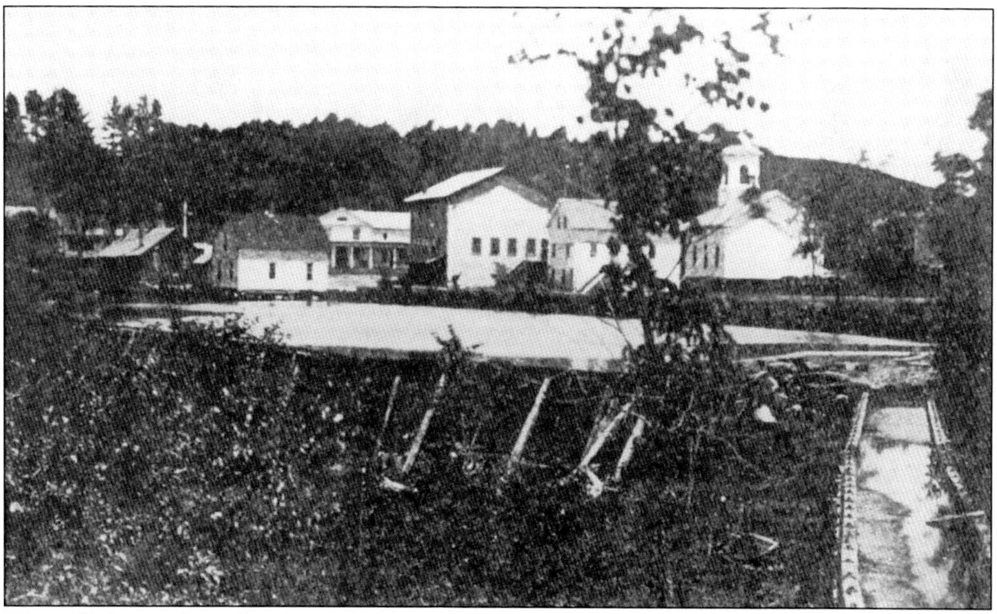
The mill dam and pond with its aqueduct to mill. This picture is looking north to the upper end of Belmont from Depot Street to Hall's store and hall, and South Church, *c.* 1875.

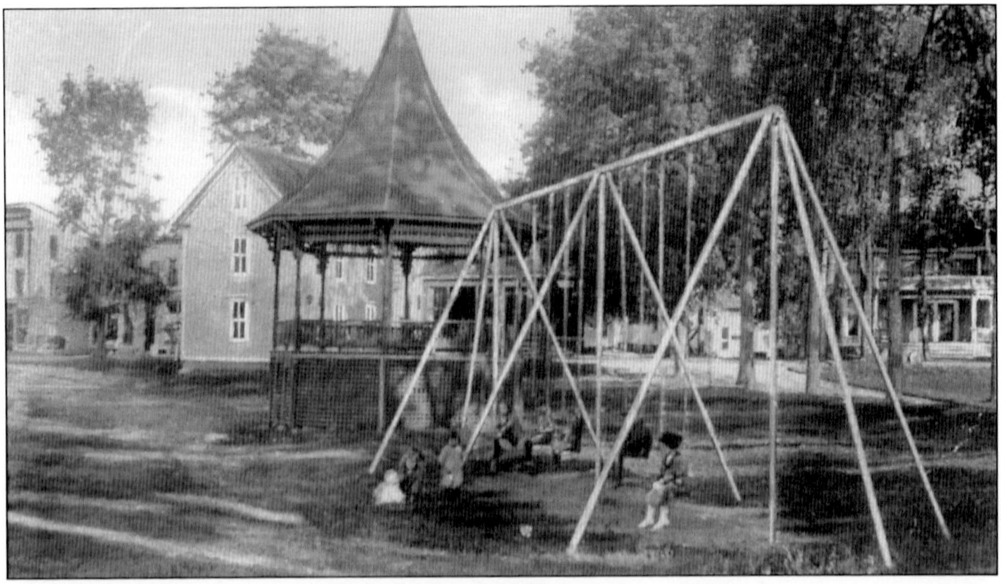

Main Street from a playground in the Belmont Mill complex, *c.* 1923.

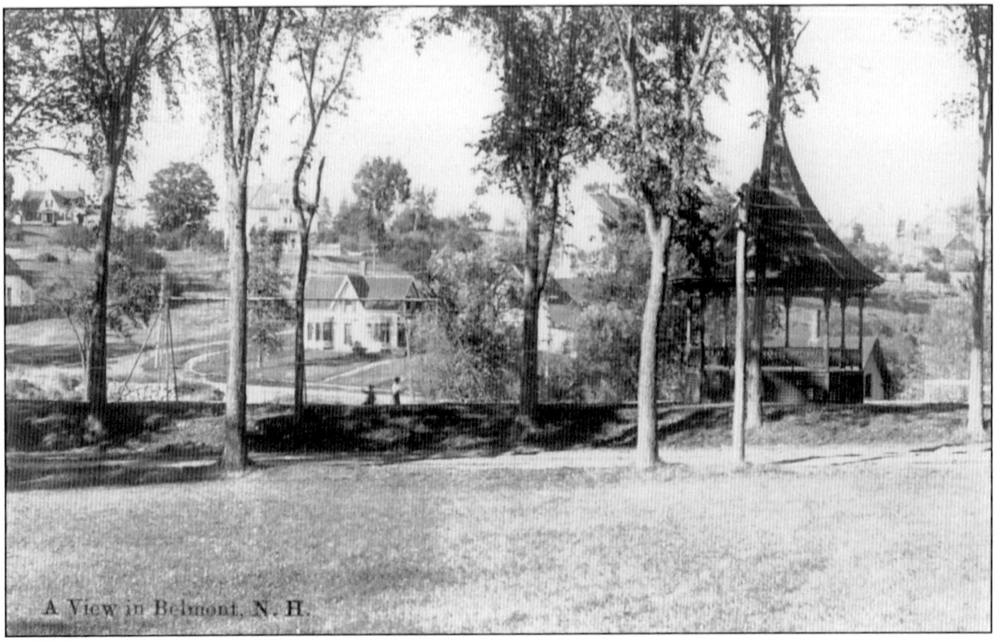

Depot Street with Johnson Street as seen from Mill Street, *c.* 1915.

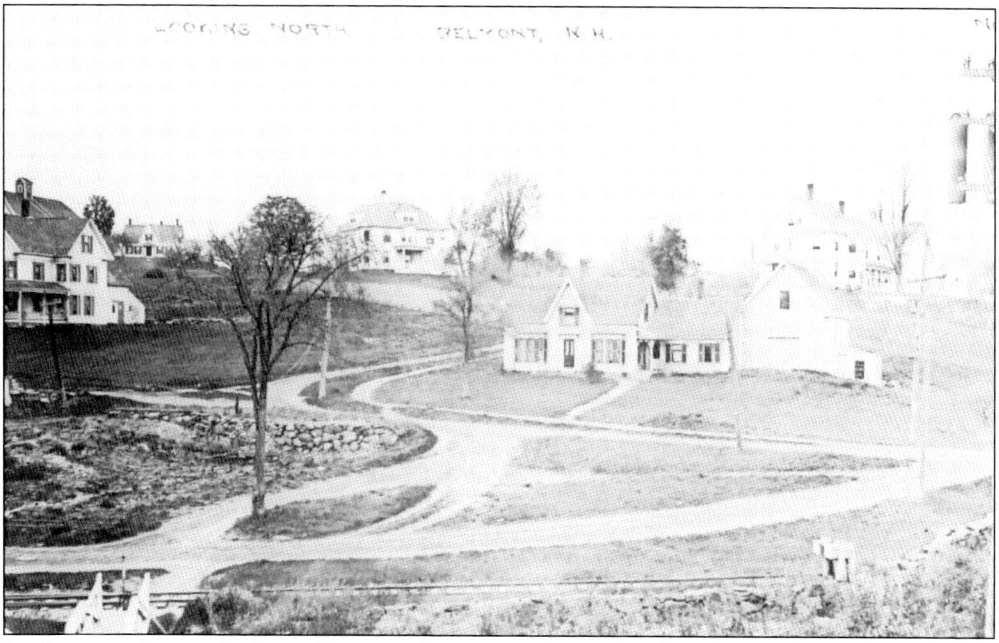

Looking north over the Tioga River at the end of the Tilton and Belmont Railroad, c. 1900.

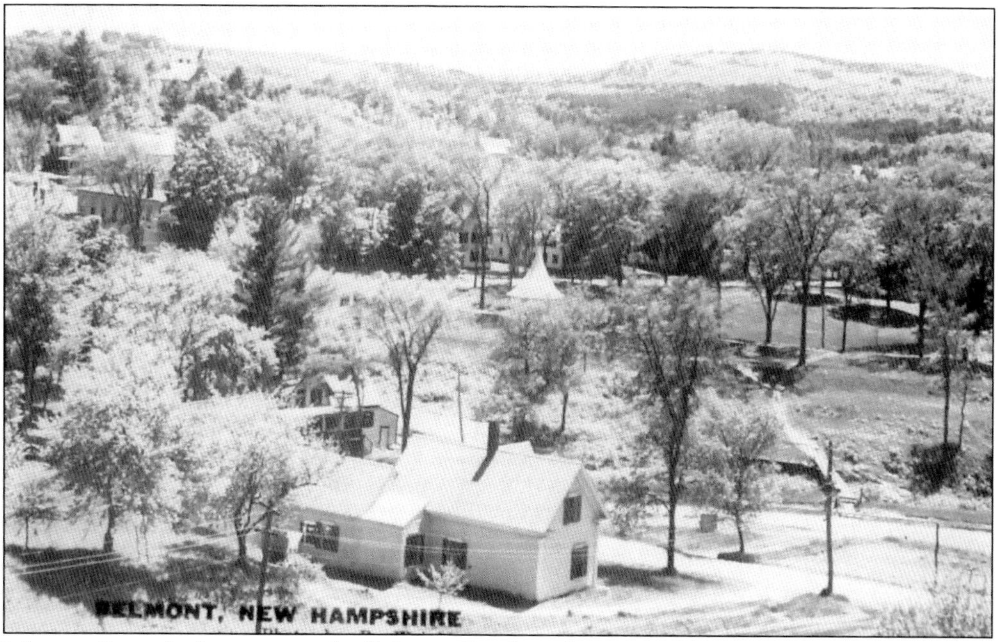

Johnson Street looking east at the Belmont Bandstand, c. 1900.

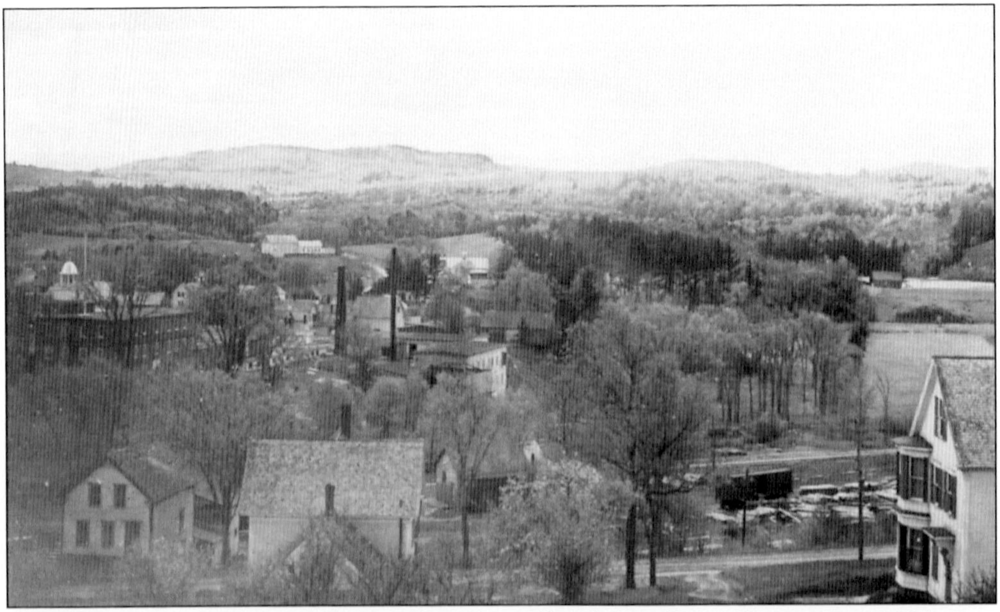

The Belmont and Tilton Railroad yard at the millyard complex on Depot Street, Belmont, c. 1900s.

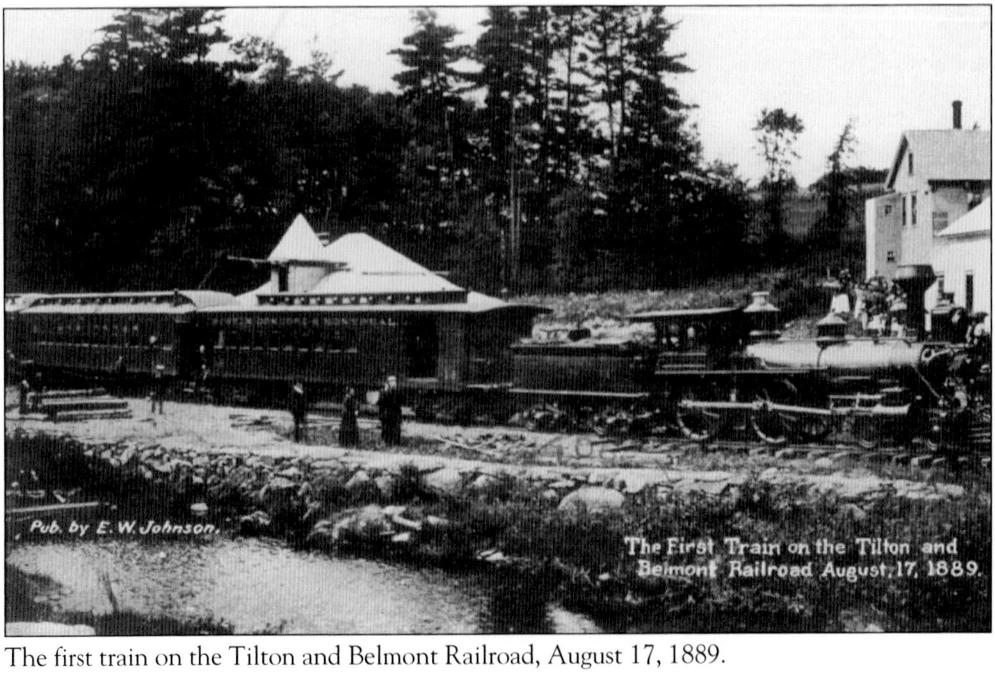

The first train on the Tilton and Belmont Railroad, August 17, 1889.

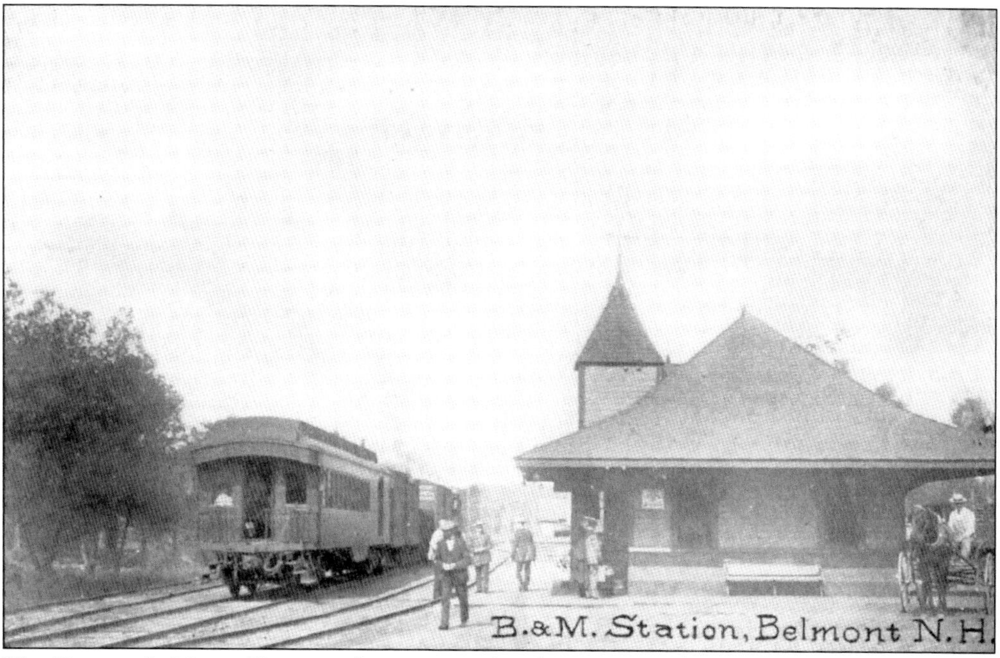

The Boston & Maine Depot with mix train heading west to the main line in Tilton, early 1900.

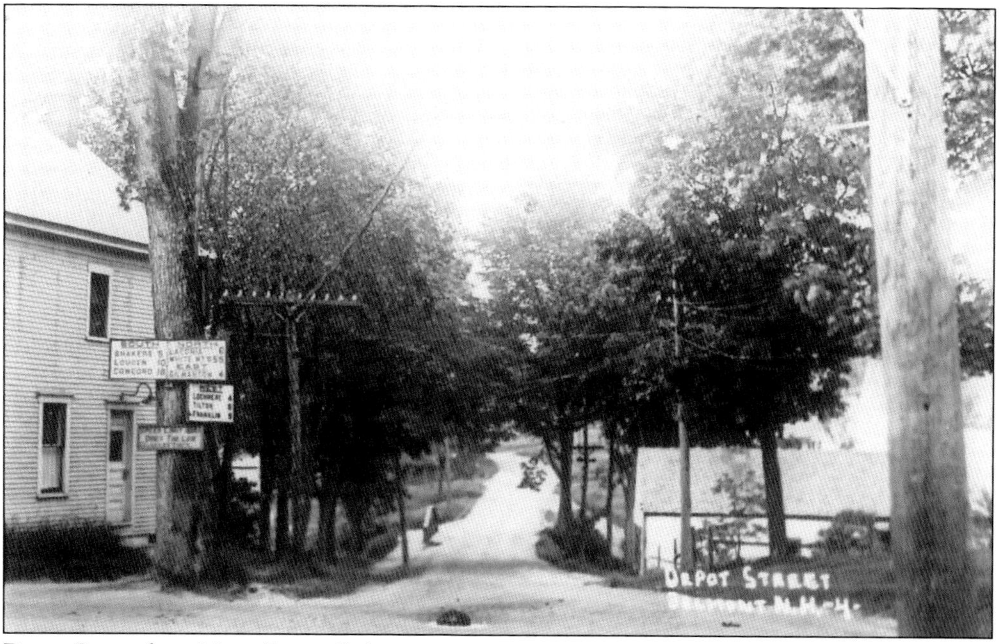

Depot Street from Main Street, Belmont.

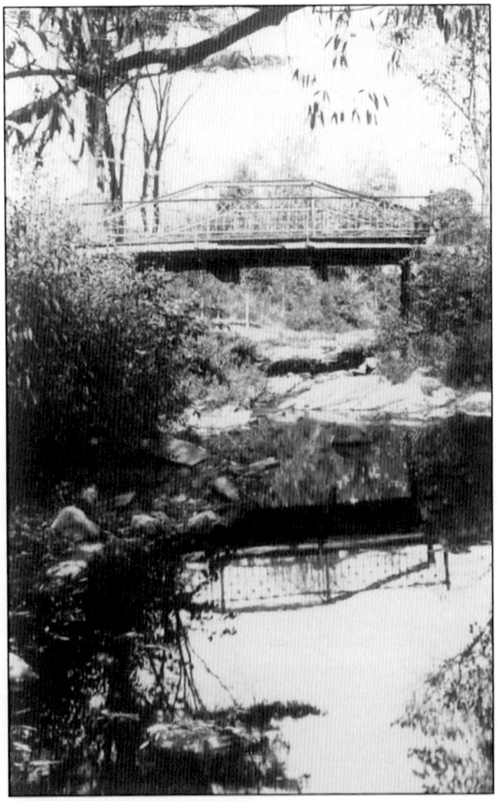

Looking north up the Tioga River at Depot Street and the steel bridge, Belmont, c. 1900.

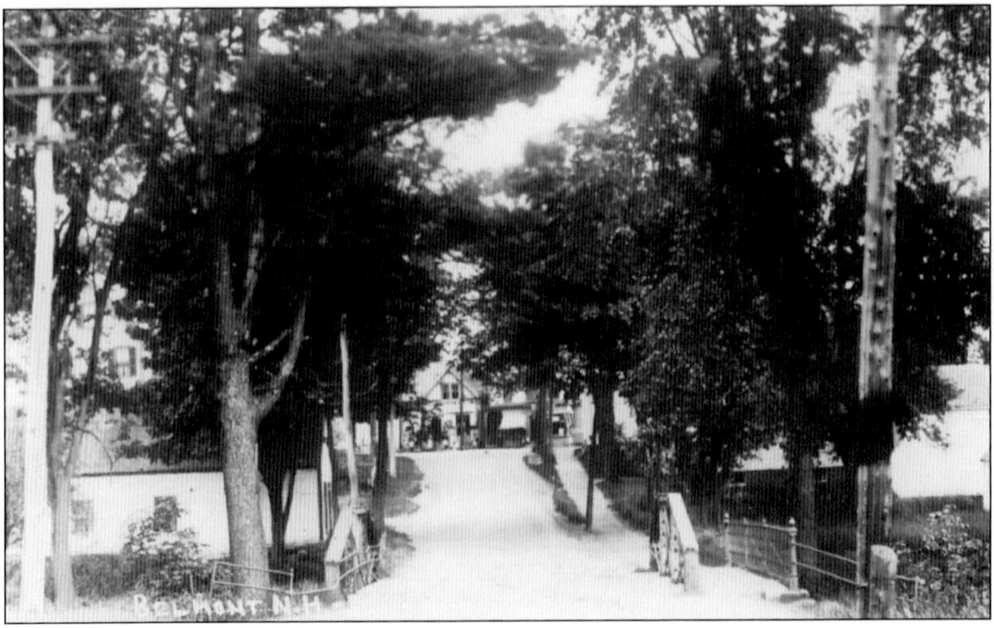

Depot Street (Route 140) and the Village Store on Main Street, Belmont.

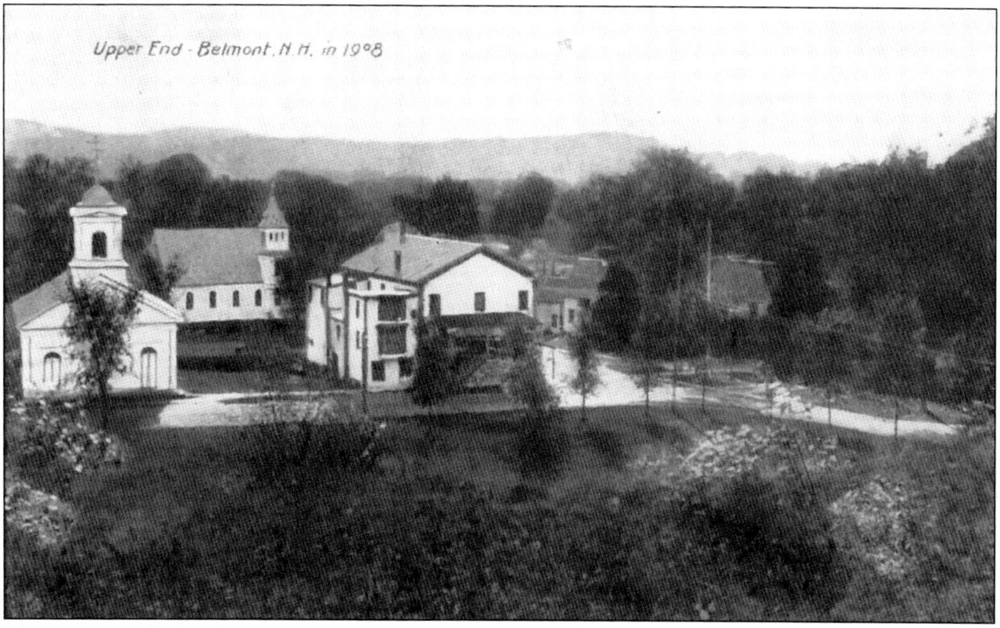

The upper end of Belmont looking south, 1908. The South Church and Catholic church can be seen to the left, with Hall's store and hall in the center.

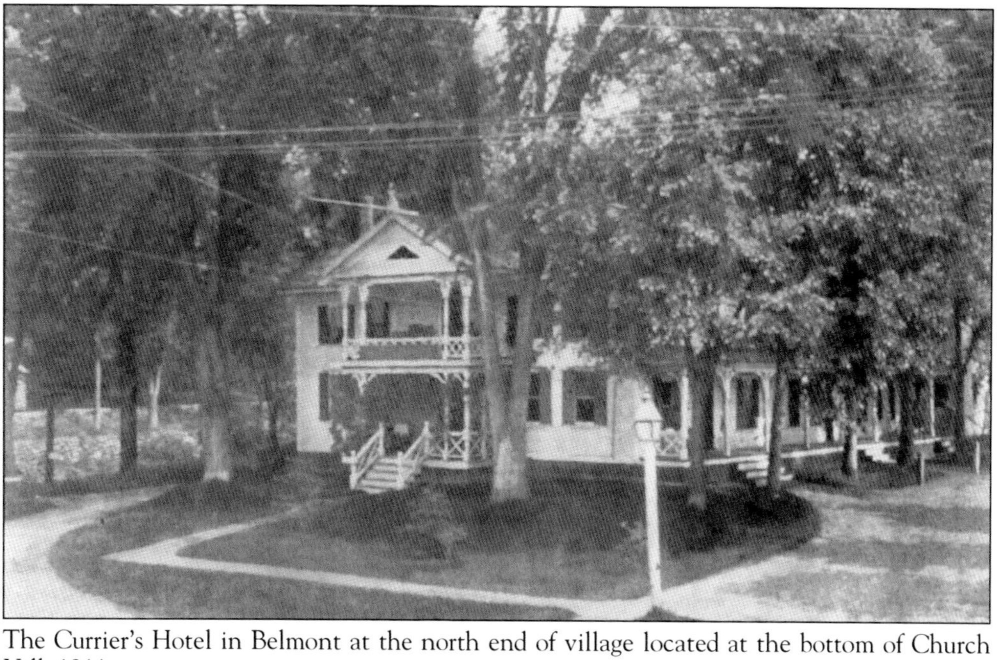

The Currier's Hotel in Belmont at the north end of village located at the bottom of Church Hill, 1911.

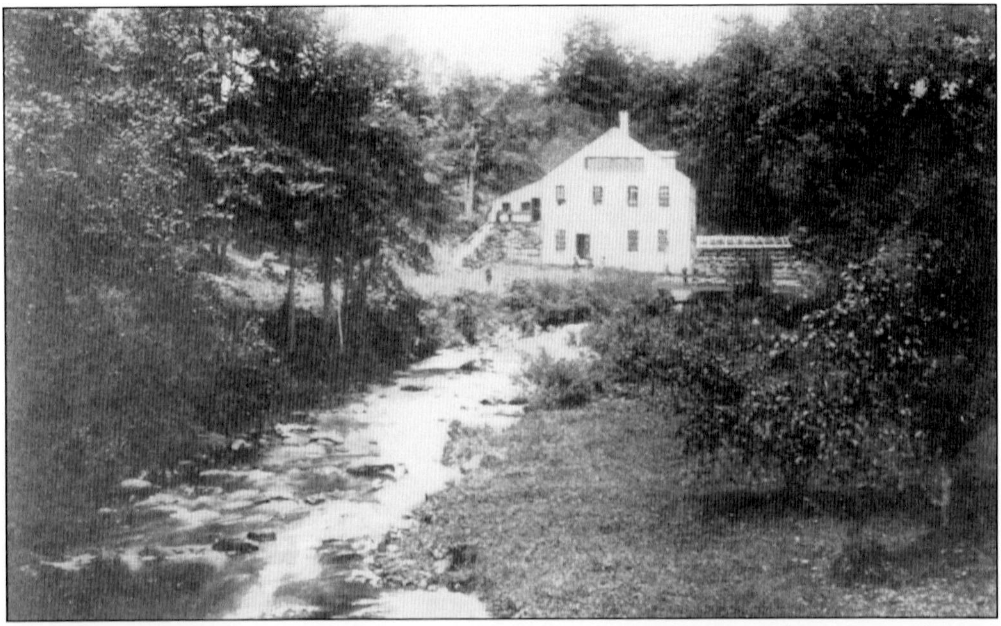

The old grist and woodworking mill looking north from Church Street. This structure burned on May 7, 1885.

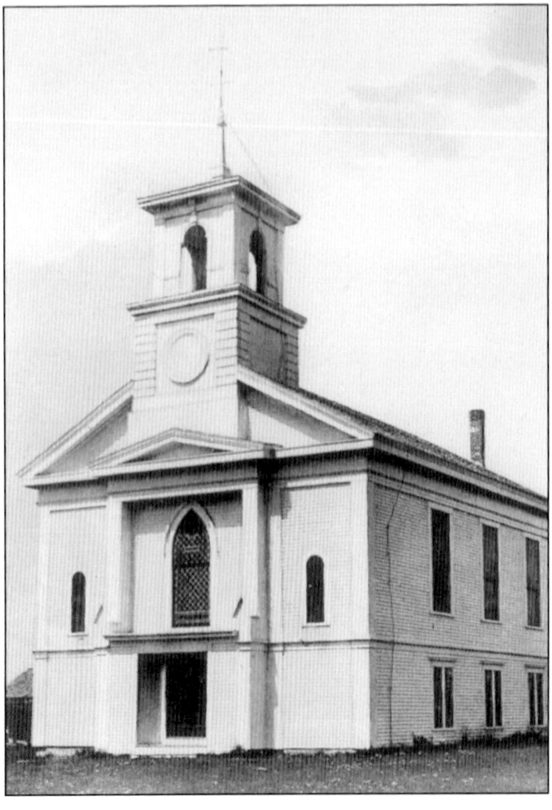

The First Baptist Church, built 1852. The building was raised in 1889 to accommodate the vestry, Sunday school, and meeting area. The structure burned, *c.* 1970.

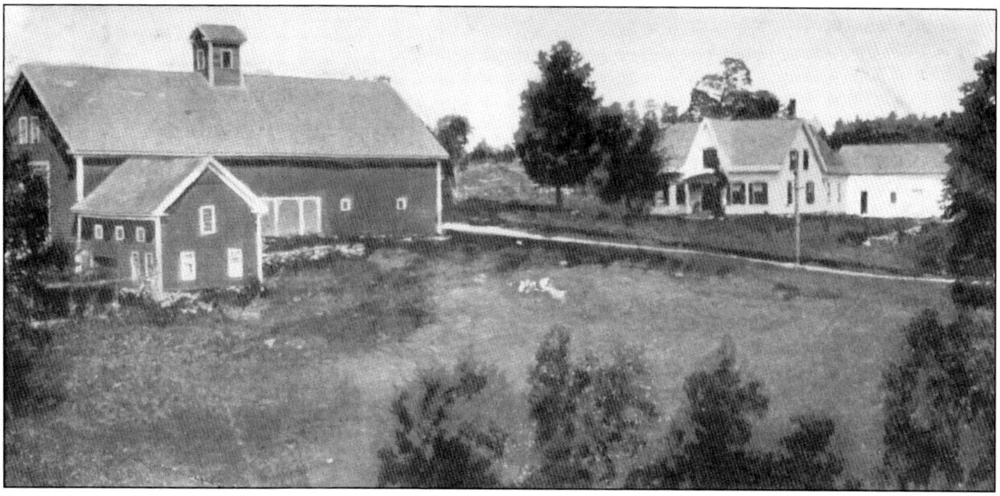

E.C. Bean's residence, *c*. 1910.

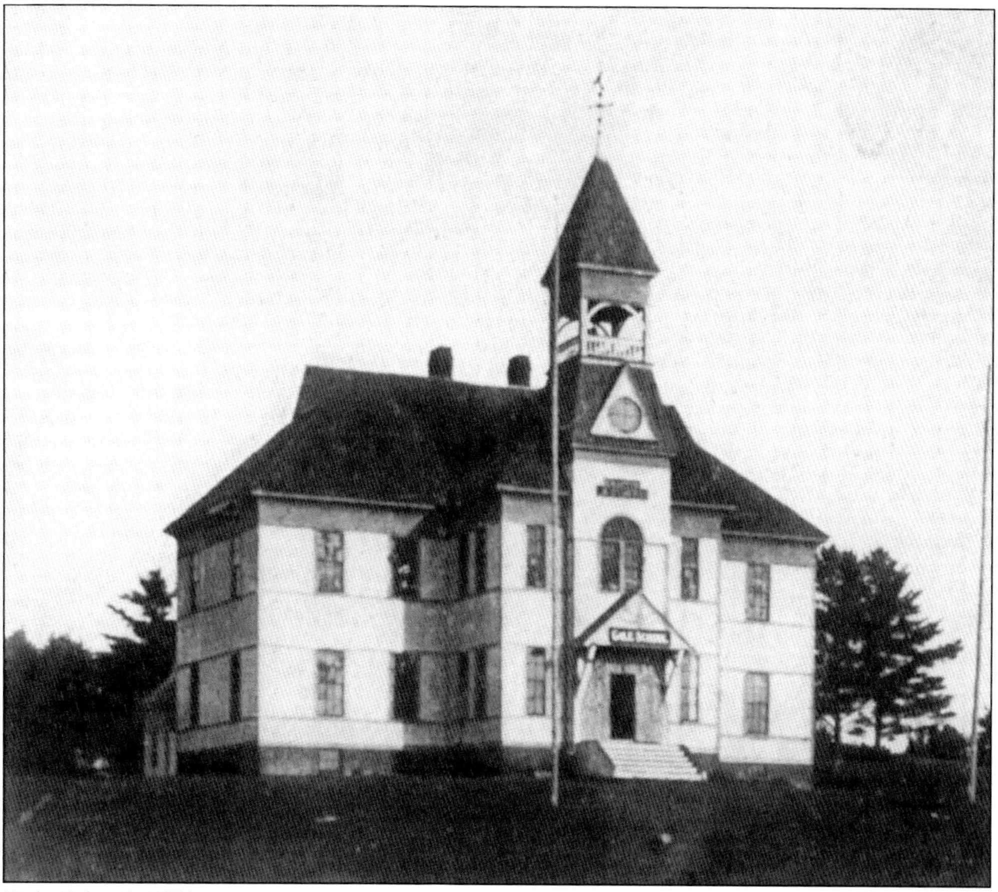

Gale School, 1894.

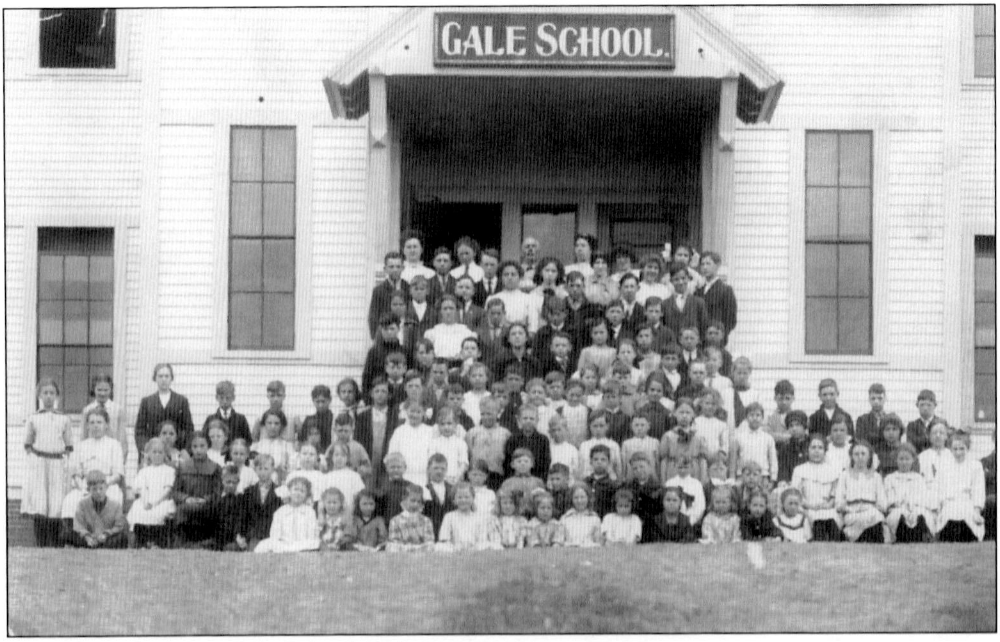

The Class of 1912 at Gale School, Belmont.

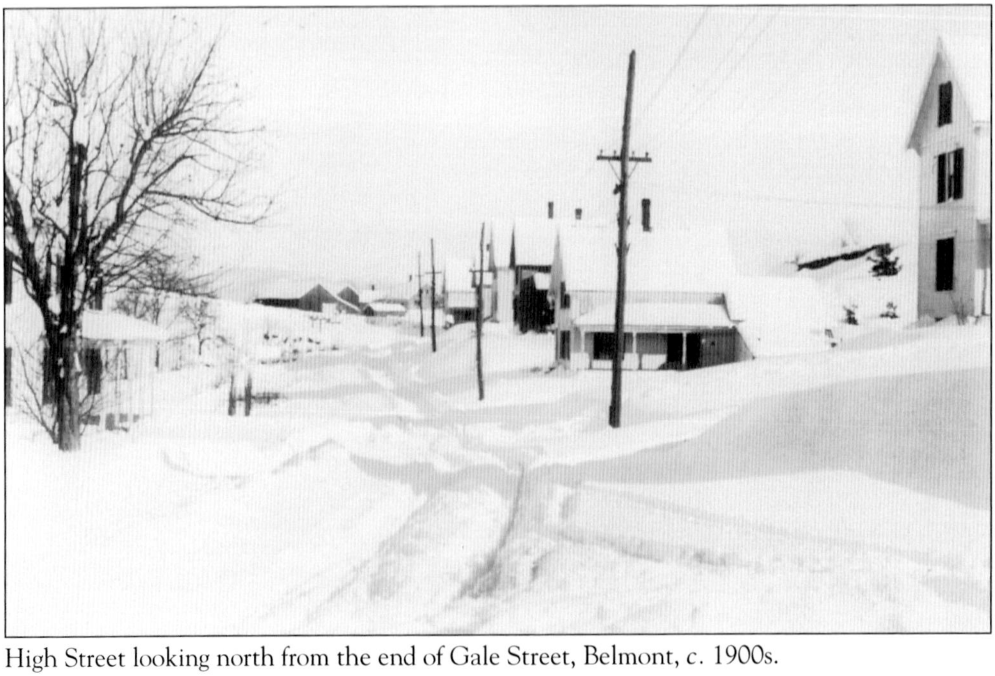
High Street looking north from the end of Gale Street, Belmont, *c.* 1900s.

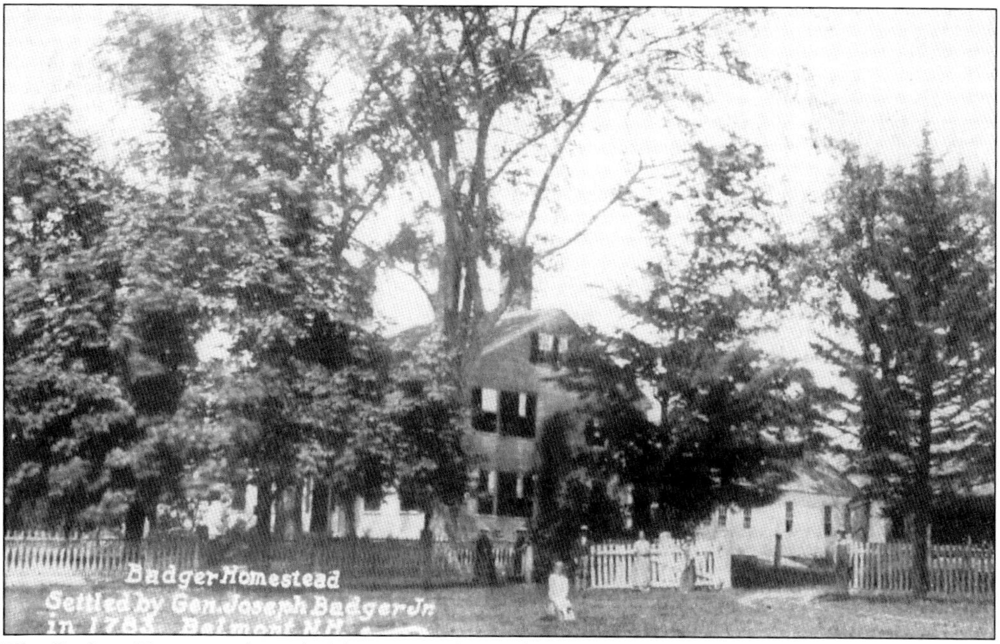

The Badger Homestead, settled by General Joseph Badger Jr. in 1783. This farm is located off Route 140 on Hackett Road going to Gilmanton Corners, Belmont.

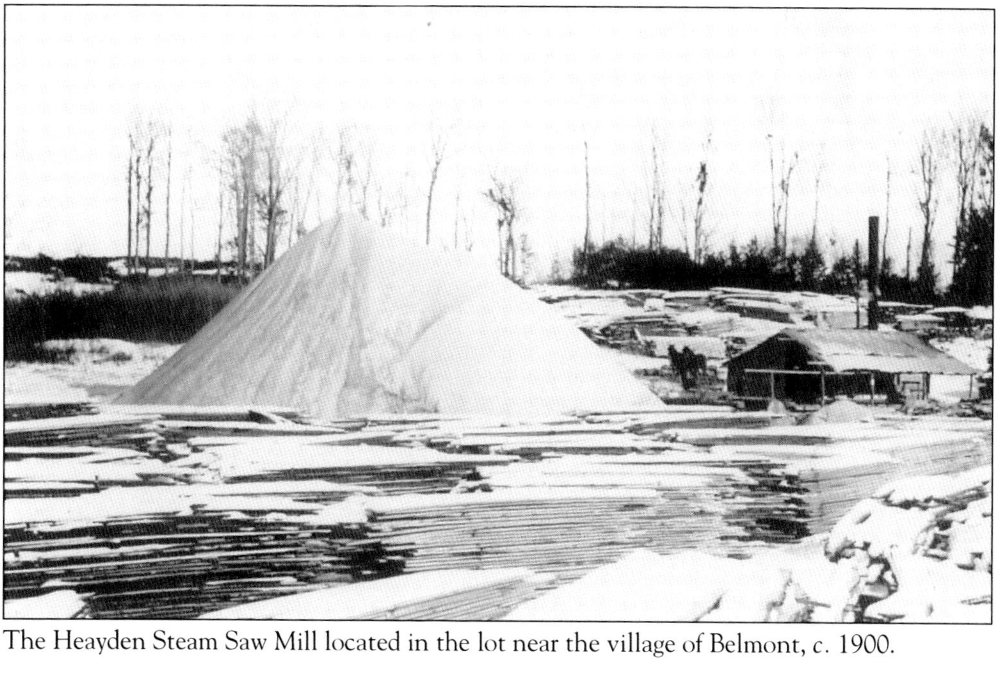
The Heayden Steam Saw Mill located in the lot near the village of Belmont, *c.* 1900.

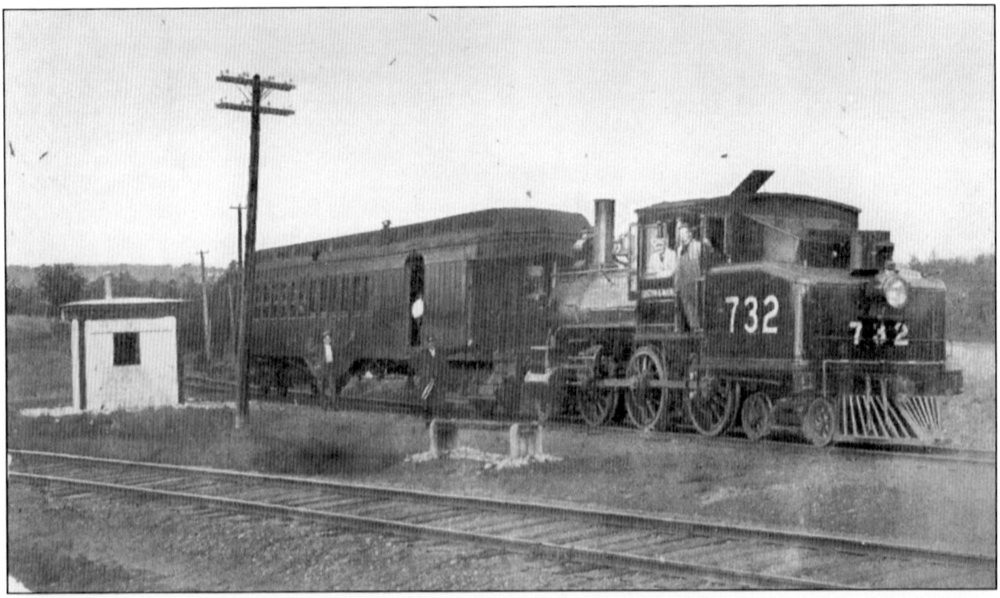

A Belmont Branch train at the Belmont and Tilton junction, 1908. This was the "B&M" No. 732; the natives referred to her as the "Back and Forth." She is shown here on the Belmont Branch. The main line heads left to Laconia, and right to Tilton.

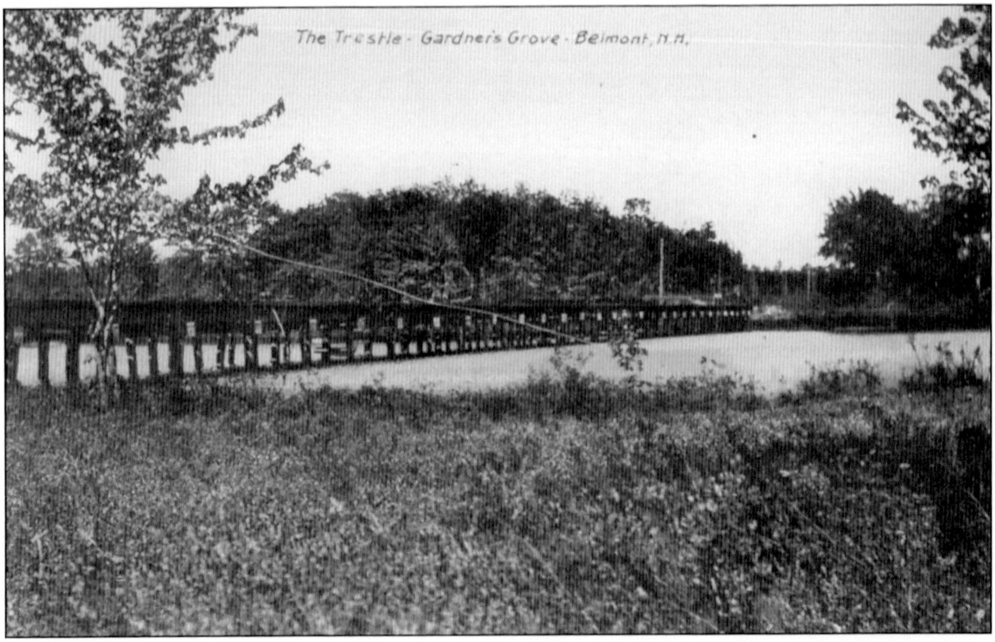

The Tilton and Belmont Railroad trestle crossing part of Silver Lake at Gardner's Grove, c. 1900.

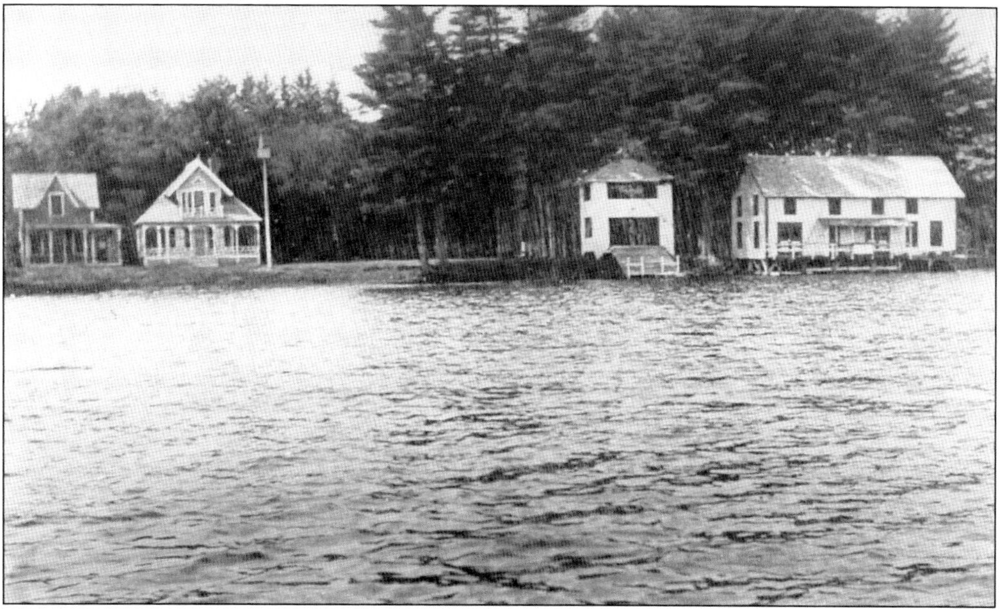

Gardner's Grove. This is about halfway between Tilton and Belmont, and near the line of the Branch Railroad. It was one of the latest offshoots from the main line of the Concord & Montreal Railroad. As the name implies, the branch connected the towns of Tilton and Belmont, and is about 7 miles in length.

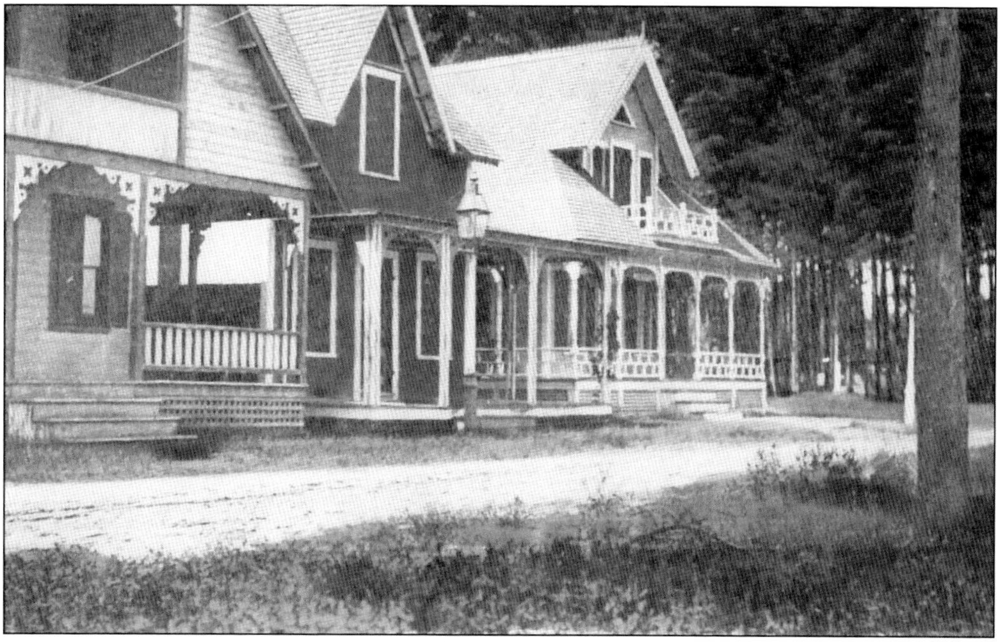

Cottage row on Silver Lake Avenue on the shore of Silver Lake in Belmont, 1908. Belmont lies well up among the foothills of the Balknap Mountain Range, and with Gilford and Gilmanton occupies an intervale section between the Winnipesaukee River and the mountains of unequalled beauty.

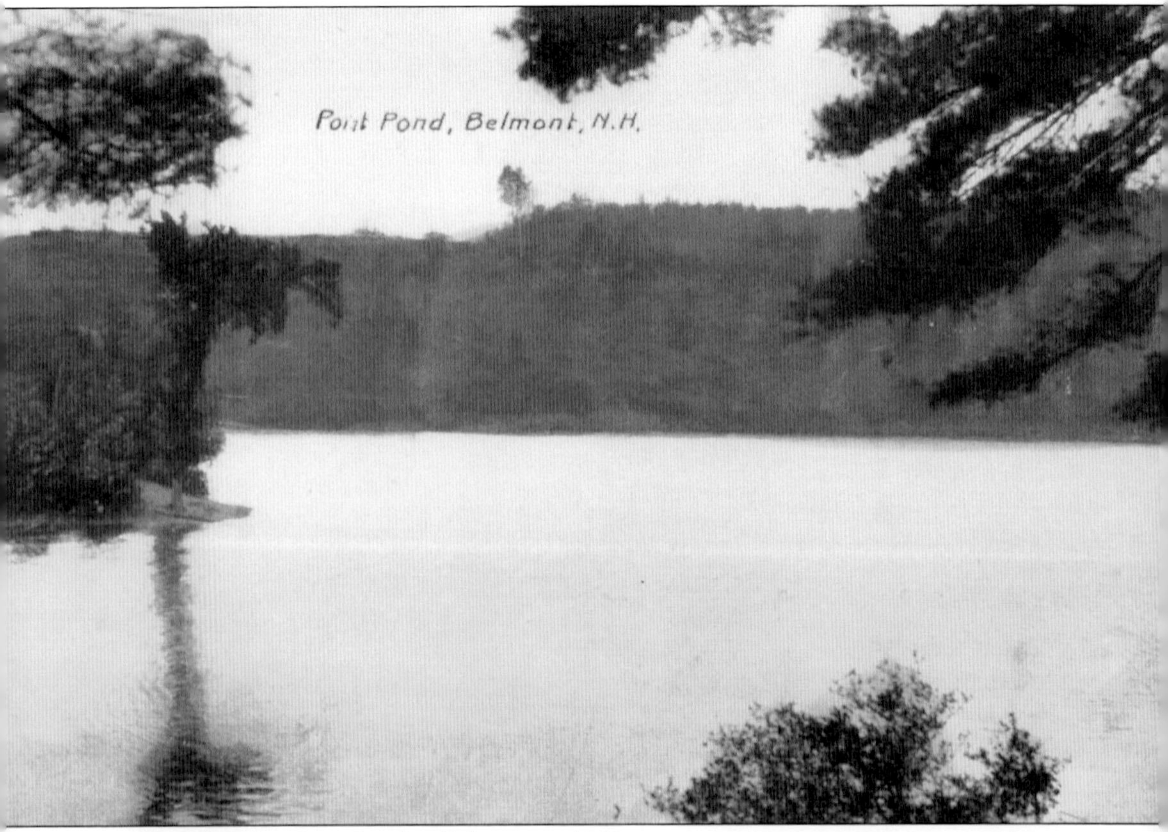

Looking east over Pout Pond in Belmont, *c.* 1900.

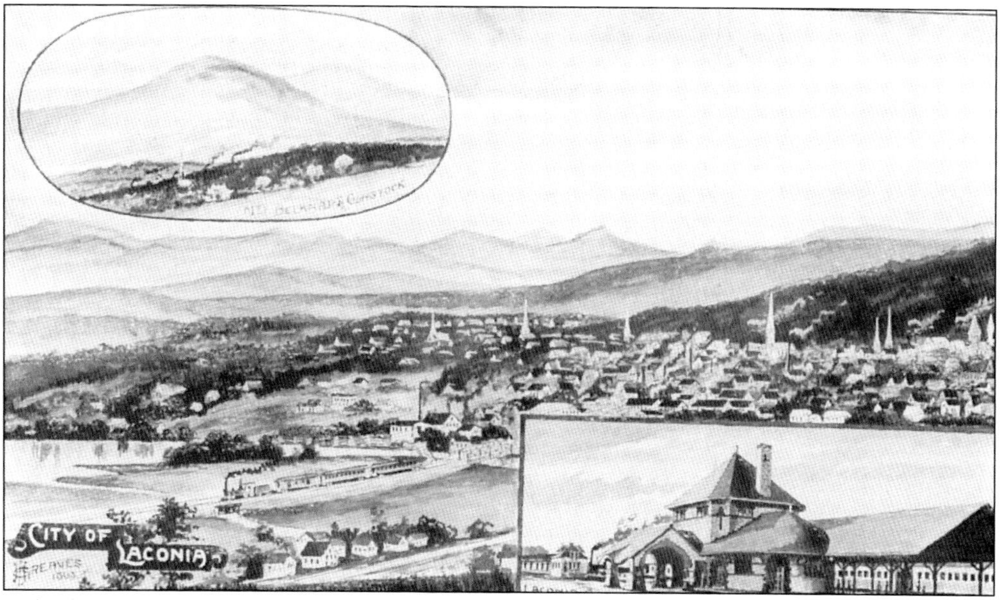

A bird's-eye view of Laconia, N.H. Along the eastern shore of Lake Winnisquam lies the town of Laconia, its northern limits being only a mile or two removed from the mouth of Lake Winnipesaukee. On the east its territory reaches into the Belknap section, and on the south joins the towns of Tilton and Winnisquam.

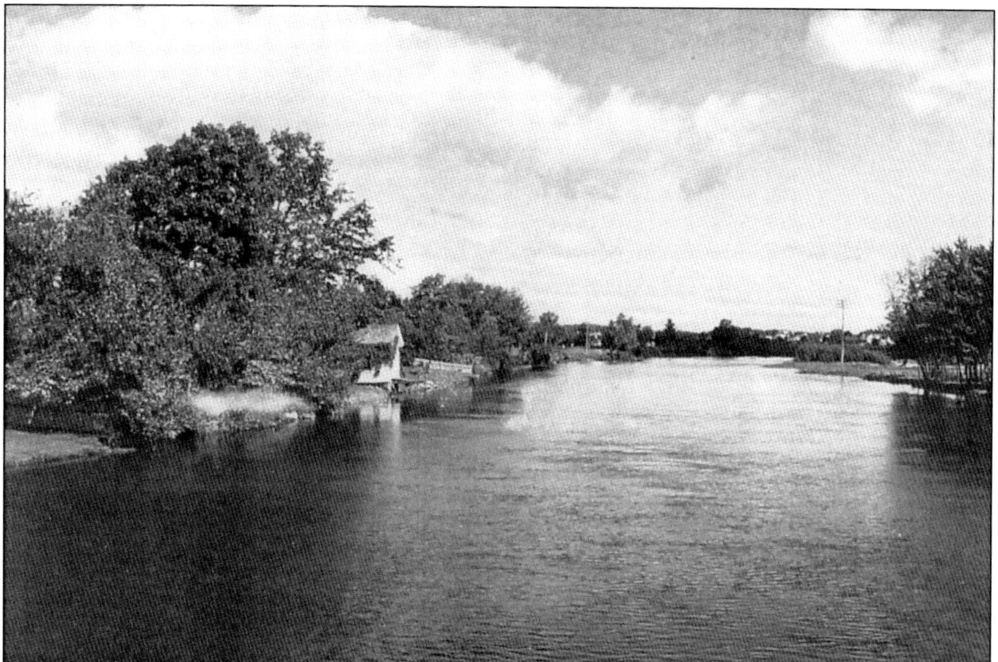

The Winnipesaukee River at Laconia. This is the major outlet for Lake Winnipesaukee which feeds into the Merrimack River at Franklin Falls.

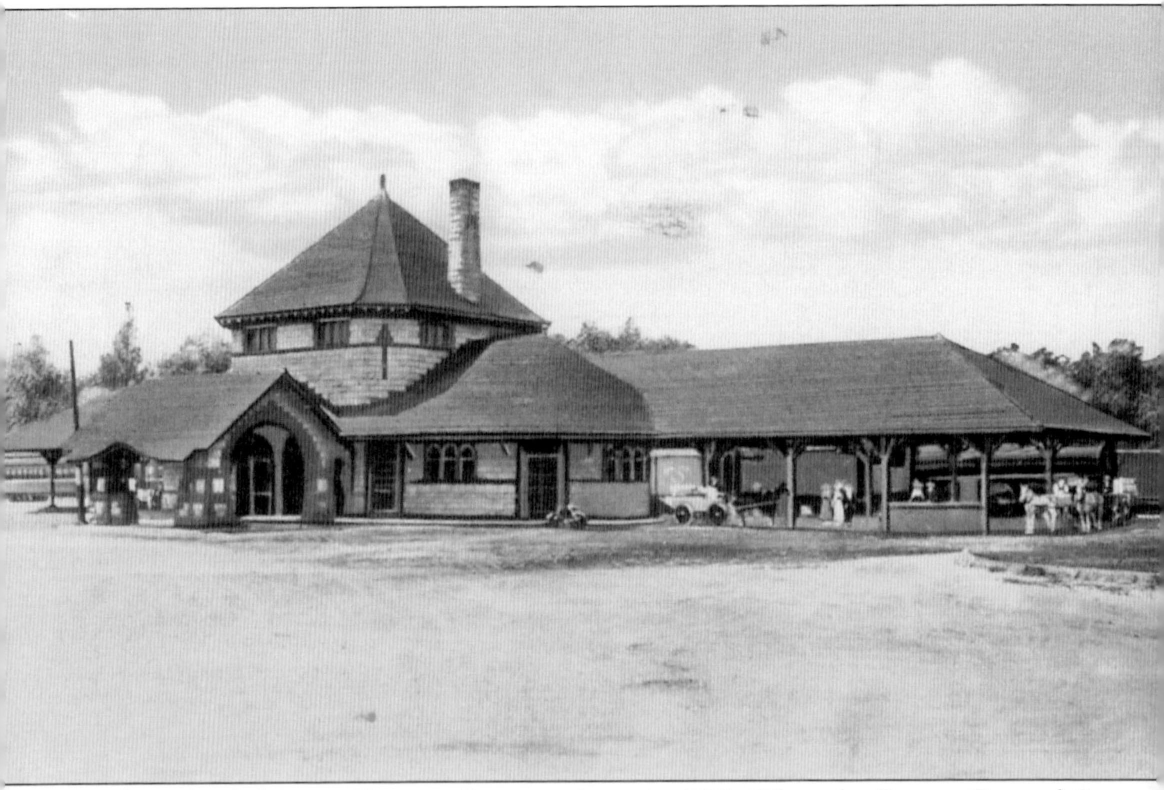

The railroad depot at Veterans Square in Laconia, 1917. When the Boston, Concord & Montreal Railroad was extended to Meredith Bridge, passengers were provided with a small wooden station, which soon became inadequate as the community grew. After the merge of the Boston, Concord, & Montreal Railroad and the Concord Railroad, to form the Concord & Montreal Railroad in 1889, the new railroad company immediately proceeded to modernize its many railroad stations. Charles A. Busiel, a prominent Laconia businessman and one of the railroads managing directors, made sure that a new station was built in his city. The city responded to this effort by widening Depot Street in order to create the present Veterans Square to better serve the heavy traffic and make this an appropriate entry to the city. On August 22, 1892, the station was dedicated and opened to the public.

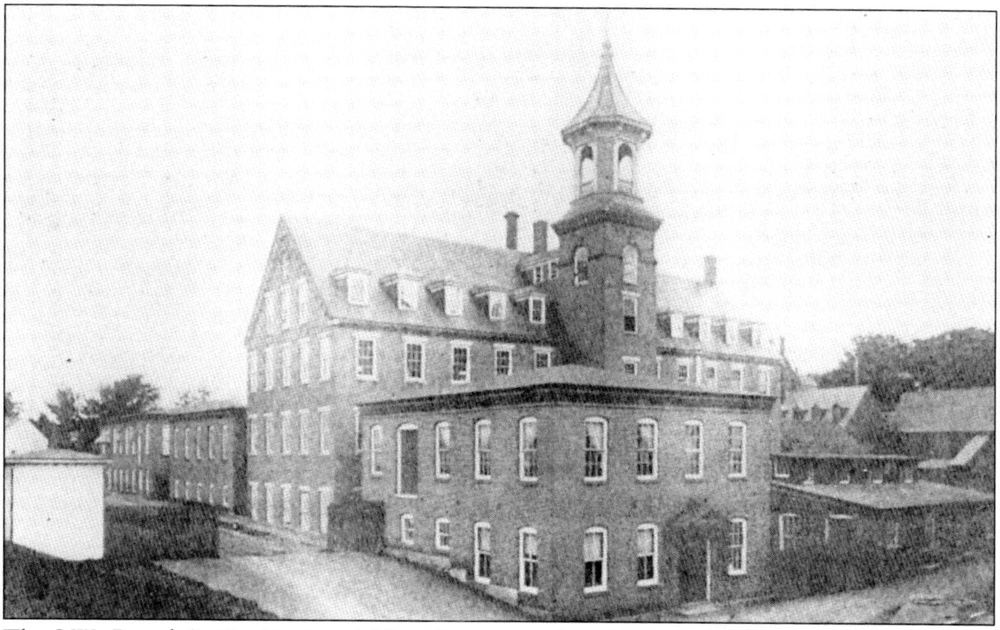

The J.W. Busiel & Co. Hosiery Mills. "Constructed in 1823, the Belknap Mill is the oldest unaltered brick textile mill in the United States. Once a hosiery mill, it houses an intact hydraulic power plant and a bell cast by George Holbrook, apprentice to Paul Revere. The Busiel Mill, built in 1853 as a hosiery mill, was later used for the manufacture of clocks, electronic relays and organs." Today it is the home of the Belknap Mill Society, Laconia.

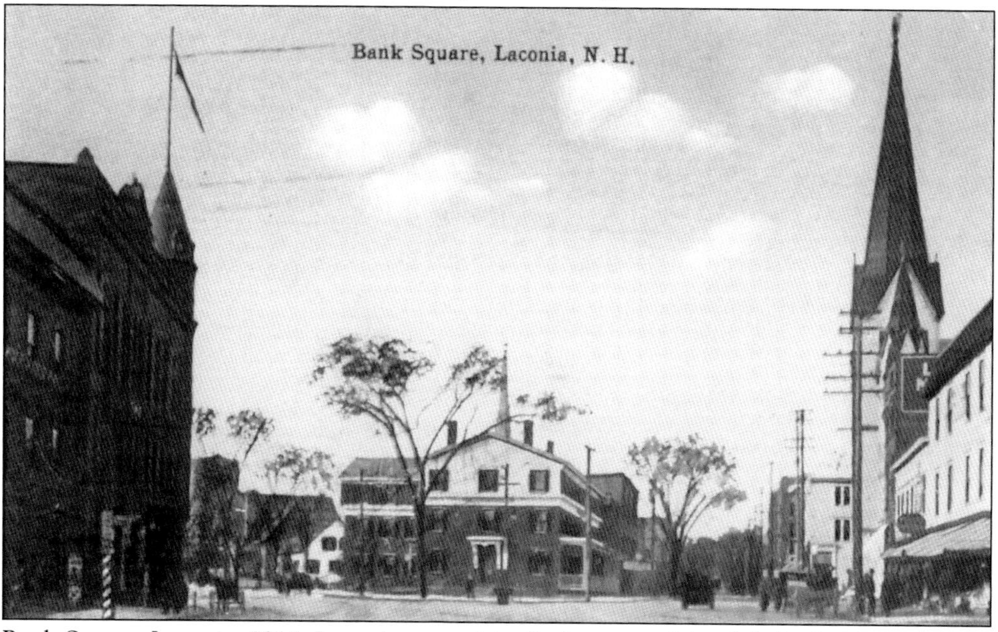

Bank Square, Laconia, 1914. Laconia was originally known as Meredith Bridge, but after the annual town meeting on March 13, 1855, this section of town separated from Meredith in July of that year, and formed the new town of Laconia. Laconia remained a town until 1893, when it received its city charter. The Honorable Charles A. Busiel, who later became governor of New Hampshire, was the city's first mayor.

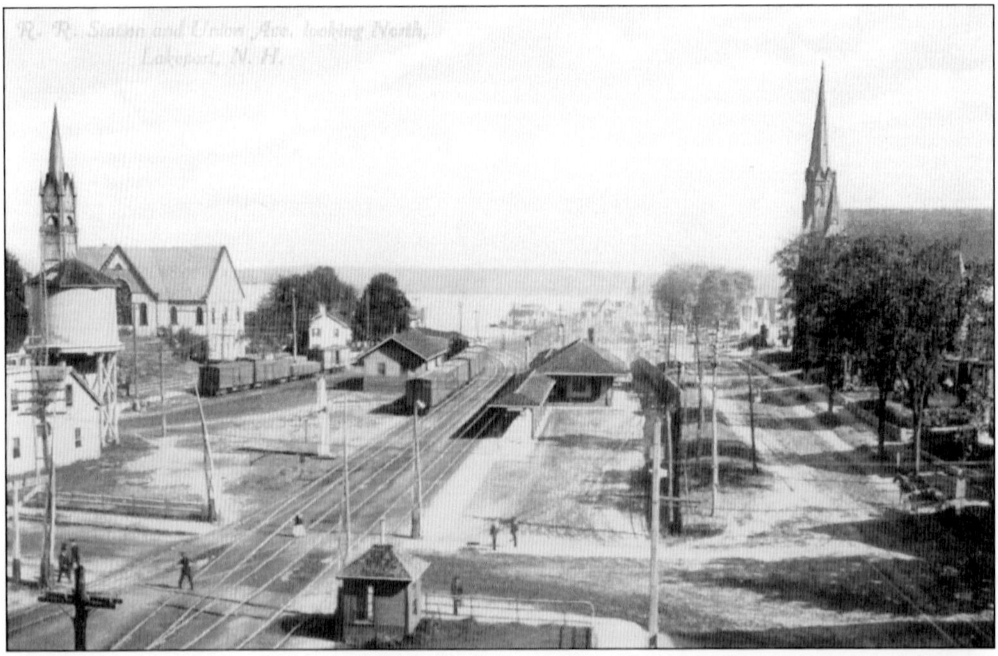

The passenger station and Union Avenue looking north onto Paugus Bay, Laconia, *c.* 1900. On August 8, 1848, the opening of the Boston, Concord & Montreal Railroad between Concord and Meredith Bridge was established and marked an important development in the growth of what is now Laconia. The following year the road was extended to Lake Village, known today as Lakeport. This event caused one of the largest celebrations these towns had ever seen and probably ever will see.

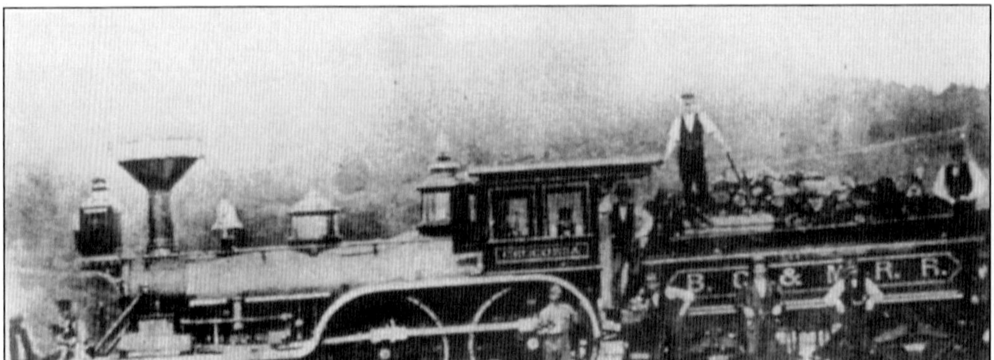

The "Chocorua," a favorite BC&M engine built in the Lake Village shops sported high drivewheels for passenger assignments, *c.* 1880s. In 1847, a charter was granted to build the Lake Shore Railroad between Laconia and Alton Bay. This 18-mile road was established so as to connect the Cocheco Road on the eastern side of New Hampshire with the Boston, Concord & Montreal Railroad at Meredith. Due to the lack of finances, the project was postponed for forty years. Finally, in 1883, the charter was granted to Mr. Charles A. Busiel and his associates. This line was finally constructed by the Concord Railroad Corporation and officially opened in Laconia on June 17, 1890.

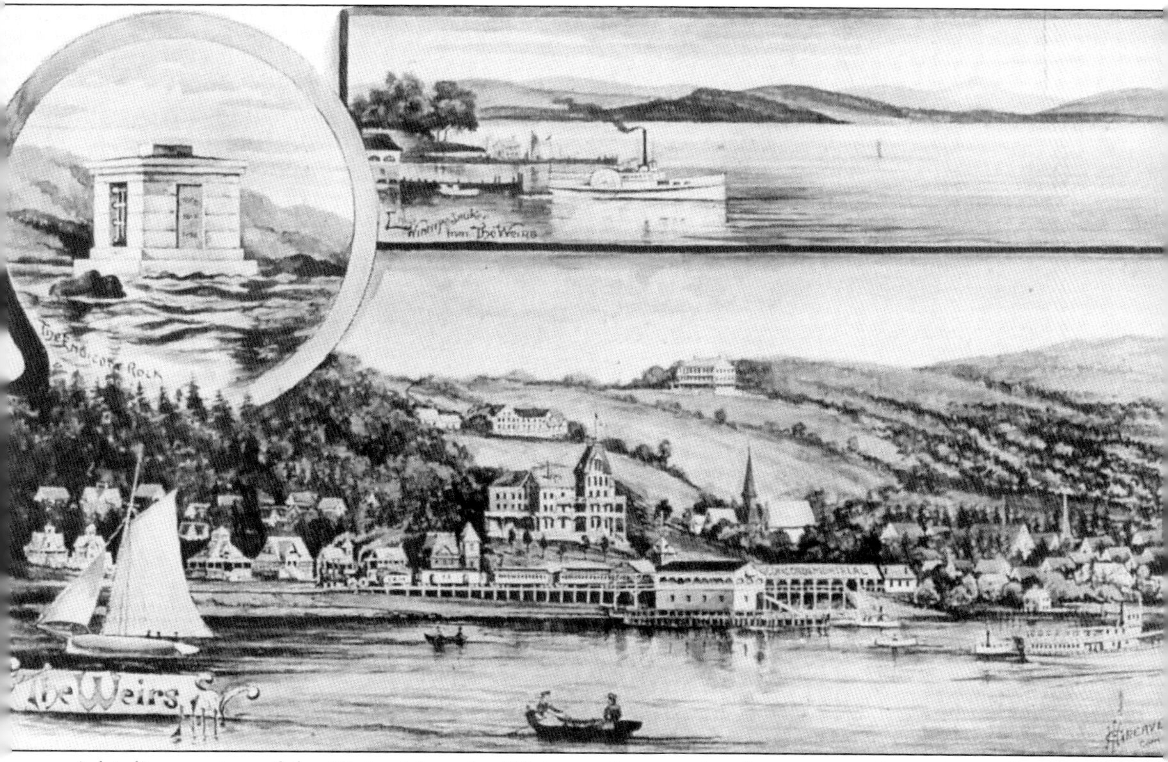

A bird's-eye view of the Weirs. Near the Weirs station, on the shore approaching the outlet of the lake, is "Endicott Rock," a large boulder 20 feet in circumference, upon which are carved the initials of the chiefs of the colonial survey of 1652, and the name and initials "John Endicott, Gov." Here also are the spacious and handsome groves and buildings of the New Hampshire Veteran's Association. This station is located on the Boston, Concord & Montreal Rail, 34 miles from Concord and 109 miles from Boston. The hotel in the center of the picture is the old Hotel Weirs, which burned in November 1924. It was one of the famous grand hotels on Lake Winnipesaukee.

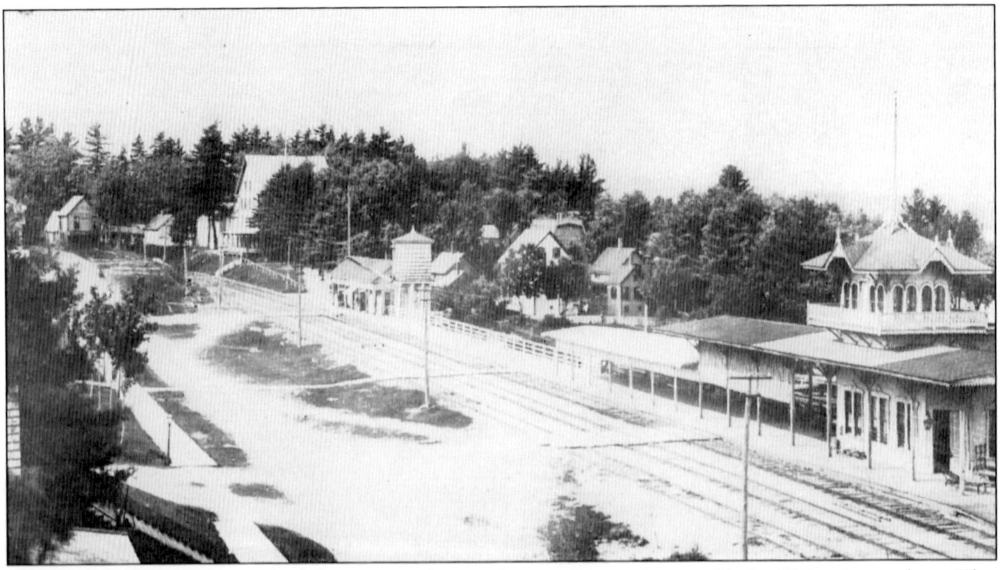

The Weirs. The Weirs railroad station is located on the west shore of Lake Winnipesaukee. The Penacook word for Weirs was "Aquedoctan," which was a large fishing place in 1652 located near Endicott Rock. The Indian village Aquadoctan was located on the hills to the north and west and was the largest village in this region. The ruins of the weirs, which were a triangular enclosure of rocks and logs used for trapping fish, could, at one time, be seen in the waters just north of Endicott Rock Monument.

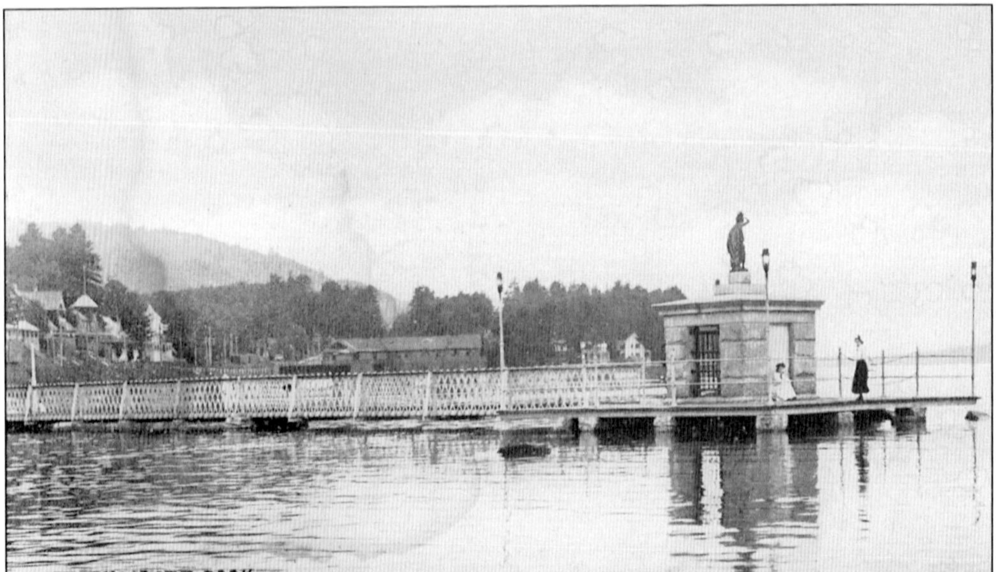

The Endicott Rock Monument. It was Captain Simon Willard and Captain Edward Johnson who were appointed commissioners by the court to determine the northernmost part of the Merrimack River. They, in turn, employed John Sherman and Jonathan Ince to ascertain and determine the latitude of "Aquedauctan," a name given the Merrimack River where it issues out of Lake Winnipisaukee. On August 1, 1652, they found that the latitude was 45 degrees, 40 miles, and 12 seconds, besides those minutes which are to be allowed for the 3 more miles north which run into the lake.

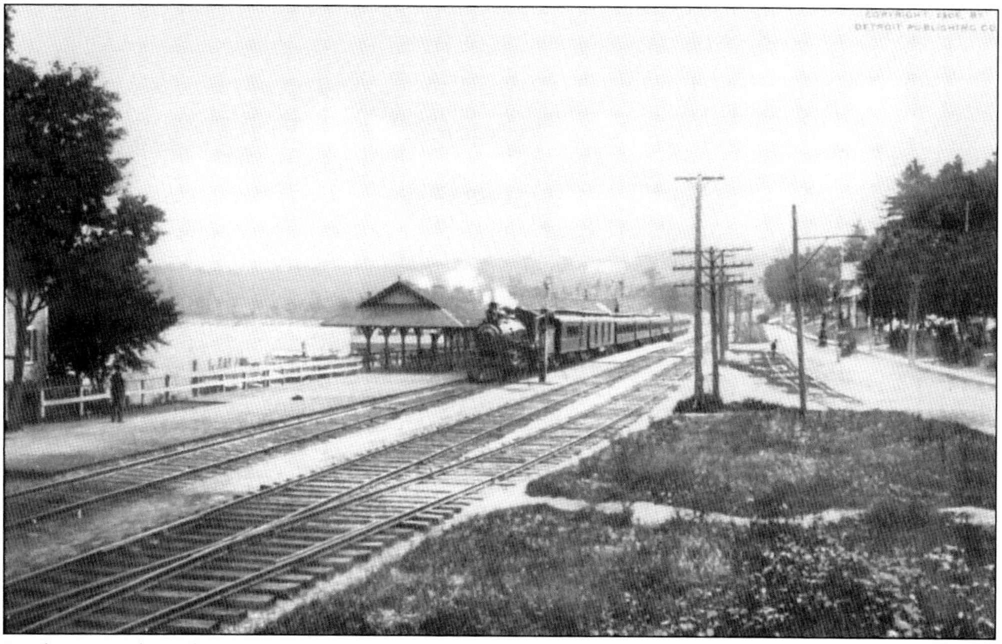

Looking south at the Weirs railroad station next to Lake Winnipesaukee, Laconia, 1906. During the second half of the nineteenth century, it was customary for railroad companies to build and own their own steamboats so as to transfer their passengers from train to boat on their trek to the grand hotels in the region.

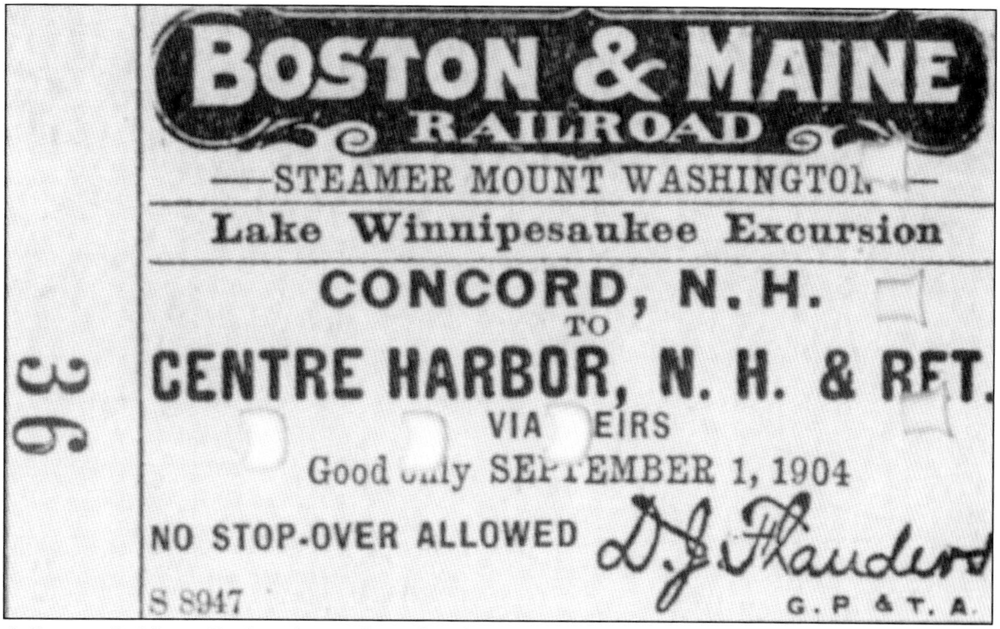

36

BOSTON & MAINE
RAILROAD
—STEAMER MOUNT WASHINGTON—
Lake Winnipesaukee Excursion
CONCORD, N.H.
TO
CENTRE HARBOR, N. H. & RET.
VIA WEIRS
Good only SEPTEMBER 1, 1904
NO STOP-OVER ALLOWED
D. J. Flanders
G. P. & T. A.
S 8947

A Boston & Maine Railroad transfer ticket from Concord to Centre Harbor, N.H., 1904.

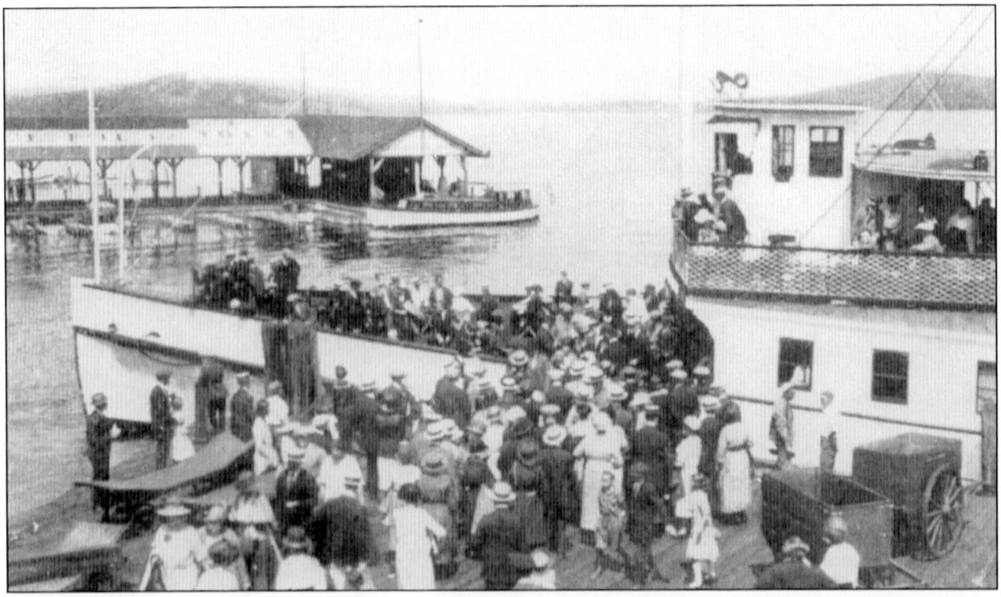

Here the passengers are loading on the B&M steamer *Mount Washington* at the Weirs station, c. 1880s. In 1872 the Boston & Maine built the *Mount* at Alton Bay, and at that time she was considered the largest, safest, and most luxurious steamer on the lake.

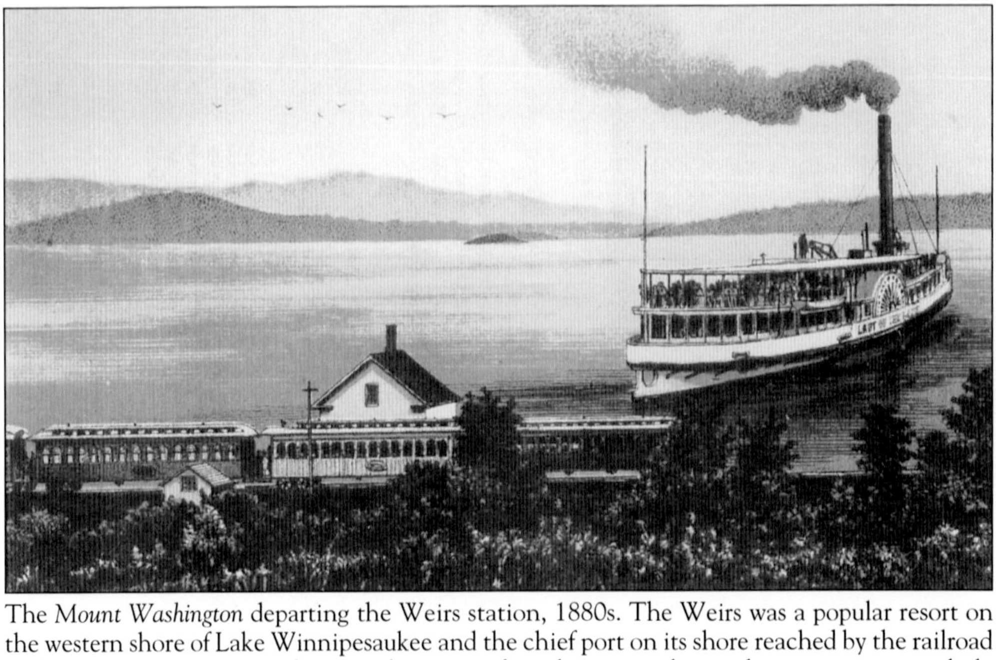

The *Mount Washington* departing the Weirs station, 1880s. The Weirs was a popular resort on the western shore of Lake Winnipesaukee and the chief port on its shore reached by the railroad and the major steamers. Today, it is the scene of much activity during the summer, particularly when seasonal boating is in full swing. The Weirs is the starting point for the M.S. *Mount Washington*.

Five

The Pemigewasset
Bristol, Ashland, Holderness, and Plymouth, New Hampshire

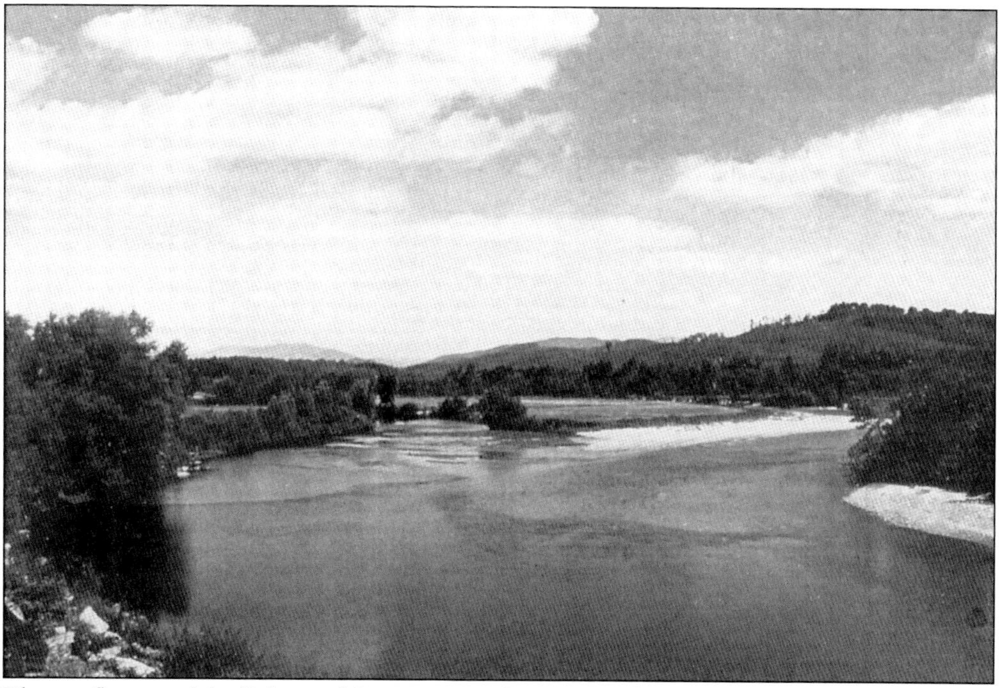

The confluence of the Baker and Pemigewasset Rivers. At Plymouth the "Pemi," as it is known locally, is joined by the Baker River, named for Captain Thomas Baker, the Indian-fighter. It rises on the eastern side of Mount Moosilauke and flows through Warren, Wentworth, Rumney, and Plymouth.

With Holderness on its east bank, the Pemigewasset flows into Ashland and then, dividing New Hampton from Bridgewater, cuts Bristol into two almost equal parts and winds along the eastern edge of Hill to join the Winnipesaukee River at Franklin Falls, known as the "Forks."

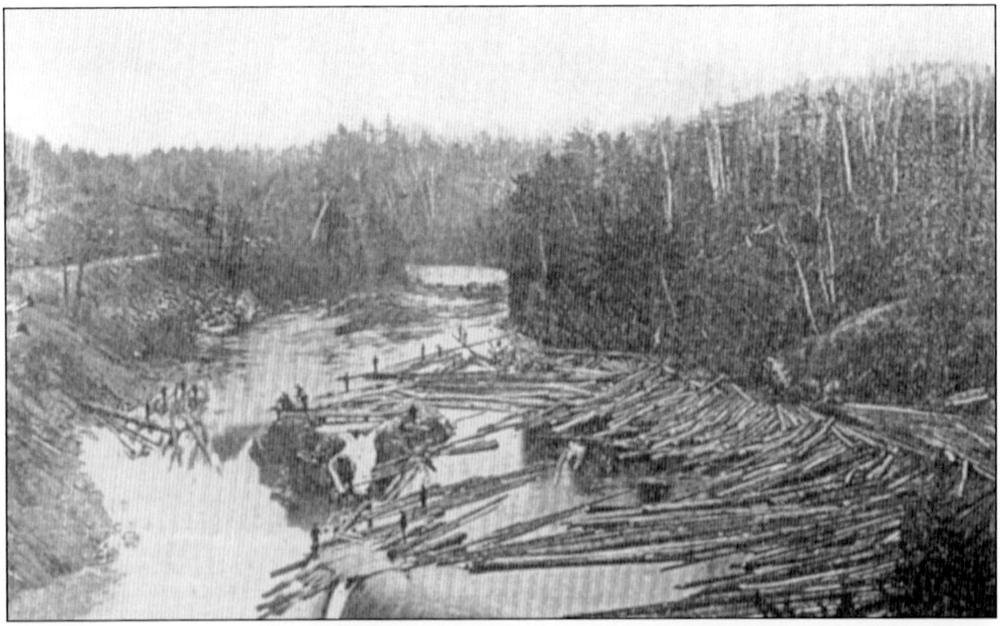

Logging at Livermore Falls in Holderness. Logging was a major industry in the area, but sawmills also dotted the shores of most waterways throughout the Lakes Region. This spot is mostly admired by the angler, for trout and some of the most beautify specimens of land-locked salmon can be caught at these falls. The state fish hatching establishment was located here for these reasons.

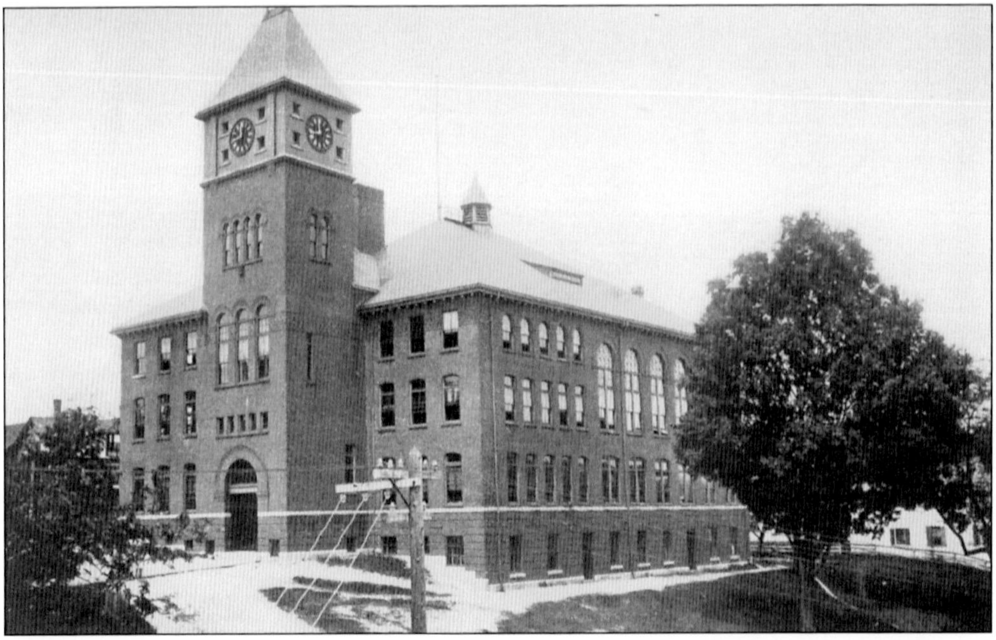

The New Hampshire State Normal School, Plymouth. This building, Rounds Hall, was dedicated on August 28, 1891. For more than 125 years, this institution has been responsible for guiding, inspiring, and motivating young adults to excel. The educational facility is now known as Plymouth State College of the University System of New Hampshire.

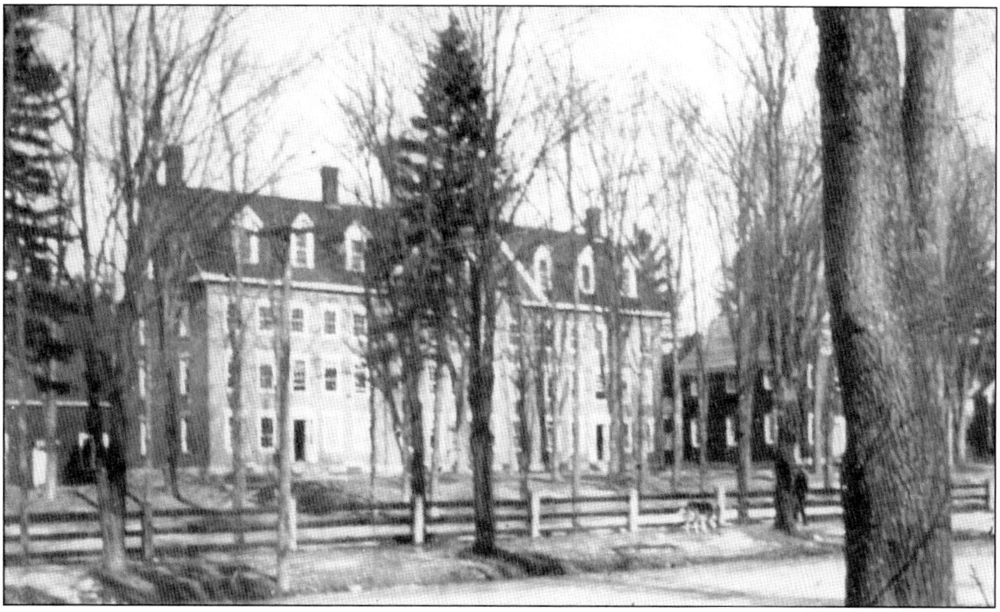

The New Hampton School in 1906. This private school, located in the center of the village of New Hampton, and housed in a row of red brick buildings of the American Georgian style, was founded in 1821 by William B. Kelley and Nathaniel Norris. Shortly after 1825, the charter of the school was amended and the school became known as the New Hampton Academical and Theological Institute. In 1853, a new charter was granted to the New Hampton Literary and Biblical Institution. Today this school is considered one of the finest in secondary education in all of New England.

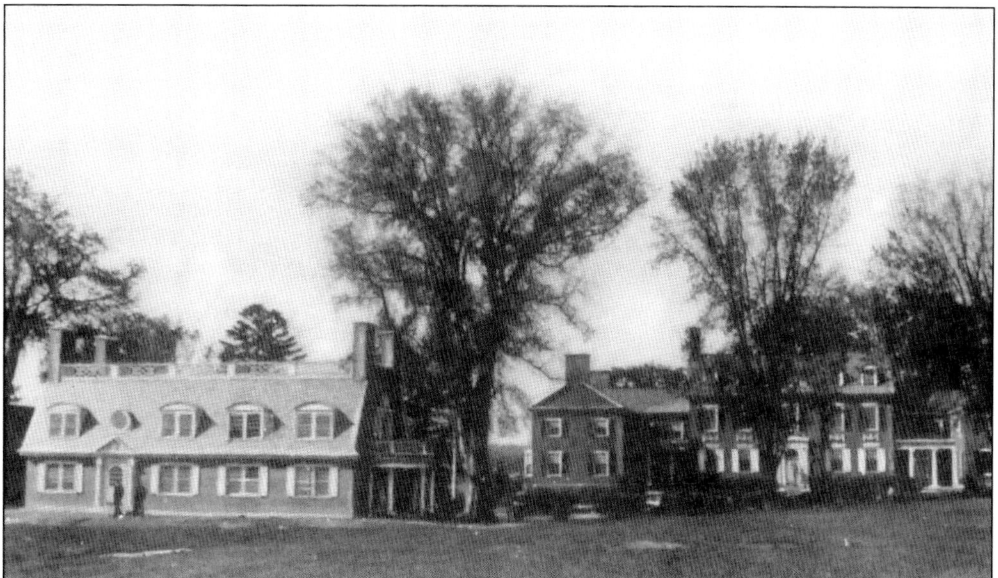

The Holderness School. This privately endowed educational institution is located in the town of Holderness on a high terrace overlooking the Pemigewasset River. The central building is a fine example of the Southern Colonial style. This secondary school is ranked high in the academic community, and attracts many students from all over the country.

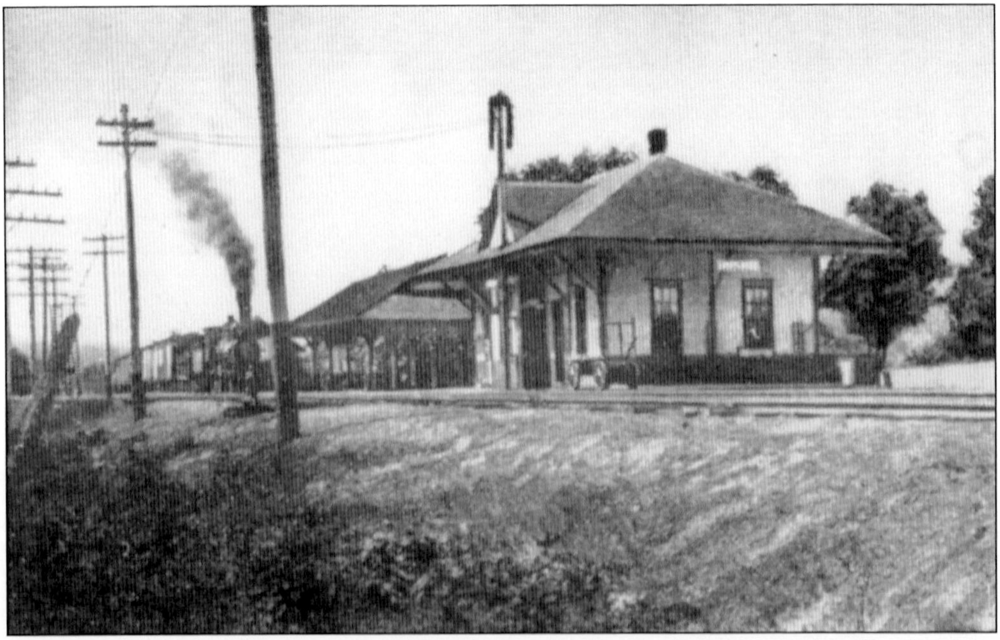

The Ashland railroad station, early 1900s. The Boston, Concord, & Montreal Railroad ran the first train from Concord to Plymouth on Friday, January 18, 1850. The regular passenger service started on Monday, January 22, with one train daily from Concord. This was due at Ashland about 11:45 am and left Ashland on the return journey to Concord about 12:30 pm. Many people will remember the long canopy at the Ashland station which provided shelter during bad weather.

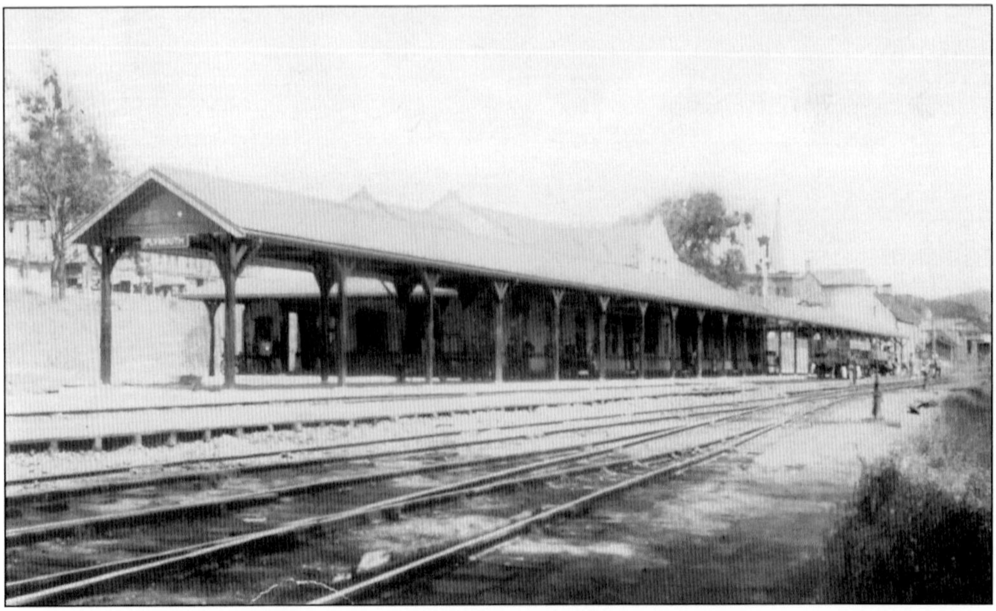

The railroad station at Plymouth, *c.* 1900. This station was a little above the Pemigewasset River, while the village was located upon a terrace reached by a sharp grade from the railroad station. Today, the village is situated in the same spot with the addition of a large college campus. This location is now the site of the new Senior Center.

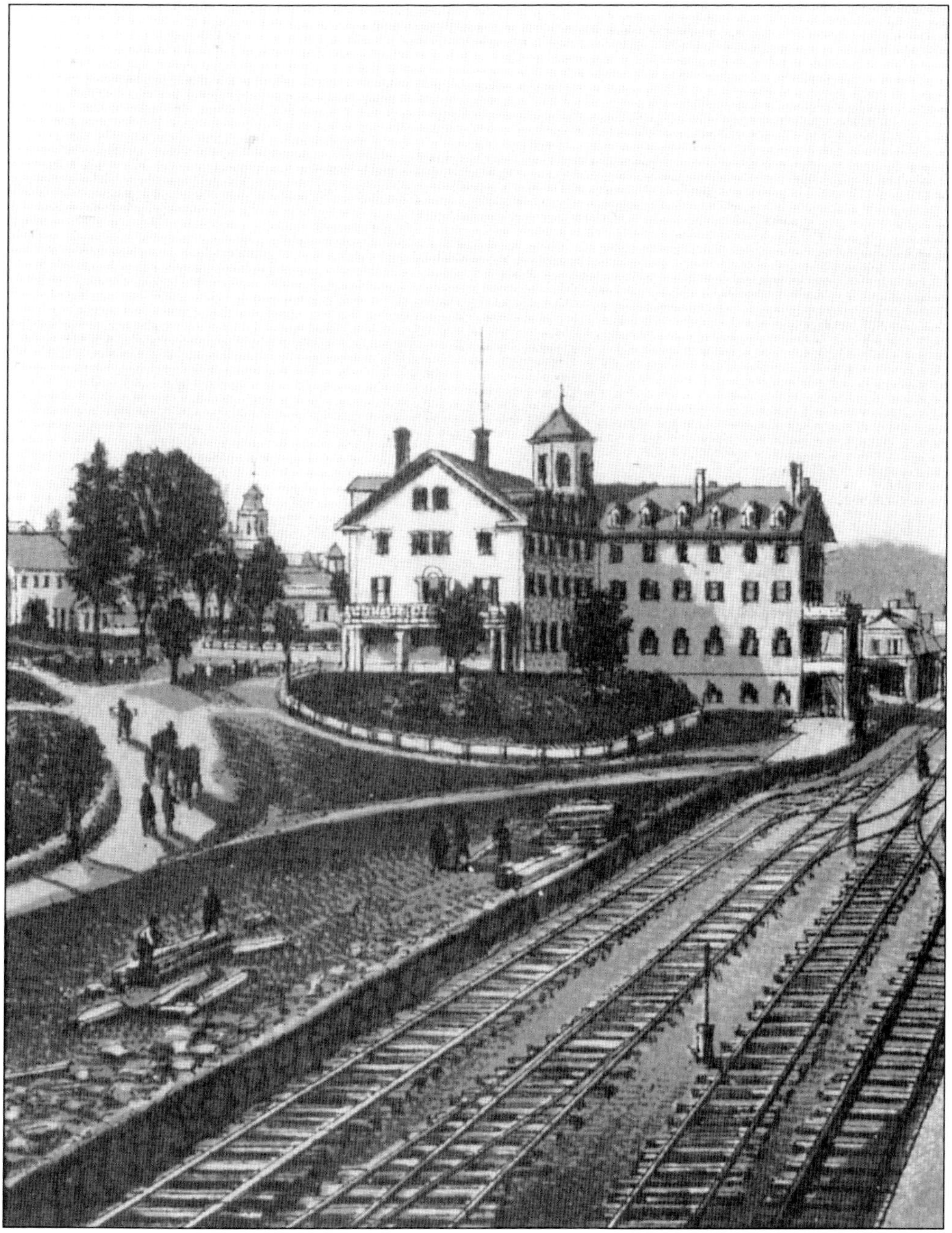

The Pemigewasset House and the Boston, Concord & Montreal Railroad Station, Plymouth, 1877. In 1850 the Boston, Concord & Montreal Railroad completed the road to Plymouth from Concord. In 1858 the BC&M leased the White Mountain Railroad which continued the road from Plymouth to Littleton. In 1869 the construction of an extension of the White Mountain Railroad beyond Littleton was undertaken, and in 1872 the track from Wing Road toward the base of Mount Washington was begun.

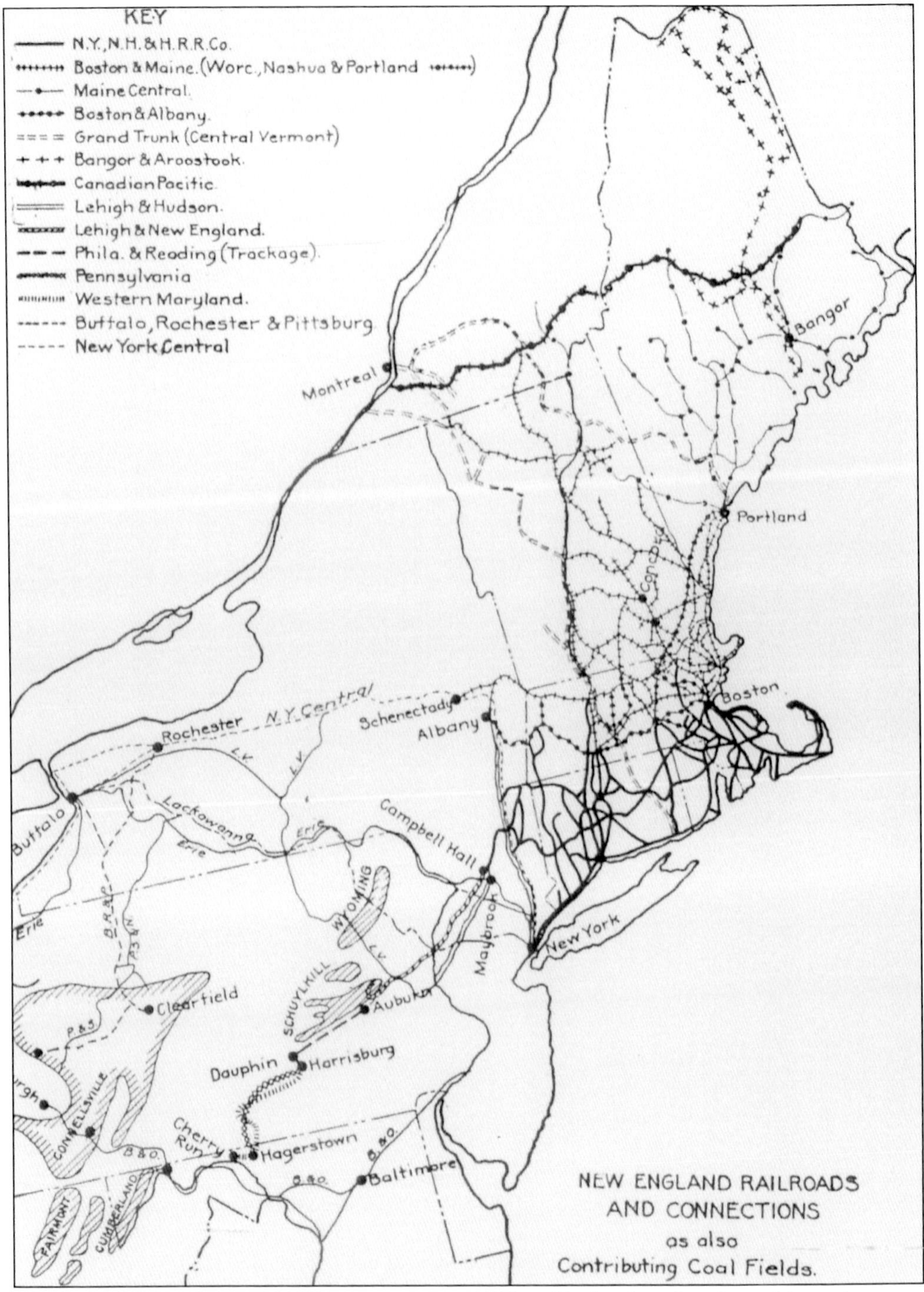

New England Roads, *c.* 1900. The importance of New Englands railroads could not be overestimated. Here are shown her roads and their connections, the routes over which many passengers traveled for a summer's vacation to the grand hotels and the routes which raw materials came to us and our finished products were delivered to the consumers. How well we remember the importance of the rail and water routes throughout New England.